Writers: Grant Morrison & Mark Millar
Penciler: Steve Yeowell
Inker: Chris Ivy
Colors: Chia-Chi Wang, Chris DeFelippo, Malibu & Digital Chameleon
Letters: Richard Starkings & Comicraft
Cover Colors: Tom Smith
Editor: Tom Brevoort

Collection Editor: Mark D. Beazley
Assistant Editor: Michael Short
Associate Editor: Jennifer Grünwald
Senior Editor, Special Projects: Jeff Youngquist
Vice President of Sales: David Gabriel
Production: Jerron Quality Color
Book Designer: Jhonson Eteng
Vice President of Creative: Tom Marvelli

Editor-in-Chief: Joe Quesada
Publisher: Dan Buckley

Special thanks to Pond Scum

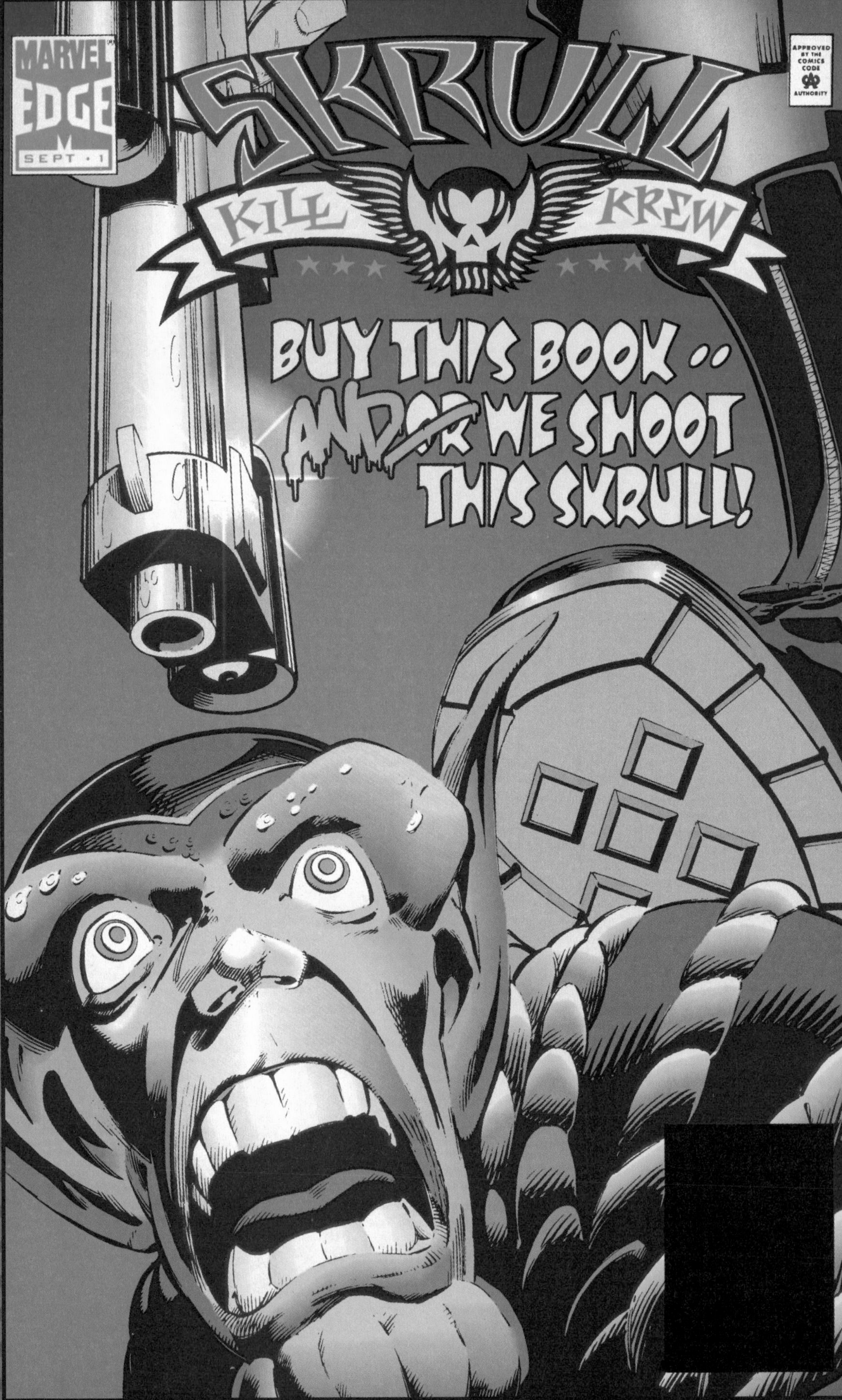
MARVEL EDGE
SEPT • 1
APPROVED BY THE COMICS CODE AUTHORITY
SKRULL
KILL KREW
BUY THIS BOOK ..
AND OR WE SHOOT
THIS SKRULL!

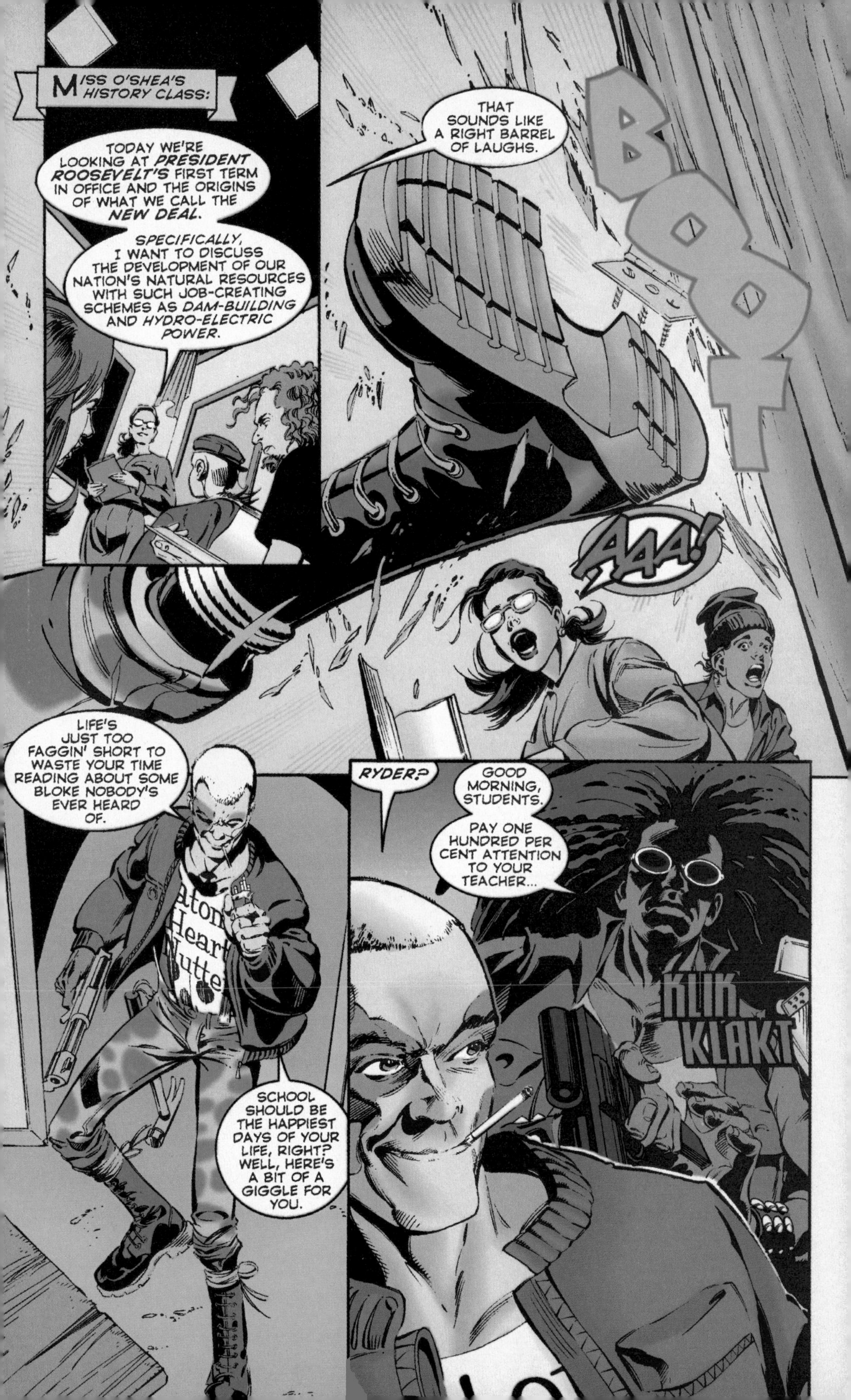
MISS O'SHEA'S HISTORY CLASS:
TODAY WE'RE LOOKING AT PRESIDENT ROOSEVELT'S FIRST TERM IN OFFICE AND THE ORIGINS OF WHAT WE CALL THE NEW DEAL.
SPECIFICALLY, I WANT TO DISCUSS THE DEVELOPMENT OF OUR NATION'S NATURAL RESOURCES WITH SUCH JOB-CREATING SCHEMES AS DAM-BUILDING AND HYDRO-ELECTRIC POWER.
THAT SOUNDS LIKE A RIGHT BARREL OF LAUGHS.
BOOT
AAA!
LIFE'S JUST TOO FAGGIN' SHORT TO WASTE YOUR TIME READING ABOUT SOME BLOKE NOBODY'S EVER HEARD OF.
SCHOOL SHOULD BE THE HAPPIEST DAYS OF YOUR LIFE, RIGHT? WELL, HERE'S A BIT OF A GIGGLE FOR YOU.
RYDER?
GOOD MORNING, STUDENTS.
PAY ONE HUNDRED PER CENT ATTENTION TO YOUR TEACHER...
KLIK KLAKT

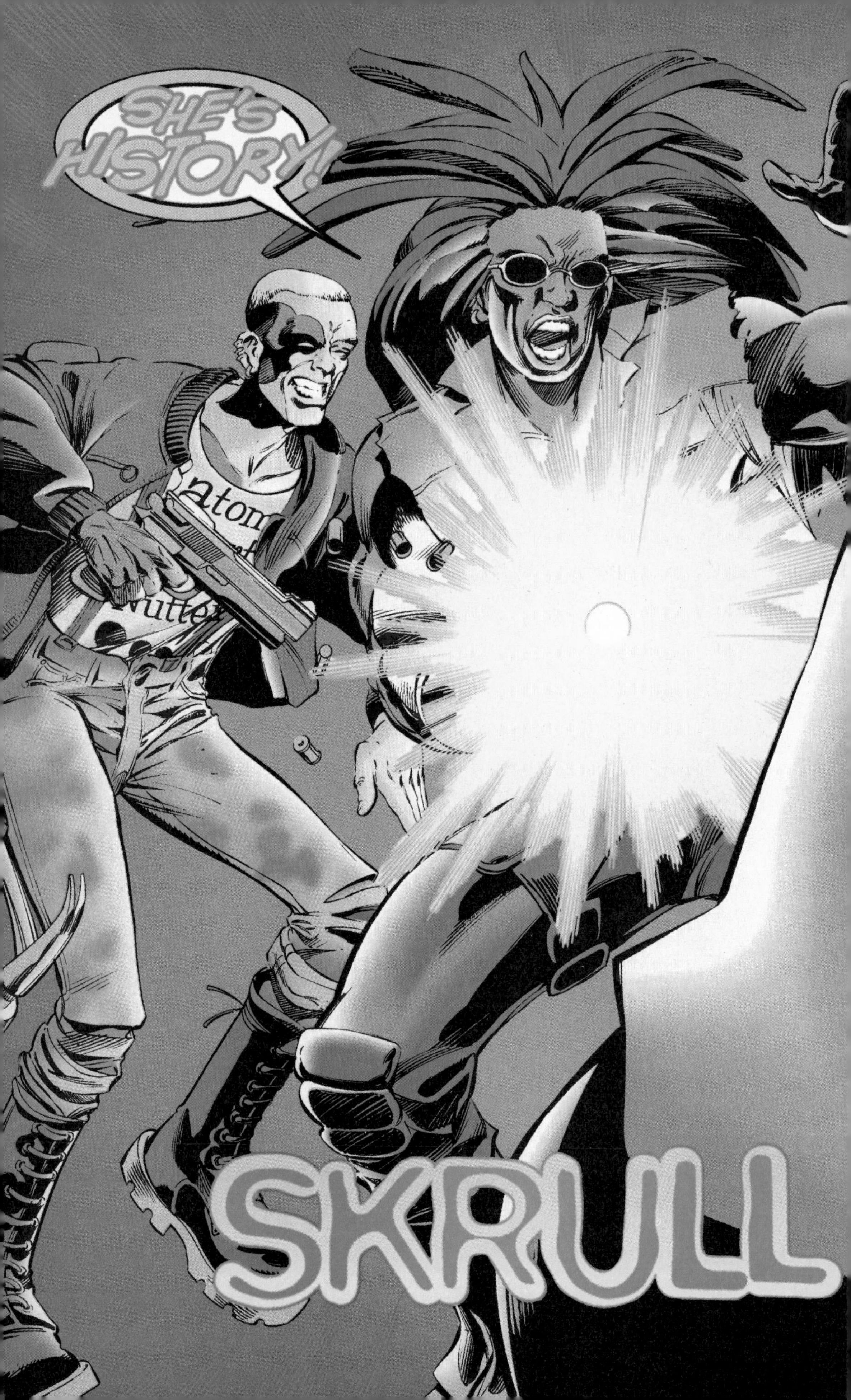
SHE'S HISTORY!
SKRULL

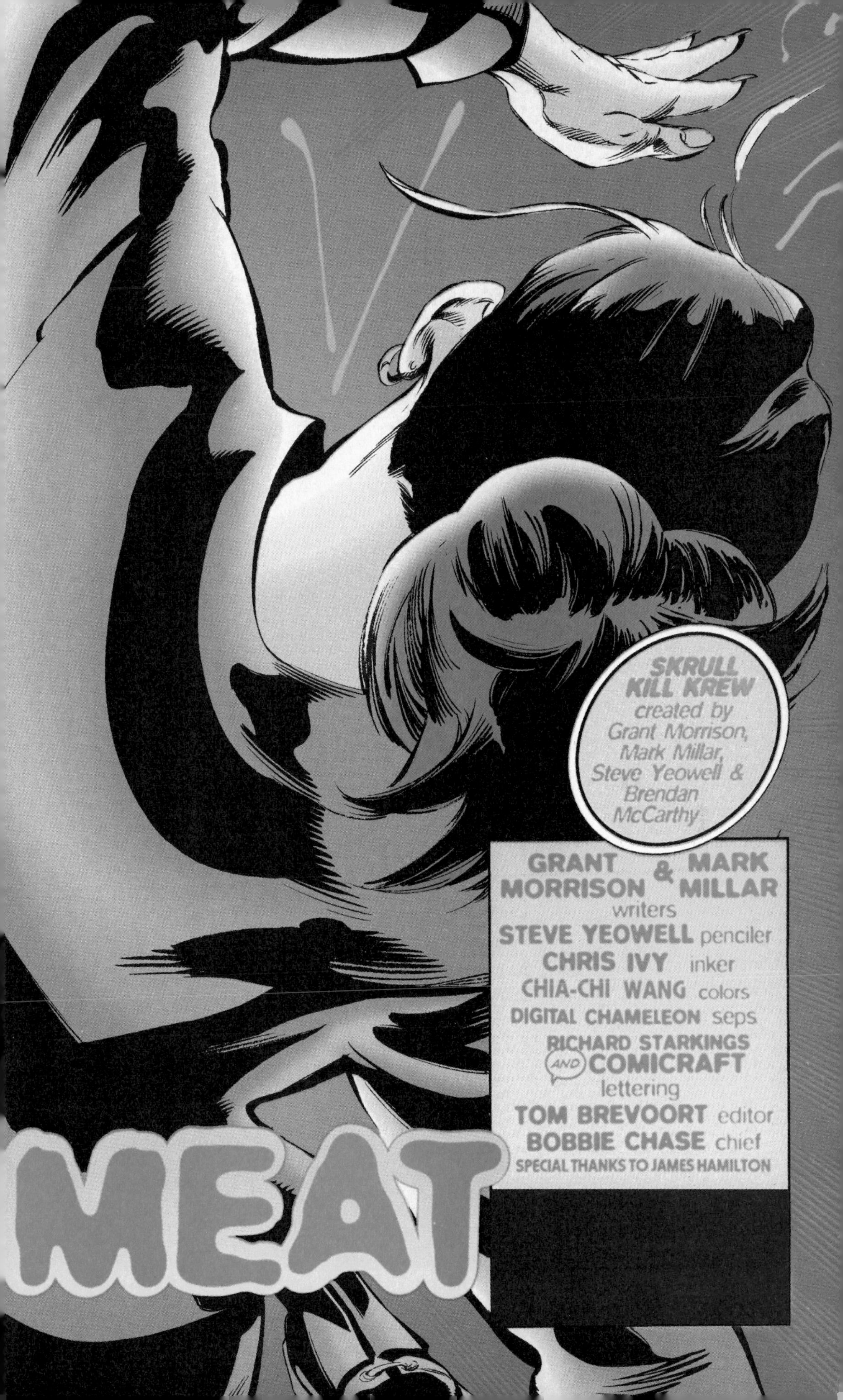
SKRULL KILL KREW created by Grant Morrison, Mark Millar, Steve Yeowell & Brendan McCarthy
GRANT MORRISON & MARK MILLAR writers
STEVE YEOWELL penciler
CHRIS IVY inker
CHIA-CHI WANG colors
DIGITAL CHAMELEON seps
RICHARD STARKINGS AND COMICRAFT lettering
TOM BREVOORT editor
BOBBIE CHASE chief
SPECIAL THANKS TO JAMES HAMILTON
MEAT

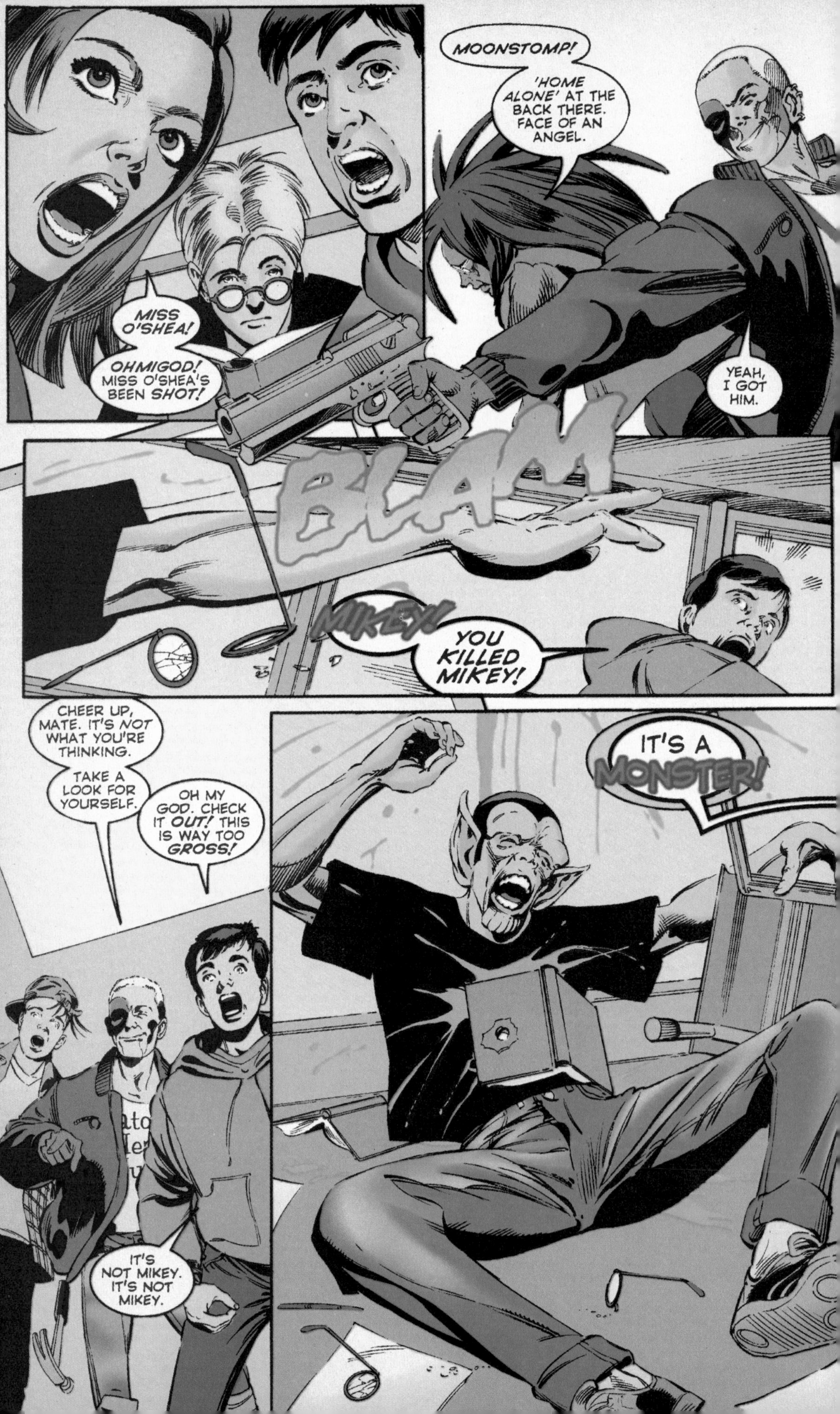
MISS O'SHEA!
OHMIGOD! MISS O'SHEA'S BEEN SHOT!
MOONSTOMP!
'HOME ALONE' AT THE BACK THERE. FACE OF AN ANGEL.
YEAH, I GOT HIM.
BLAM
MIKEY!
YOU KILLED MIKEY!
CHEER UP, MATE. IT'S NOT WHAT YOU'RE THINKING.
TAKE A LOOK FOR YOURSELF.
OH MY GOD. CHECK IT OUT! THIS IS WAY TOO GROSS!
IT'S NOT MIKEY. IT'S NOT MIKEY.
IT'S A MONSTER!

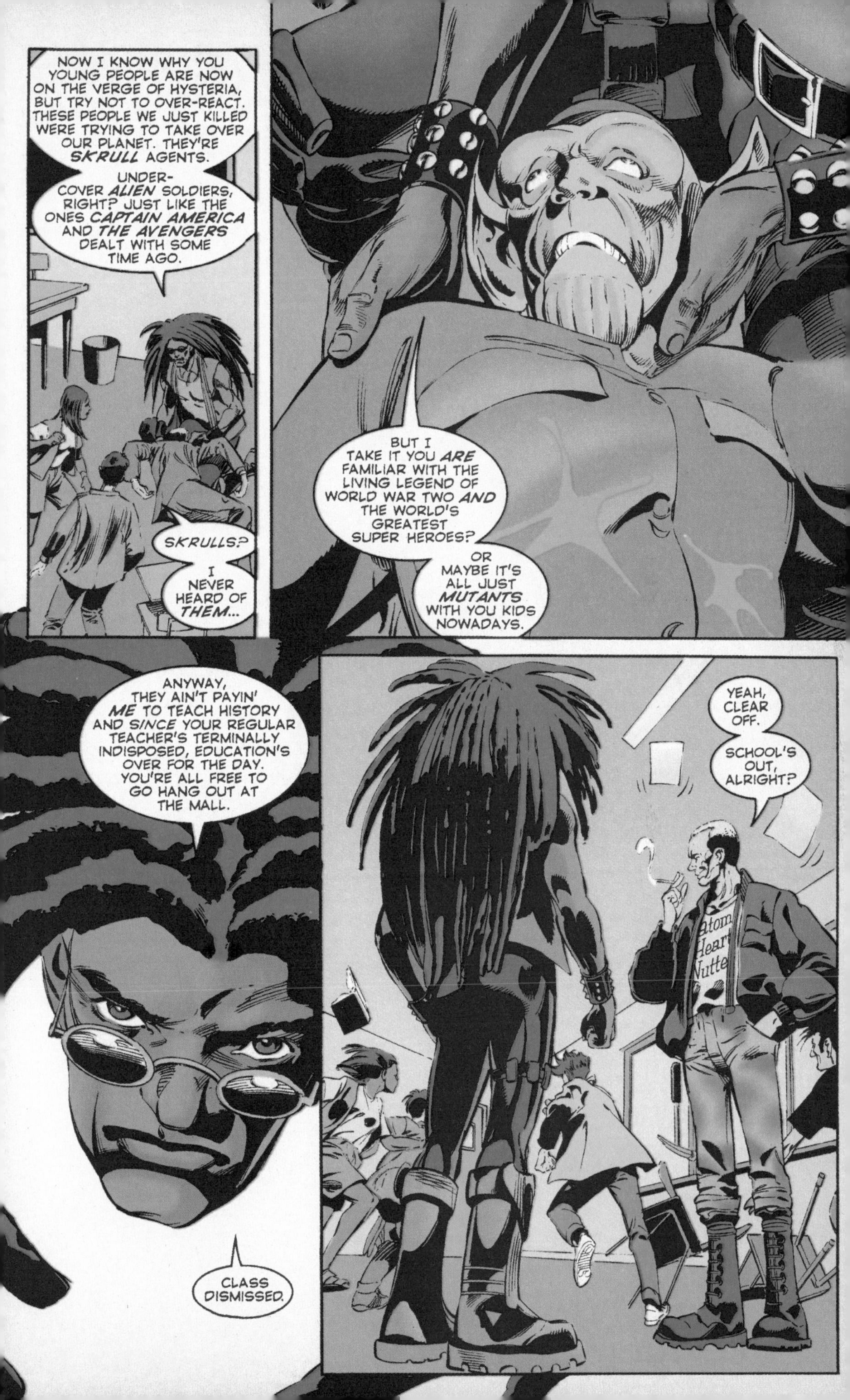

NOW I KNOW WHY YOU YOUNG PEOPLE ARE NOW ON THE VERGE OF HYSTERIA, BUT TRY NOT TO OVER-REACT. THESE PEOPLE WE JUST KILLED WERE TRYING TO TAKE OVER OUR PLANET. THEY'RE SKRULL AGENTS.
UNDER-COVER ALIEN SOLDIERS, RIGHT? JUST LIKE THE ONES CAPTAIN AMERICA AND THE AVENGERS DEALT WITH SOME TIME AGO.
SKRULLS?
I NEVER HEARD OF THEM...
BUT I TAKE IT YOU ARE FAMILIAR WITH THE LIVING LEGEND OF WORLD WAR TWO AND THE WORLD'S GREATEST SUPER HEROES?
OR MAYBE IT'S ALL JUST MUTANTS WITH YOU KIDS NOWADAYS.
ANYWAY, THEY AIN'T PAYIN' ME TO TEACH HISTORY AND SINCE YOUR REGULAR TEACHER'S TERMINALLY INDISPOSED, EDUCATION'S OVER FOR THE DAY. YOU'RE ALL FREE TO GO HANG OUT AT THE MALL.
CLASS DISMISSED.
YEAH, CLEAR OFF.
SCHOOL'S OUT, ALRIGHT?

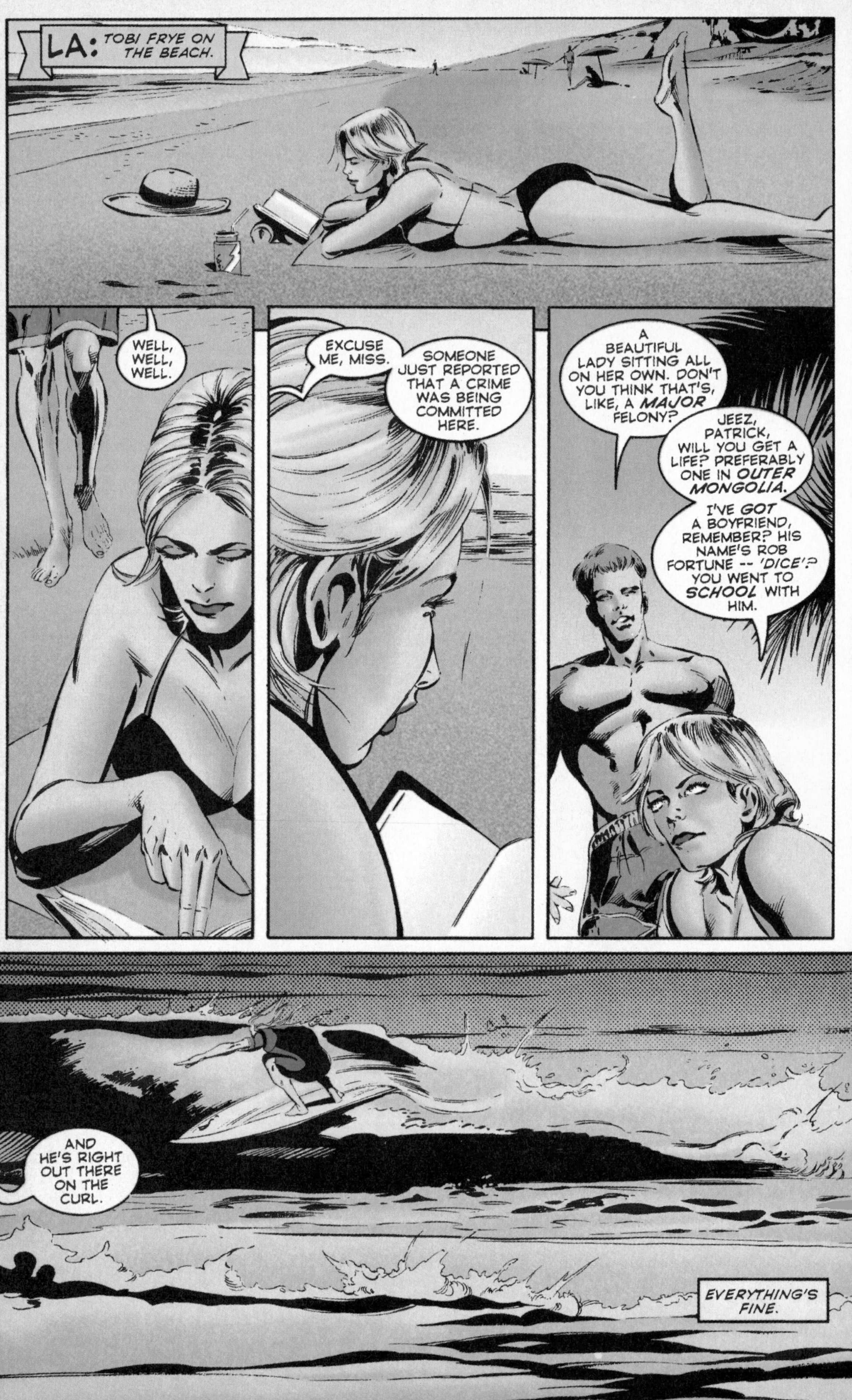
LA: TOBI FRYE ON THE BEACH.
WELL, WELL, WELL.
EXCUSE ME, MISS.
SOMEONE JUST REPORTED THAT A CRIME WAS BEING COMMITTED HERE.
A BEAUTIFUL LADY SITTING ALL ON HER OWN. DON'T YOU THINK THAT'S, LIKE, A MAJOR FELONY?
JEEZ, PATRICK, WILL YOU GET A LIFE? PREFERABLY ONE IN OUTER MONGOLIA.
I'VE GOT A BOYFRIEND, REMEMBER? HIS NAME'S ROB FORTUNE -- 'DICE'? YOU WENT TO SCHOOL WITH HIM.
AND HE'S RIGHT OUT THERE ON THE CURL.
EVERYTHING'S FINE.

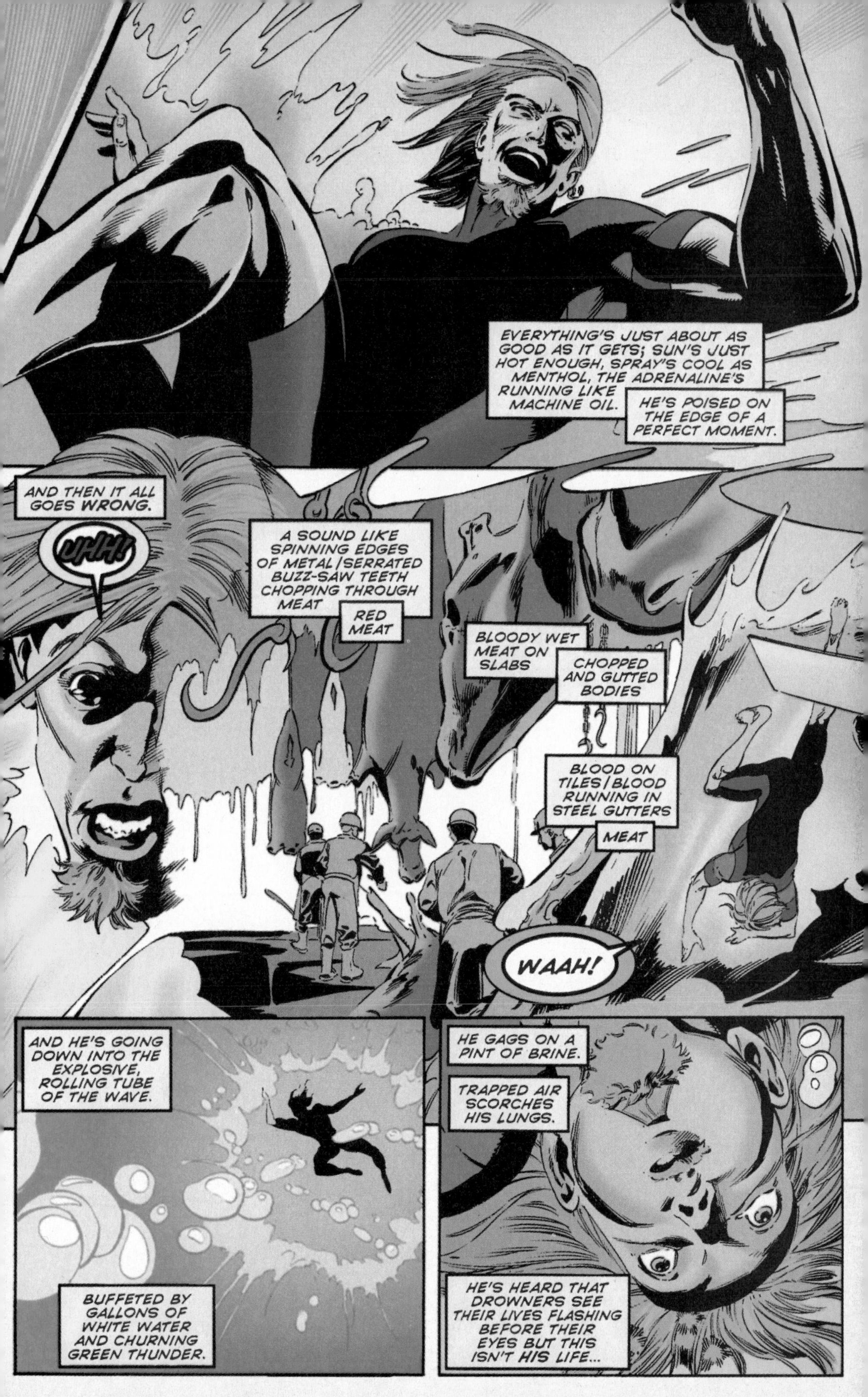
EVERYTHING'S JUST ABOUT AS GOOD AS IT GETS; SUN'S JUST HOT ENOUGH, SPRAY'S COOL AS MENTHOL, THE ADRENALINE'S RUNNING LIKE MACHINE OIL.
HE'S POISED ON THE EDGE OF A PERFECT MOMENT.
AND THEN IT ALL GOES WRONG.
UHH!
A SOUND LIKE SPINNING EDGES OF METAL/SERRATED BUZZ-SAW TEETH CHOPPING THROUGH MEAT
RED MEAT
BLOODY WET MEAT ON SLABS
CHOPPED AND GUTTED BODIES
BLOOD ON TILES/BLOOD RUNNING IN STEEL GUTTERS
MEAT
WAAH!
AND HE'S GOING DOWN INTO THE EXPLOSIVE, ROLLING TUBE OF THE WAVE.
BUFFETED BY GALLONS OF WHITE WATER AND CHURNING GREEN THUNDER.
HE GAGS ON A PINT OF BRINE.
TRAPPED AIR SCORCHES HIS LUNGS.
HE'S HEARD THAT DROWNERS SEE THEIR LIVES FLASHING BEFORE THEIR EYES BUT THIS ISN'T HIS LIFE...

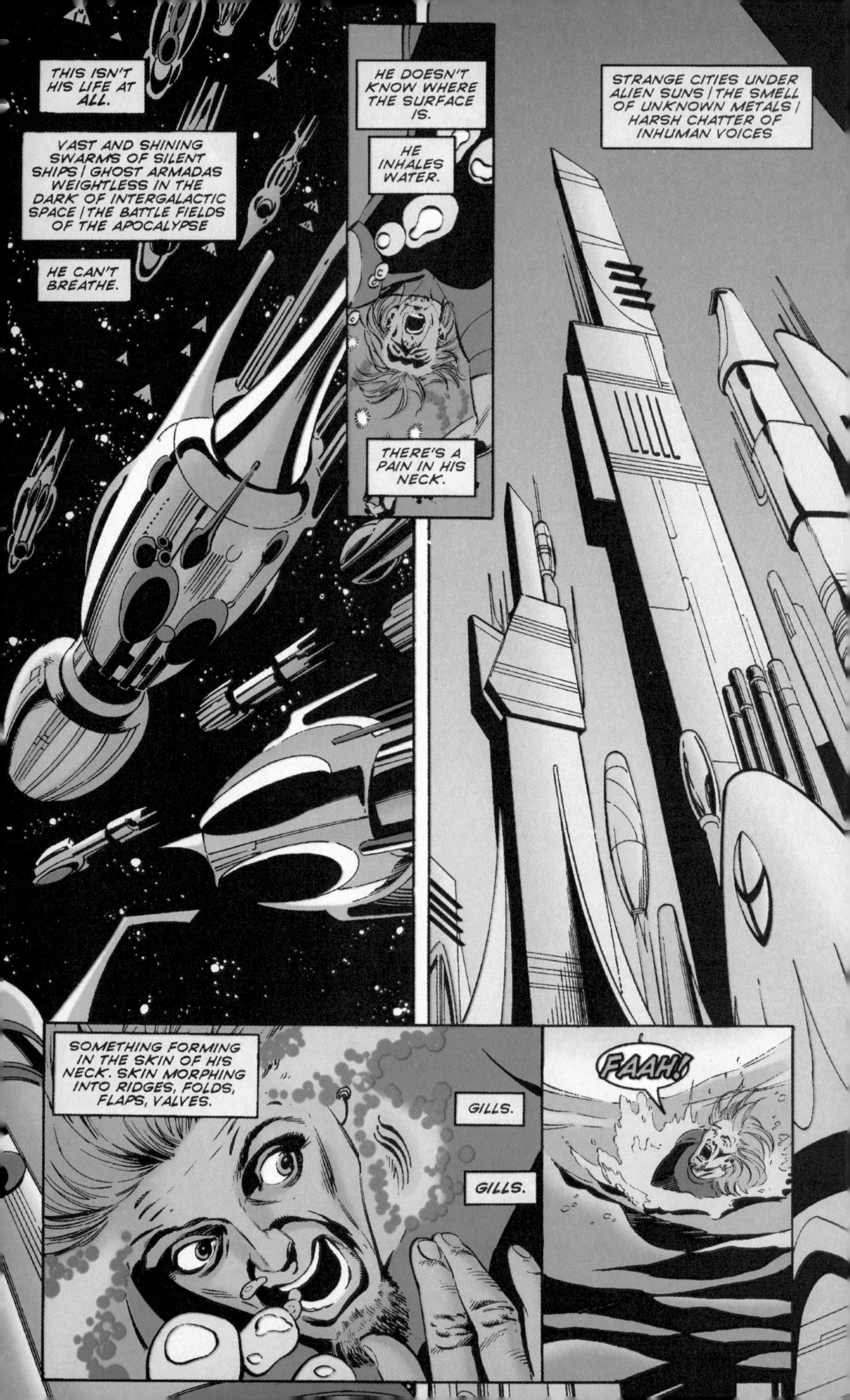
THIS ISN'T HIS LIFE AT ALL.
VAST AND SHINING SWARMS OF SILENT SHIPS | GHOST ARMADAS WEIGHTLESS IN THE DARK OF INTERGALACTIC SPACE | THE BATTLE FIELDS OF THE APOCALYPSE
HE CAN'T BREATHE.
HE DOESN'T KNOW WHERE THE SURFACE IS.
HE INHALES WATER.
THERE'S A PAIN IN HIS NECK.
STRANGE CITIES UNDER ALIEN SUNS | THE SMELL OF UNKNOWN METALS | HARSH CHATTER OF INHUMAN VOICES
SOMETHING FORMING IN THE SKIN OF HIS NECK. SKIN MORPHING INTO RIDGES, FOLDS, FLAPS, VALVES.
GILLS.
GILLS.
FAAH!

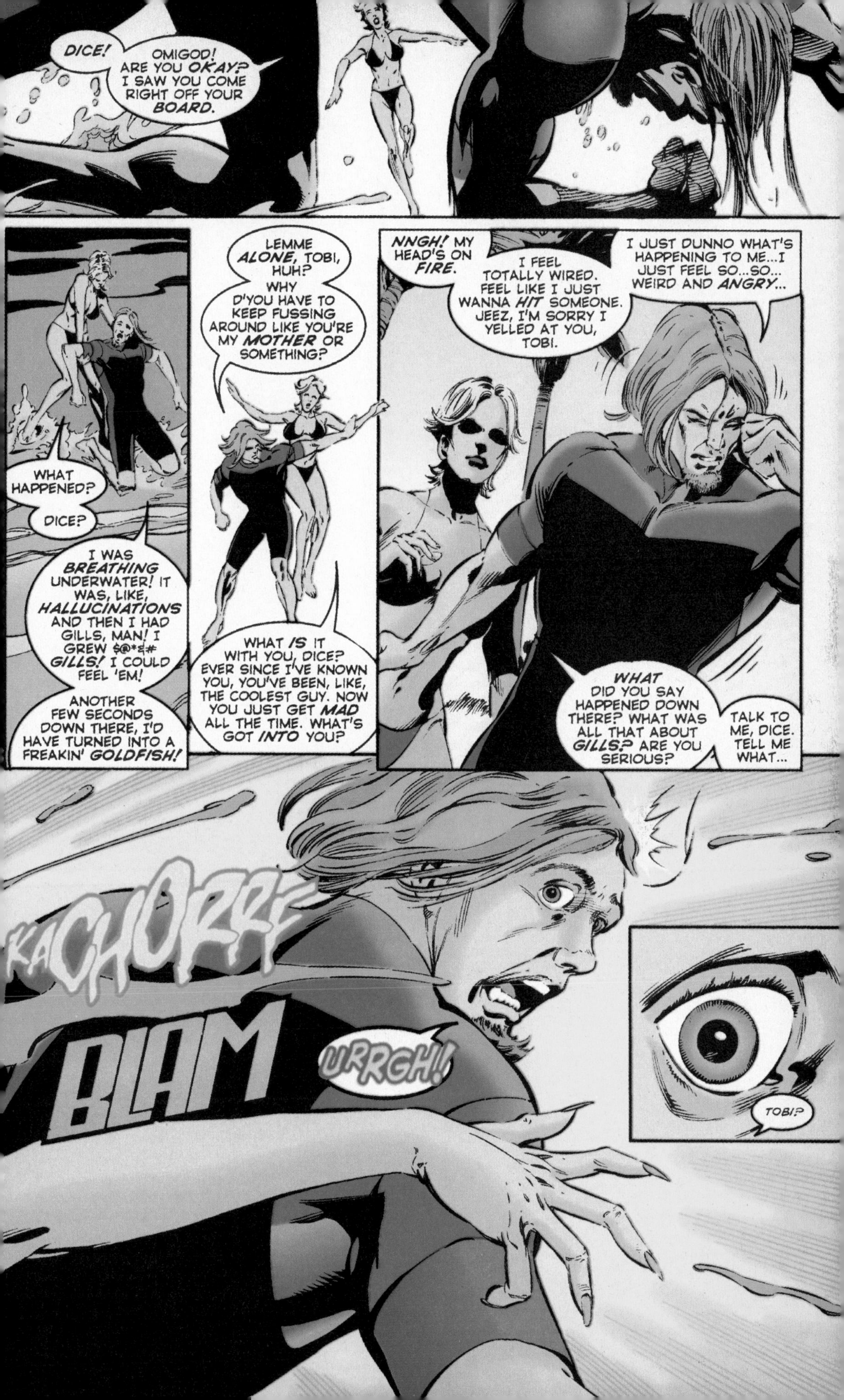
DICE!
OMIGOD! ARE YOU OKAY? I SAW YOU COME RIGHT OFF YOUR BOARD.
WHAT HAPPENED?
DICE?
I WAS BREATHING UNDERWATER! IT WAS, LIKE, HALLUCINATIONS AND THEN I HAD GILLS, MAN! I GREW $@*&# GILLS! I COULD FEEL 'EM!
ANOTHER FEW SECONDS DOWN THERE, I'D HAVE TURNED INTO A FREAKIN' GOLDFISH!
LEMME ALONE, TOBI, HUH? WHY D'YOU HAVE TO KEEP FUSSING AROUND LIKE YOU'RE MY MOTHER OR SOMETHING?
WHAT IS IT WITH YOU, DICE? EVER SINCE I'VE KNOWN YOU, YOU'VE BEEN, LIKE, THE COOLEST GUY. NOW YOU JUST GET MAD ALL THE TIME. WHAT'S GOT INTO YOU?
NNGH! MY HEAD'S ON FIRE.
I FEEL TOTALLY WIRED. FEEL LIKE I JUST WANNA HIT SOMEONE. JEEZ, I'M SORRY I YELLED AT YOU, TOBI.
I JUST DUNNO WHAT'S HAPPENING TO ME...I JUST FEEL SO...SO... WEIRD AND ANGRY...
WHAT DID YOU SAY HAPPENED DOWN THERE? WHAT WAS ALL THAT ABOUT GILLS? ARE YOU SERIOUS?
TALK TO ME, DICE. TELL ME WHAT...
KACHORRE
BLAM
URRGH!
TOBI?

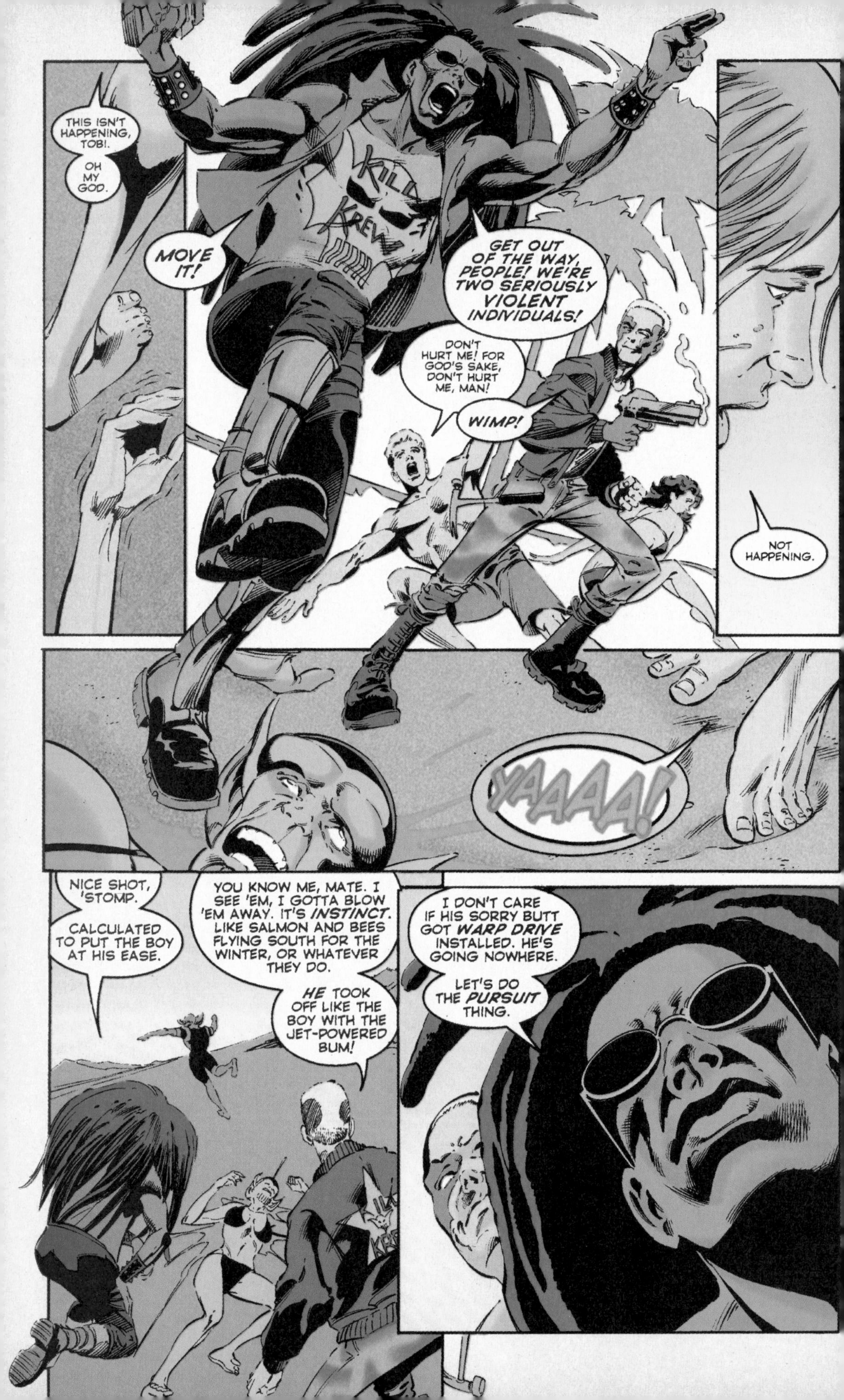
THIS ISN'T HAPPENING, TOBI.
OH MY GOD.
MOVE IT!
GET OUT OF THE WAY, PEOPLE! WE'RE TWO SERIOUSLY VIOLENT INDIVIDUALS!
DON'T HURT ME! FOR GOD'S SAKE, DON'T HURT ME, MAN!
WIMP!
NOT HAPPENING.
YAAAA!
NICE SHOT, 'STOMP.
CALCULATED TO PUT THE BOY AT HIS EASE.
YOU KNOW ME, MATE. I SEE 'EM, I GOTTA BLOW 'EM AWAY. IT'S INSTINCT. LIKE SALMON AND BEES FLYING SOUTH FOR THE WINTER, OR WHATEVER THEY DO.
HE TOOK OFF LIKE THE BOY WITH THE JET-POWERED BUM!
I DON'T CARE IF HIS SORRY BUTT GOT WARP DRIVE INSTALLED. HE'S GOING NOWHERE.
LET'S DO THE PURSUIT THING.

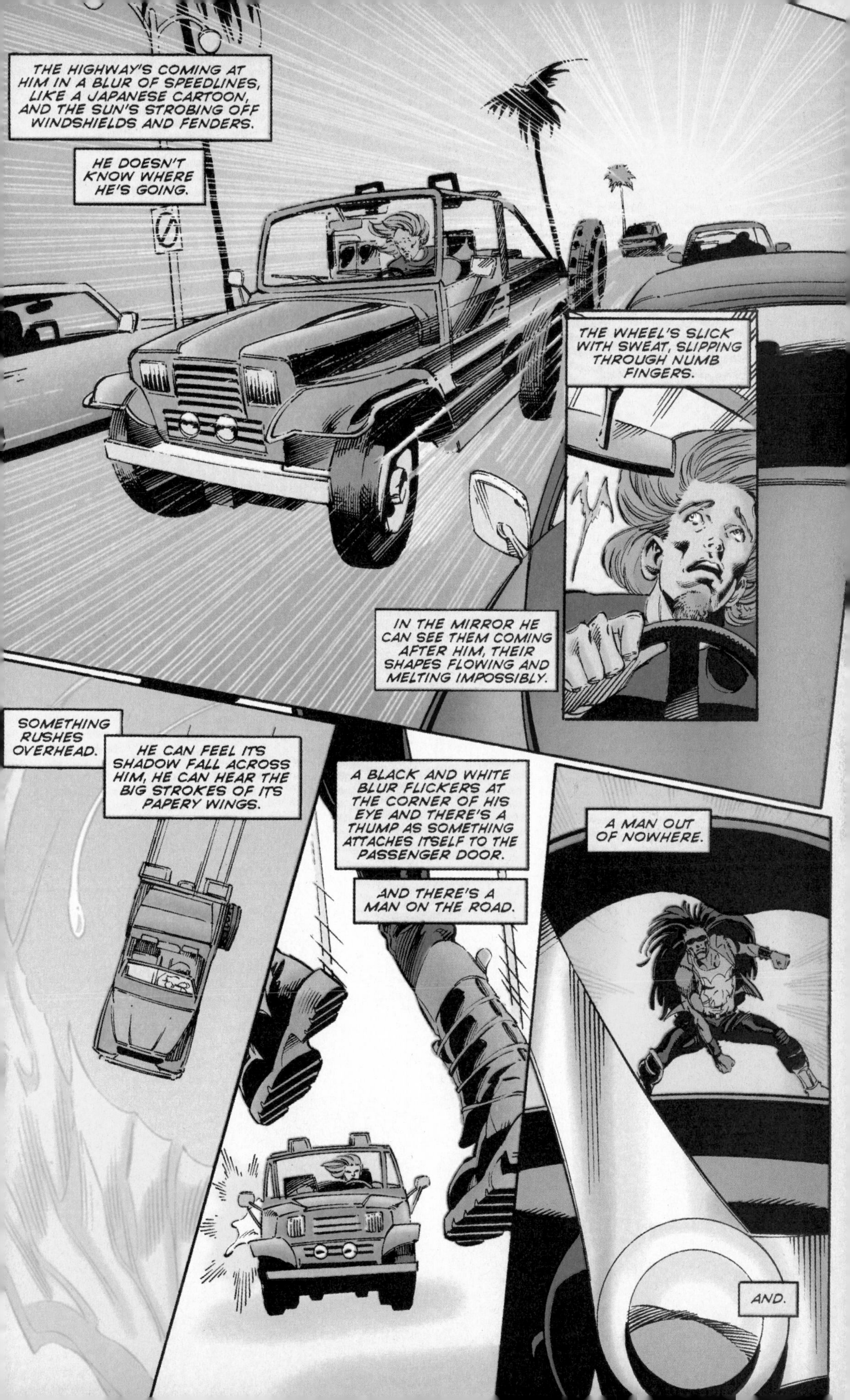
THE HIGHWAY'S COMING AT HIM IN A BLUR OF SPEEDLINES, LIKE A JAPANESE CARTOON, AND THE SUN'S STROBING OFF WINDSHIELDS AND FENDERS.
HE DOESN'T KNOW WHERE HE'S GOING.
THE WHEEL'S SLICK WITH SWEAT, SLIPPING THROUGH NUMB FINGERS.
IN THE MIRROR HE CAN SEE THEM COMING AFTER HIM, THEIR SHAPES FLOWING AND MELTING IMPOSSIBLY.
SOMETHING RUSHES OVERHEAD.
HE CAN FEEL ITS SHADOW FALL ACROSS HIM, HE CAN HEAR THE BIG STROKES OF ITS PAPERY WINGS.
A BLACK AND WHITE BLUR FLICKERS AT THE CORNER OF HIS EYE AND THERE'S A THUMP AS SOMETHING ATTACHES ITSELF TO THE PASSENGER DOOR.
AND THERE'S A MAN ON THE ROAD.
A MAN OUT OF NOWHERE.
AND.

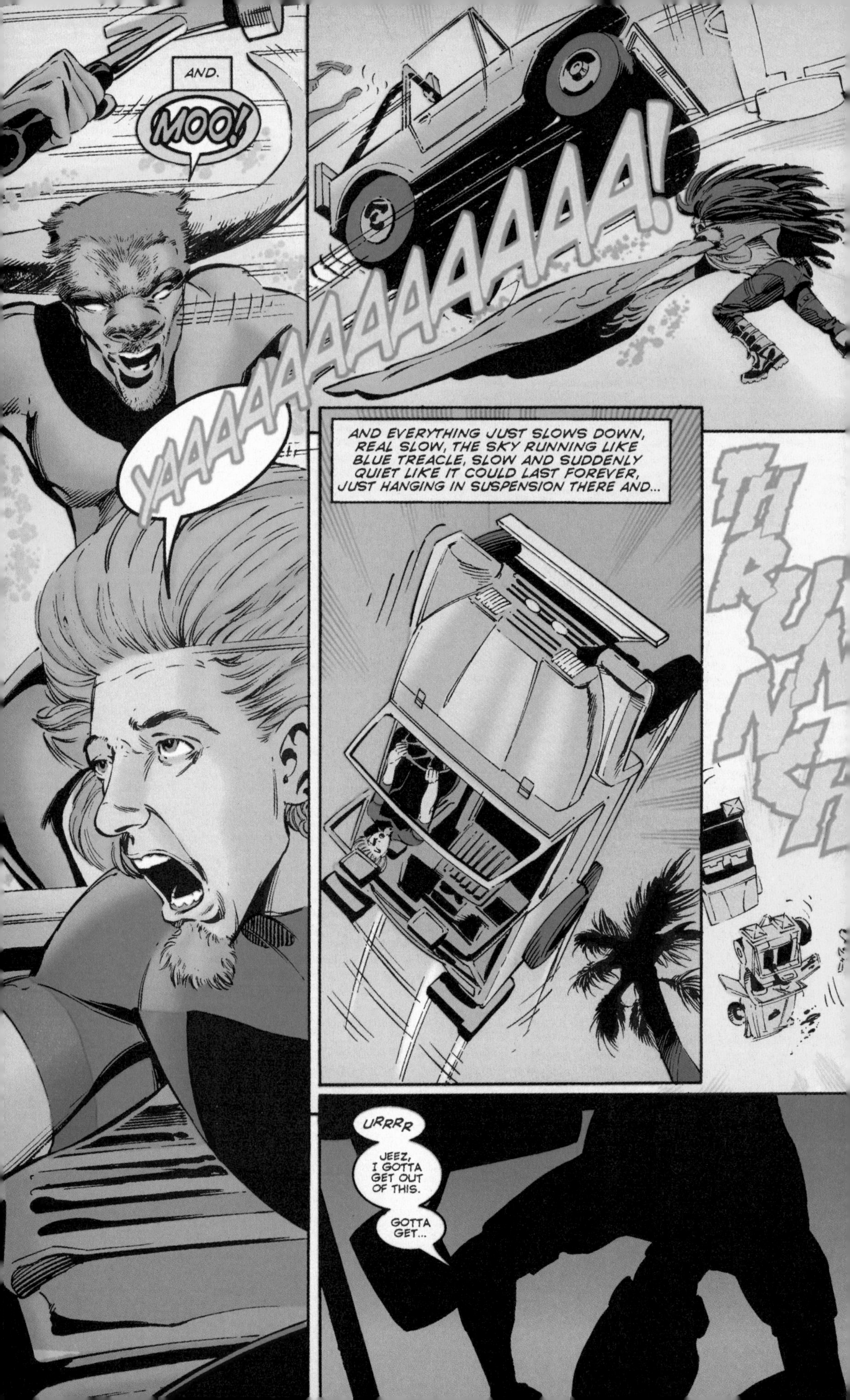
AND.
MOO!
YAAAAAAAAAAAAAA!
AND EVERYTHING JUST SLOWS DOWN, REAL SLOW, THE SKY RUNNING LIKE BLUE TREACLE, SLOW AND SUDDENLY QUIET LIKE IT COULD LAST FOREVER, JUST HANGING IN SUSPENSION THERE AND...
URRRR
JEEZ, I GOTTA GET OUT OF THIS.
GOTTA GET...

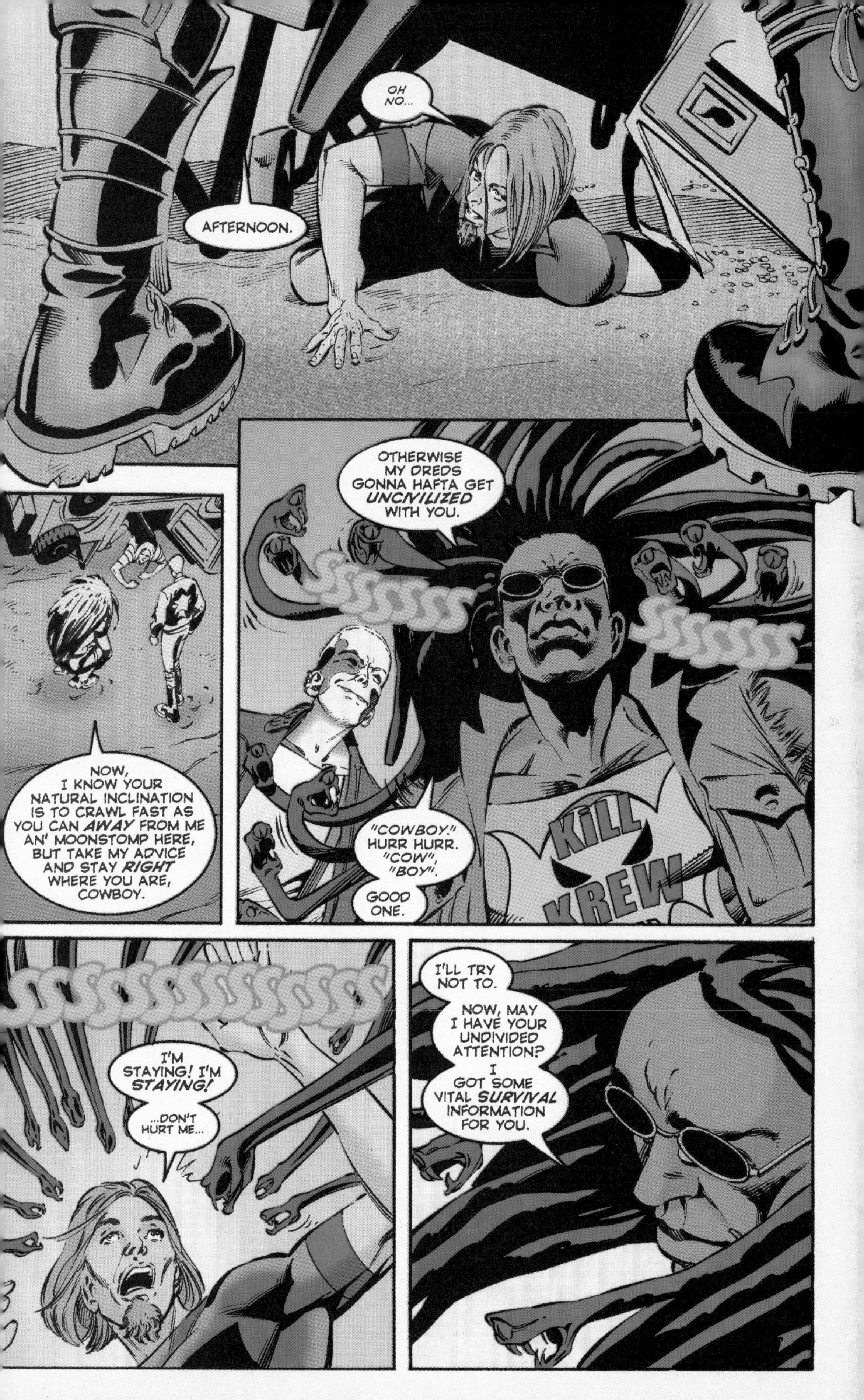

OH NO...
AFTERNOON.
OTHERWISE MY DREDS GONNA HAFTA GET UNCIVILIZED WITH YOU.
SSSSSS
SSSSSS
NOW, I KNOW YOUR NATURAL INCLINATION IS TO CRAWL FAST AS YOU CAN AWAY FROM ME AN' MOONSTOMP HERE, BUT TAKE MY ADVICE AND STAY RIGHT WHERE YOU ARE, COWBOY.
"COWBOY." HURR HURR. "COW", "BOY".
GOOD ONE.
KILL KREW
SSSSSSSSSSSSSS
I'M STAYING! I'M STAYING!
...DON'T HURT ME...
I'LL TRY NOT TO.
NOW, MAY I HAVE YOUR UNDIVIDED ATTENTION?
I GOT SOME VITAL SURVIVAL INFORMATION FOR YOU.

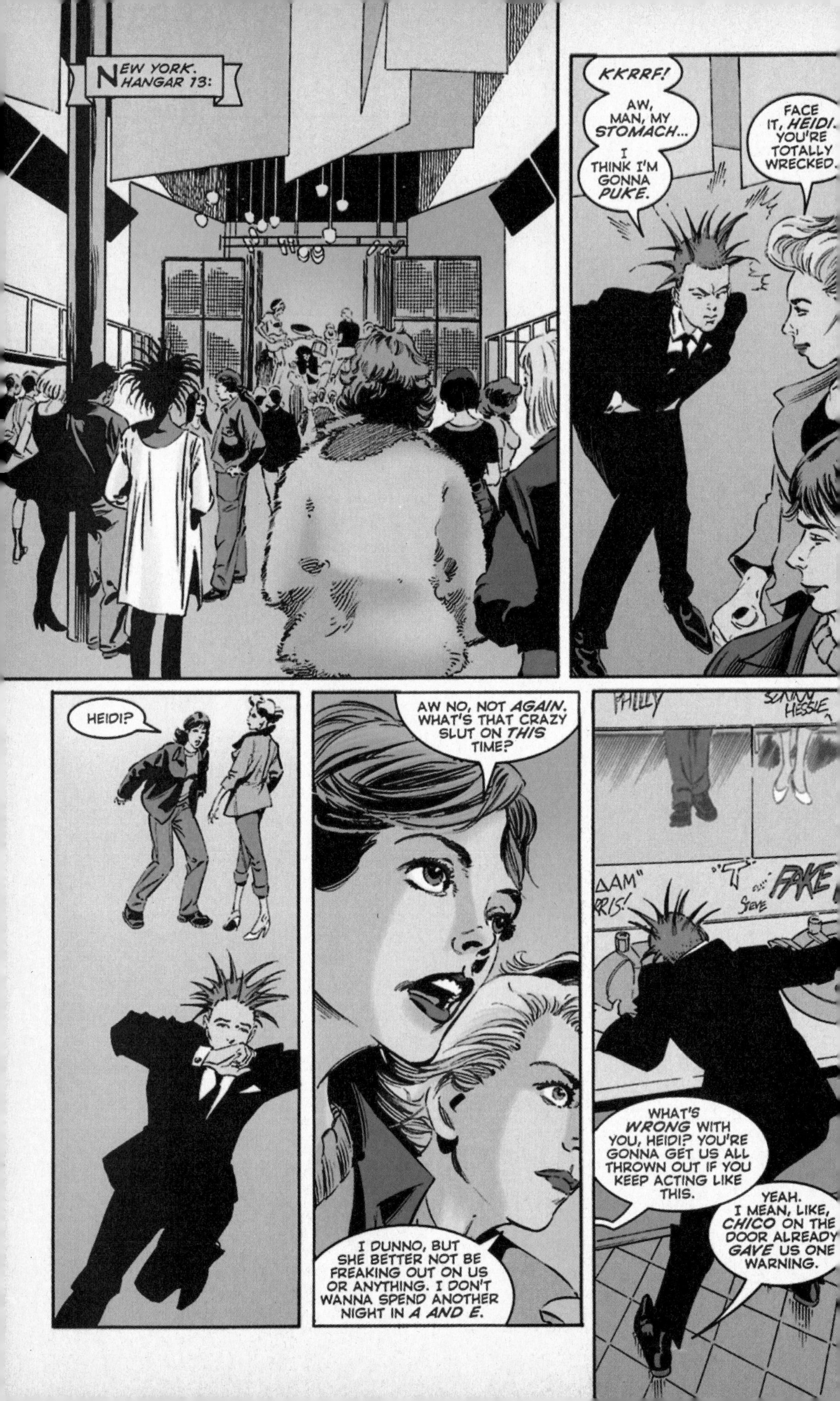

NEW YORK. HANGAR 13:
KKRRF!
AW, MAN, MY STOMACH...
I THINK I'M GONNA PUKE.
FACE IT, HEIDI. YOU'RE TOTALLY WRECKED.
HEIDI?
AW NO, NOT AGAIN. WHAT'S THAT CRAZY SLUT ON THIS TIME?
I DUNNO, BUT SHE BETTER NOT BE FREAKING OUT ON US OR ANYTHING. I DON'T WANNA SPEND ANOTHER NIGHT IN A AND E.
PHILLY
HESSIE
FAKE
STEVE
WHAT'S WRONG WITH YOU, HEIDI? YOU'RE GONNA GET US ALL THROWN OUT IF YOU KEEP ACTING LIKE THIS.
YEAH. I MEAN, LIKE, CHICO ON THE DOOR ALREADY GAVE US ONE WARNING.

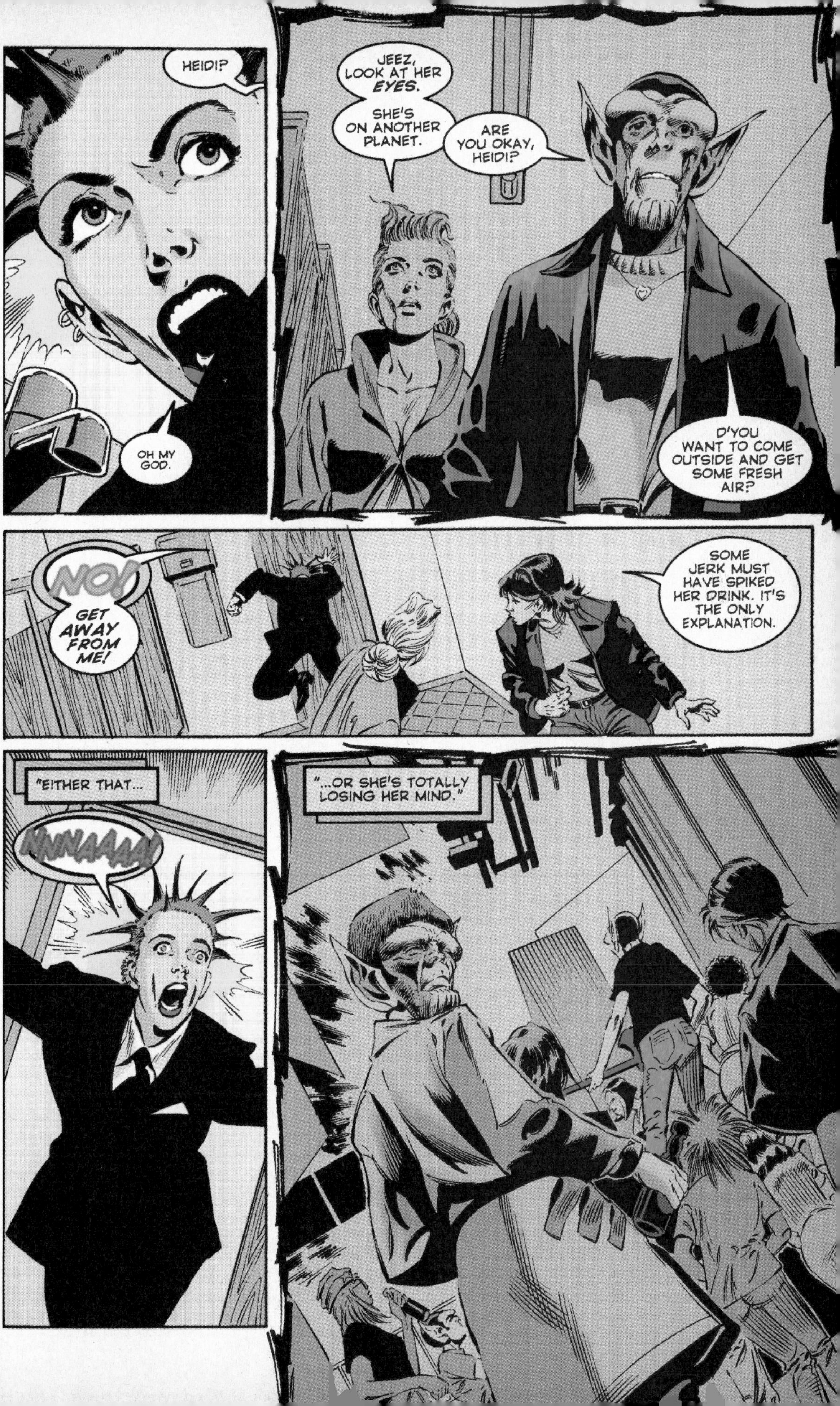
HEIDI?
OH MY GOD.
JEEZ, LOOK AT HER *EYES.*
SHE'S ON ANOTHER PLANET.
ARE YOU OKAY, HEIDI?
D'YOU WANT TO COME OUTSIDE AND GET SOME FRESH AIR?
NO!
GET *AWAY* FROM ME!
SOME JERK MUST HAVE SPIKED HER DRINK. IT'S THE ONLY EXPLANATION.
"EITHER THAT...
NNNAAAA!
"...OR SHE'S TOTALLY LOSING HER MIND."

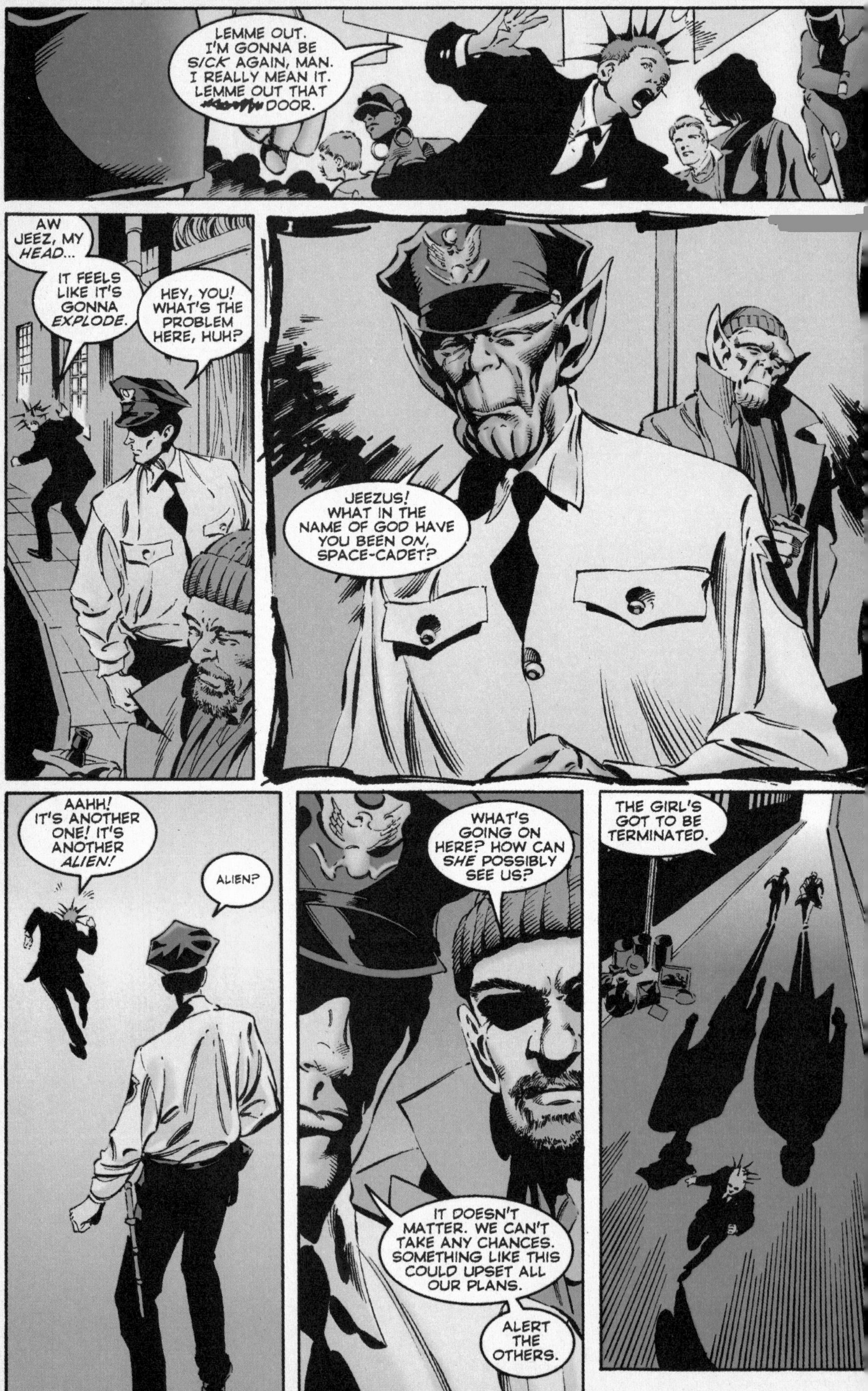

LEMME OUT. I'M GONNA BE SICK AGAIN, MAN. I REALLY MEAN IT. LEMME OUT THAT [redacted] DOOR.
AW JEEZ, MY HEAD...
IT FEELS LIKE IT'S GONNA EXPLODE.
HEY, YOU! WHAT'S THE PROBLEM HERE, HUH?
JEEZUS! WHAT IN THE NAME OF GOD HAVE YOU BEEN ON, SPACE-CADET?
AAHH! IT'S ANOTHER ONE! IT'S ANOTHER ALIEN!
ALIEN?
WHAT'S GOING ON HERE? HOW CAN SHE POSSIBLY SEE US?
IT DOESN'T MATTER. WE CAN'T TAKE ANY CHANCES. SOMETHING LIKE THIS COULD UPSET ALL OUR PLANS.
ALERT THE OTHERS.
THE GIRL'S GOT TO BE TERMINATED.

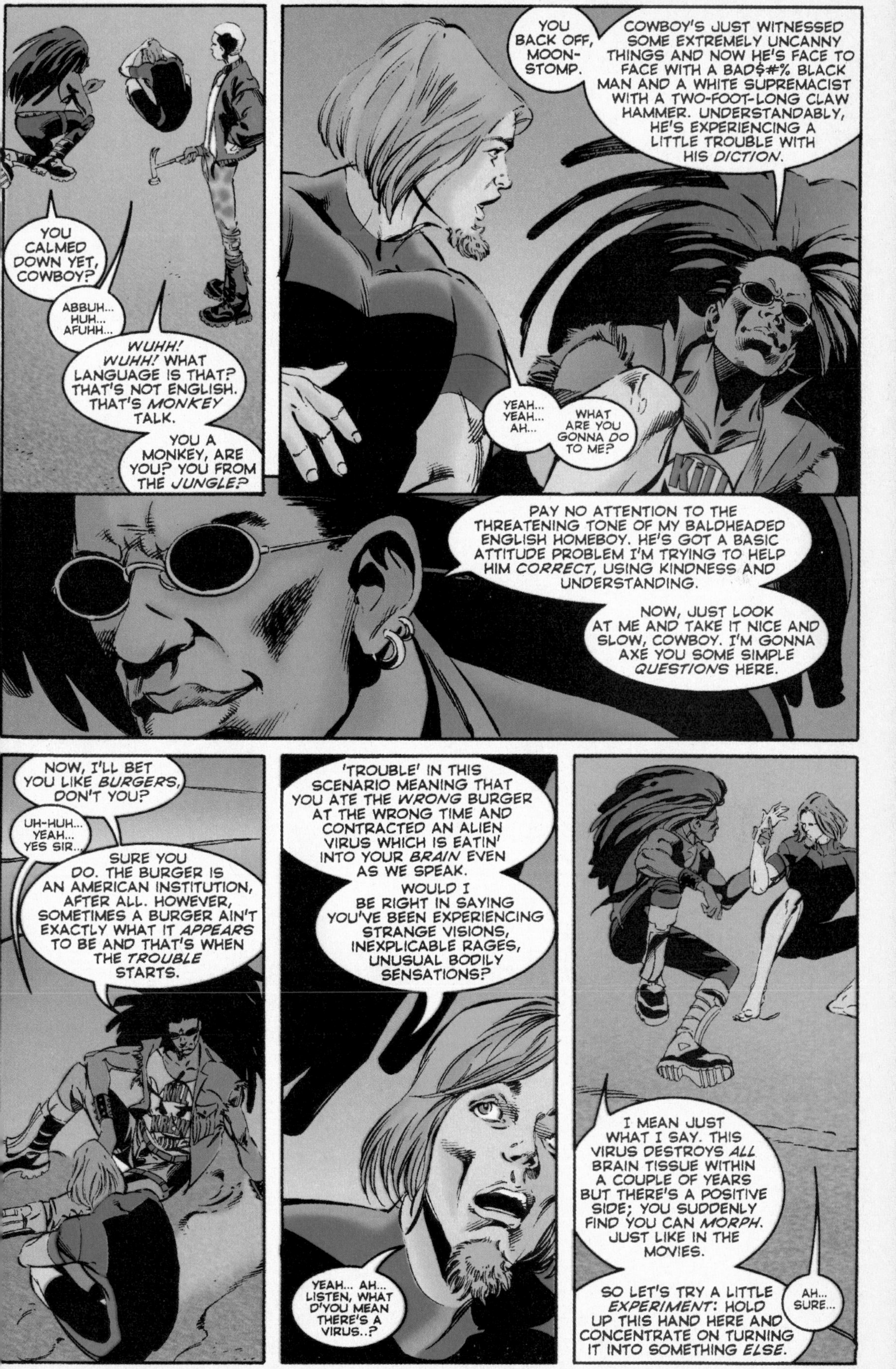
YOU CALMED DOWN YET, COWBOY?
ABBUH... HUH... AFUHH...
WUHH! WUHH! WHAT LANGUAGE IS THAT? THAT'S NOT ENGLISH. THAT'S MONKEY TALK.
YOU A MONKEY, ARE YOU? YOU FROM THE JUNGLE?
YOU BACK OFF, MOON-STOMP.
COWBOY'S JUST WITNESSED SOME EXTREMELY UNCANNY THINGS AND NOW HE'S FACE TO FACE WITH A BAD$#% BLACK MAN AND A WHITE SUPREMACIST WITH A TWO-FOOT-LONG CLAW HAMMER. UNDERSTANDABLY, HE'S EXPERIENCING A LITTLE TROUBLE WITH HIS DICTION.
YEAH... YEAH... AH...
WHAT ARE YOU GONNA DO TO ME?
PAY NO ATTENTION TO THE THREATENING TONE OF MY BALDHEADED ENGLISH HOMEBOY. HE'S GOT A BASIC ATTITUDE PROBLEM I'M TRYING TO HELP HIM CORRECT, USING KINDNESS AND UNDERSTANDING.
NOW, JUST LOOK AT ME AND TAKE IT NICE AND SLOW, COWBOY. I'M GONNA AXE YOU SOME SIMPLE QUESTIONS HERE.
NOW, I'LL BET YOU LIKE BURGERS, DON'T YOU?
UH-HUH... YEAH... YES SIR...
SURE YOU DO. THE BURGER IS AN AMERICAN INSTITUTION, AFTER ALL. HOWEVER, SOMETIMES A BURGER AIN'T EXACTLY WHAT IT APPEARS TO BE AND THAT'S WHEN THE TROUBLE STARTS.
'TROUBLE' IN THIS SCENARIO MEANING THAT YOU ATE THE WRONG BURGER AT THE WRONG TIME AND CONTRACTED AN ALIEN VIRUS WHICH IS EATIN' INTO YOUR BRAIN EVEN AS WE SPEAK.
WOULD I BE RIGHT IN SAYING YOU'VE BEEN EXPERIENCING STRANGE VISIONS, INEXPLICABLE RAGES, UNUSUAL BODILY SENSATIONS?
YEAH... AH... LISTEN, WHAT D'YOU MEAN THERE'S A VIRUS..?
I MEAN JUST WHAT I SAY. THIS VIRUS DESTROYS ALL BRAIN TISSUE WITHIN A COUPLE OF YEARS BUT THERE'S A POSITIVE SIDE; YOU SUDDENLY FIND YOU CAN MORPH. JUST LIKE IN THE MOVIES.
SO LET'S TRY A LITTLE EXPERIMENT: HOLD UP THIS HAND HERE AND CONCENTRATE ON TURNING IT INTO SOMETHING ELSE.
AH... SURE...

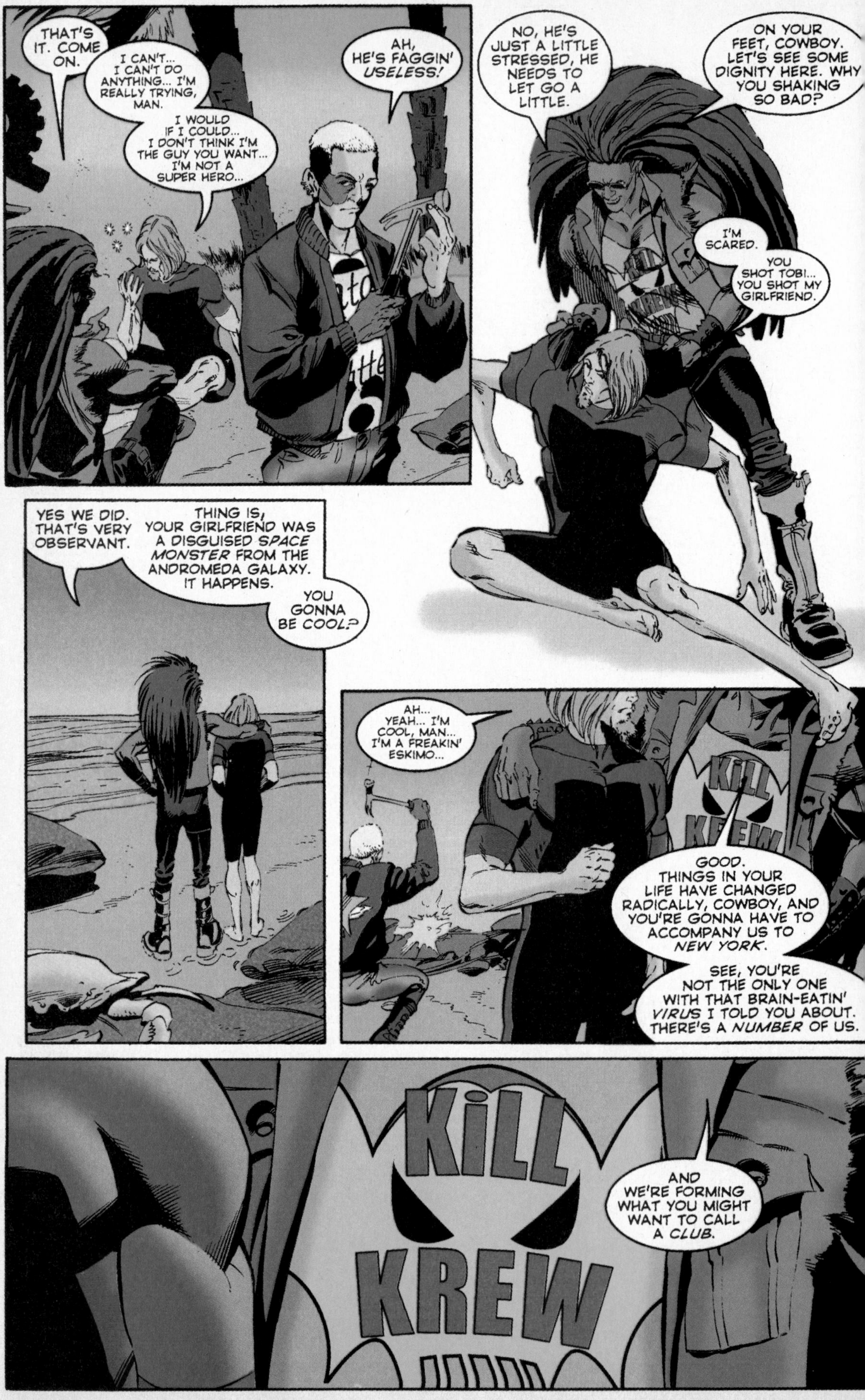

THAT'S IT. COME ON.
I CAN'T... I CAN'T DO ANYTHING... I'M REALLY TRYING, MAN.
I WOULD IF I COULD... I DON'T THINK I'M THE GUY YOU WANT... I'M NOT A SUPER HERO...
AH, HE'S FAGGIN' USELESS!
NO, HE'S JUST A LITTLE STRESSED, HE NEEDS TO LET GO A LITTLE.
ON YOUR FEET, COWBOY. LET'S SEE SOME DIGNITY HERE. WHY YOU SHAKING SO BAD?
I'M SCARED.
YOU SHOT TOBI... YOU SHOT MY GIRLFRIEND.
YES WE DID. THAT'S VERY OBSERVANT.
THING IS, YOUR GIRLFRIEND WAS A DISGUISED SPACE MONSTER FROM THE ANDROMEDA GALAXY. IT HAPPENS.
YOU GONNA BE COOL?
AH... YEAH... I'M COOL, MAN... I'M A FREAKIN' ESKIMO...
KILL KREW
GOOD. THINGS IN YOUR LIFE HAVE CHANGED RADICALLY, COWBOY, AND YOU'RE GONNA HAVE TO ACCOMPANY US TO NEW YORK.
SEE, YOU'RE NOT THE ONLY ONE WITH THAT BRAIN-EATIN' VIRUS I TOLD YOU ABOUT. THERE'S A NUMBER OF US.
KILL KREW
AND WE'RE FORMING WHAT YOU MIGHT WANT TO CALL A CLUB.

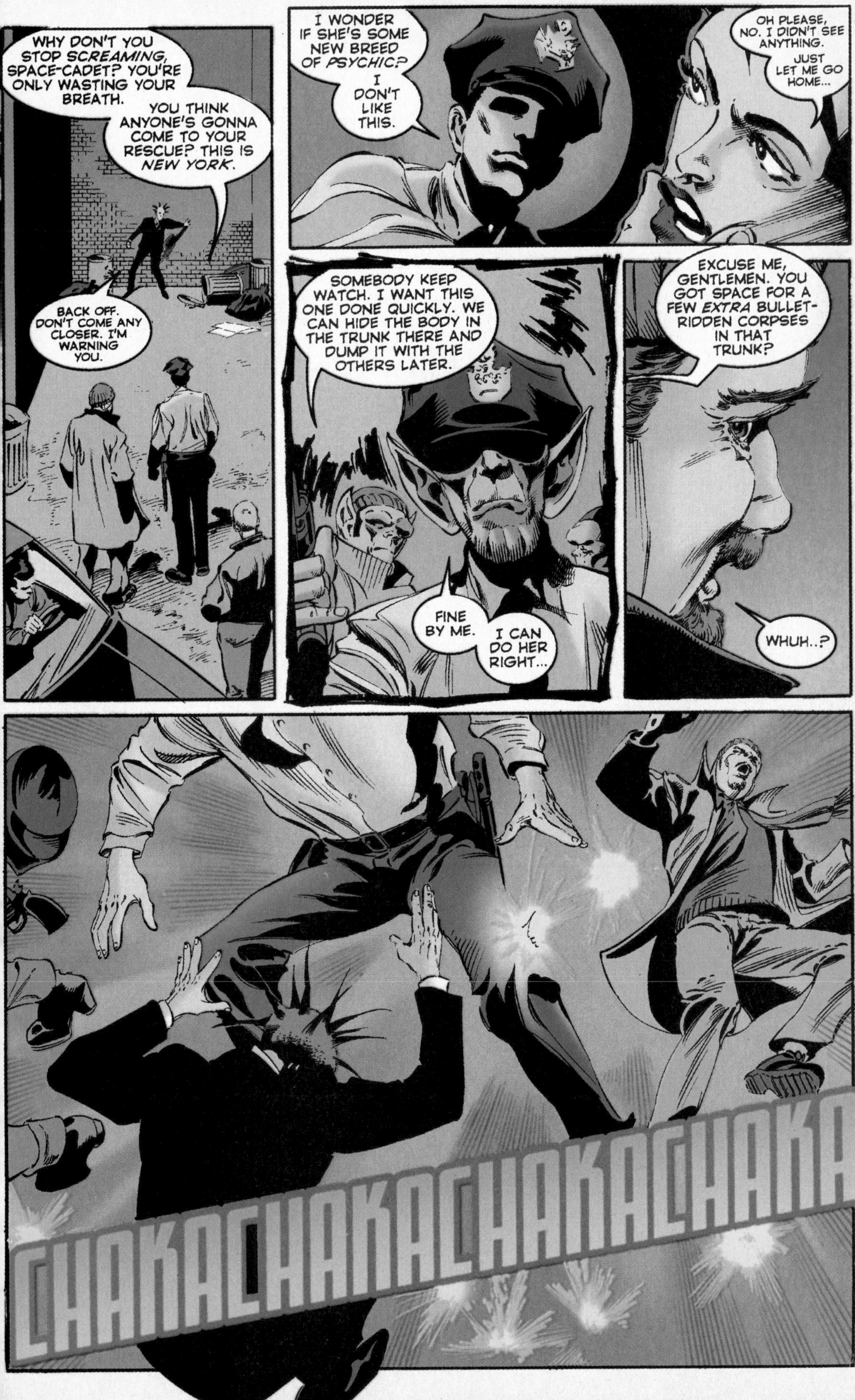
WHY DON'T YOU STOP SCREAMING, SPACE-CADET? YOU'RE ONLY WASTING YOUR BREATH.
YOU THINK ANYONE'S GONNA COME TO YOUR RESCUE? THIS IS NEW YORK.
BACK OFF. DON'T COME ANY CLOSER. I'M WARNING YOU.
I WONDER IF SHE'S SOME NEW BREED OF PSYCHIC?
I DON'T LIKE THIS.
OH PLEASE, NO. I DIDN'T SEE ANYTHING.
JUST LET ME GO HOME...
SOMEBODY KEEP WATCH. I WANT THIS ONE DONE QUICKLY. WE CAN HIDE THE BODY IN THE TRUNK THERE AND DUMP IT WITH THE OTHERS LATER.
FINE BY ME.
I CAN DO HER RIGHT...
EXCUSE ME, GENTLEMEN. YOU GOT SPACE FOR A FEW EXTRA BULLET-RIDDEN CORPSES IN THAT TRUNK?
WHUH..?
CHAKACHAKACHAKACHAKA

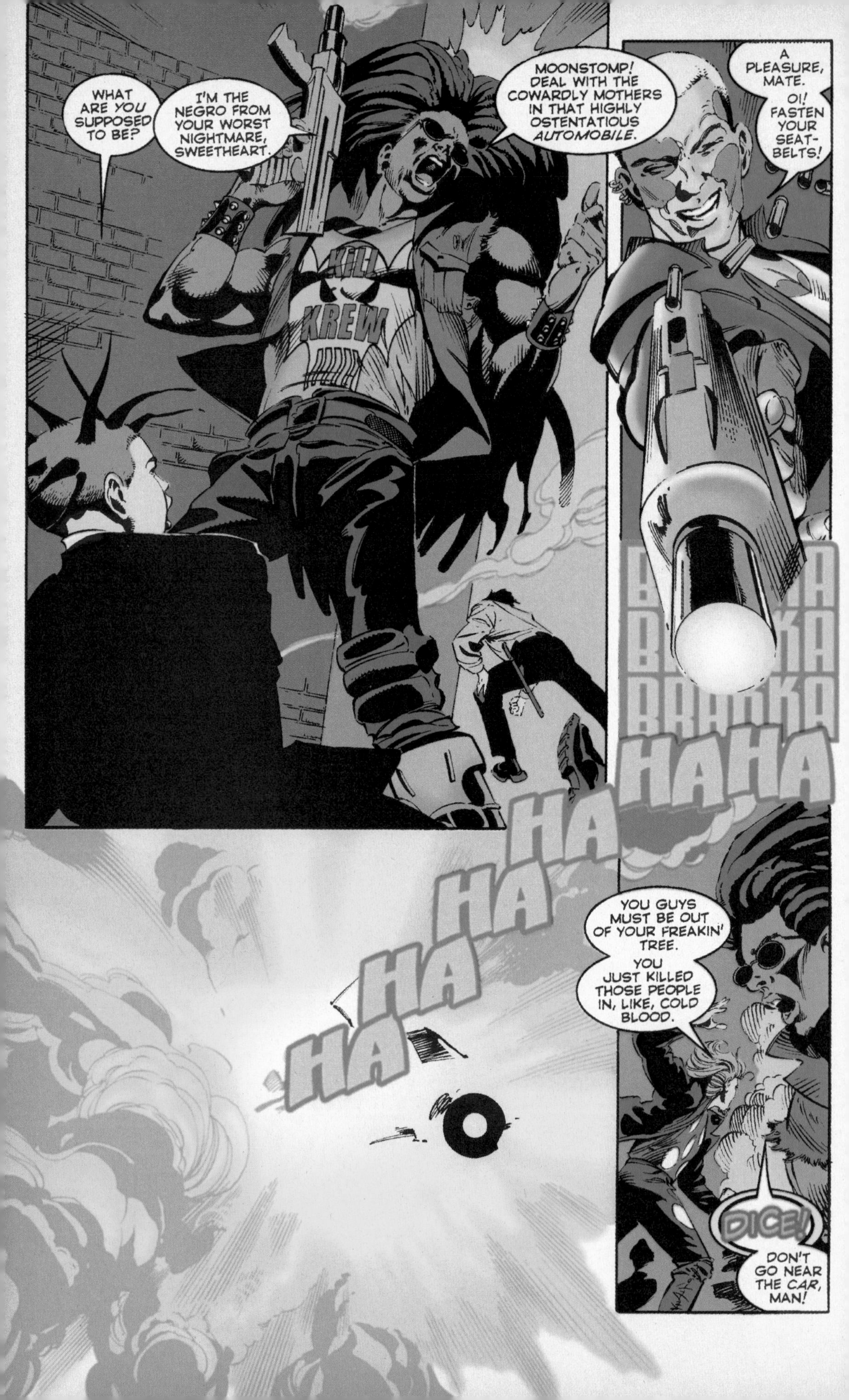

WHAT ARE YOU SUPPOSED TO BE?
I'M THE NEGRO FROM YOUR WORST NIGHTMARE, SWEETHEART.
MOONSTOMP! DEAL WITH THE COWARDLY MOTHERS IN THAT HIGHLY OSTENTATIOUS AUTOMOBILE.
KILL KREW
A PLEASURE, MATE.
OI! FASTEN YOUR SEAT-BELTS!
BRAKKA
HAHAHAHAHAHA
YOU GUYS MUST BE OUT OF YOUR FREAKIN' TREE.
YOU JUST KILLED THOSE PEOPLE IN, LIKE, COLD BLOOD.
DICE!
DON'T GO NEAR THE CAR, MAN!

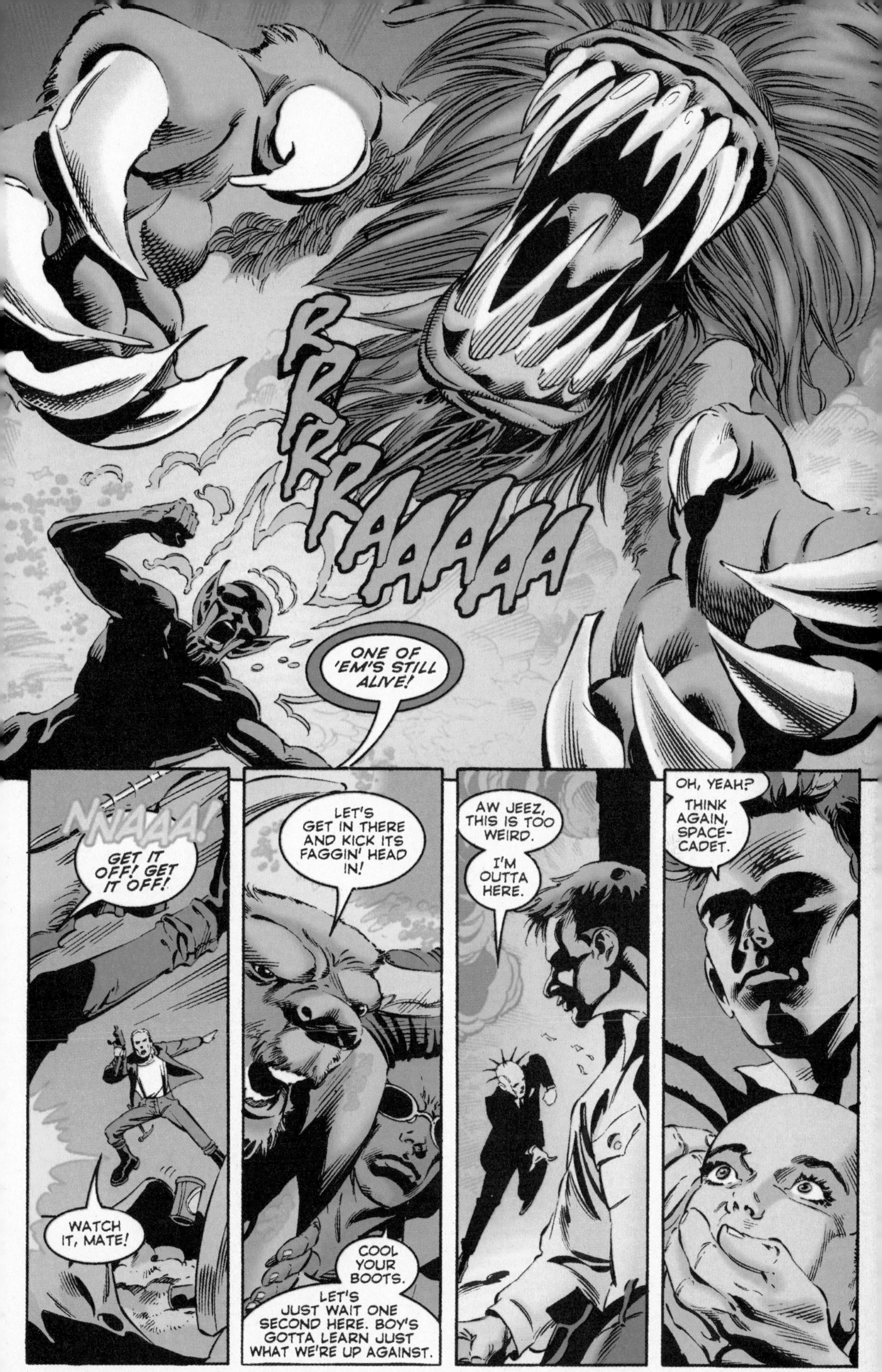
RRRRAAAAAA
ONE OF 'EM'S STILL ALIVE!
NNAAA!
GET IT OFF! GET IT OFF!
WATCH IT, MATE!
LET'S GET IN THERE AND KICK ITS FAGGIN' HEAD IN!
COOL YOUR BOOTS.
LET'S JUST WAIT ONE SECOND HERE. BOY'S GOTTA LEARN JUST WHAT WE'RE UP AGAINST.
AW JEEZ, THIS IS TOO WEIRD.
I'M OUTTA HERE.
OH, YEAH?
THINK AGAIN, SPACE-CADET.

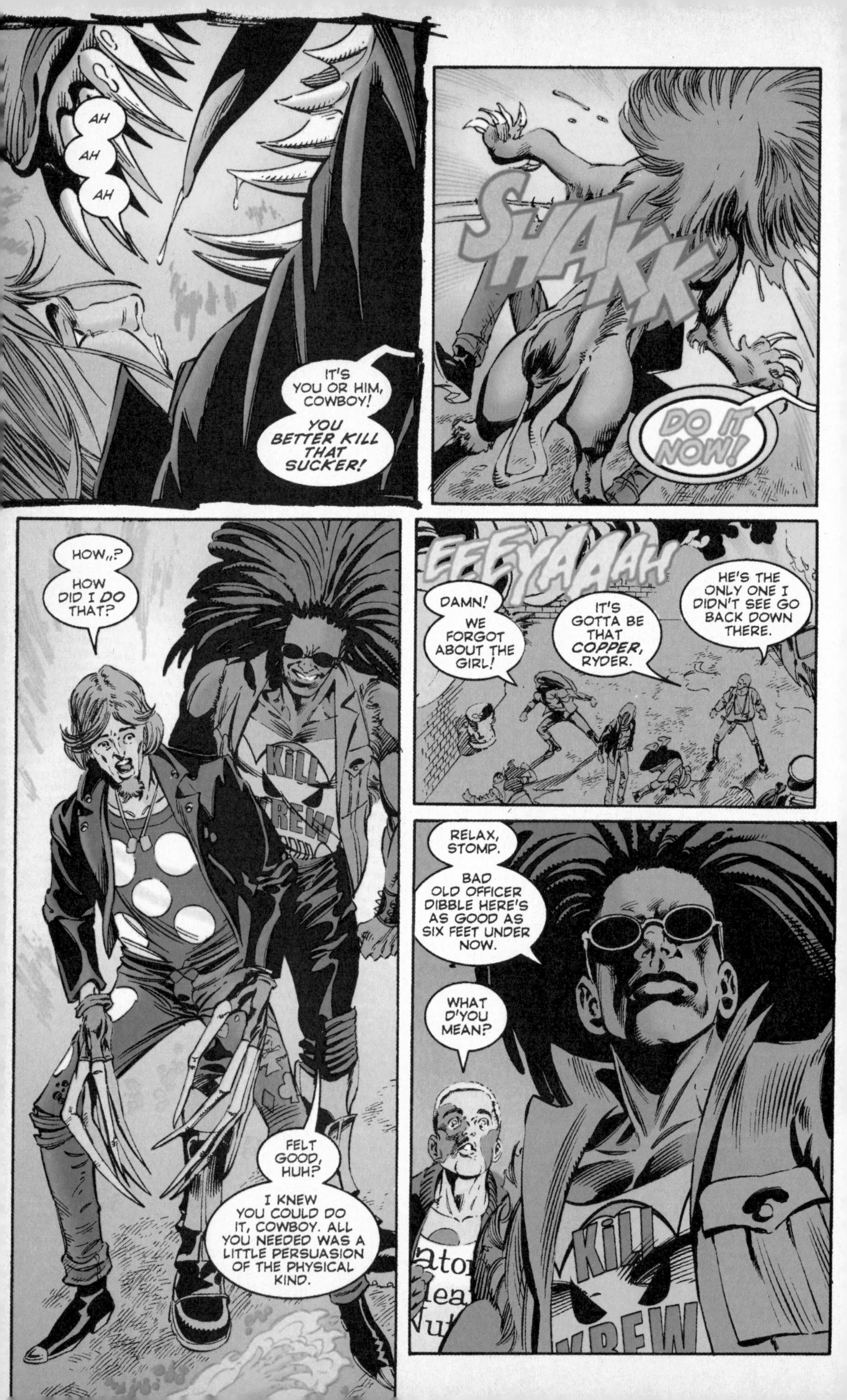
AH
AH
AH
IT'S YOU OR HIM, COWBOY!
YOU BETTER KILL THAT SUCKER!
SHAKK
DO IT NOW!
HOW..?
HOW DID I DO THAT?
FELT GOOD, HUH?
I KNEW YOU COULD DO IT, COWBOY. ALL YOU NEEDED WAS A LITTLE PERSUASION OF THE PHYSICAL KIND.
KILL KREW
EEEYAAAH
DAMN!
WE FORGOT ABOUT THE GIRL!
IT'S GOTTA BE THAT COPPER, RYDER.
HE'S THE ONLY ONE I DIDN'T SEE GO BACK DOWN THERE.
RELAX, STOMP.
BAD OLD OFFICER DIBBLE HERE'S AS GOOD AS SIX FEET UNDER NOW.
WHAT D'YOU MEAN?
KILL KREW

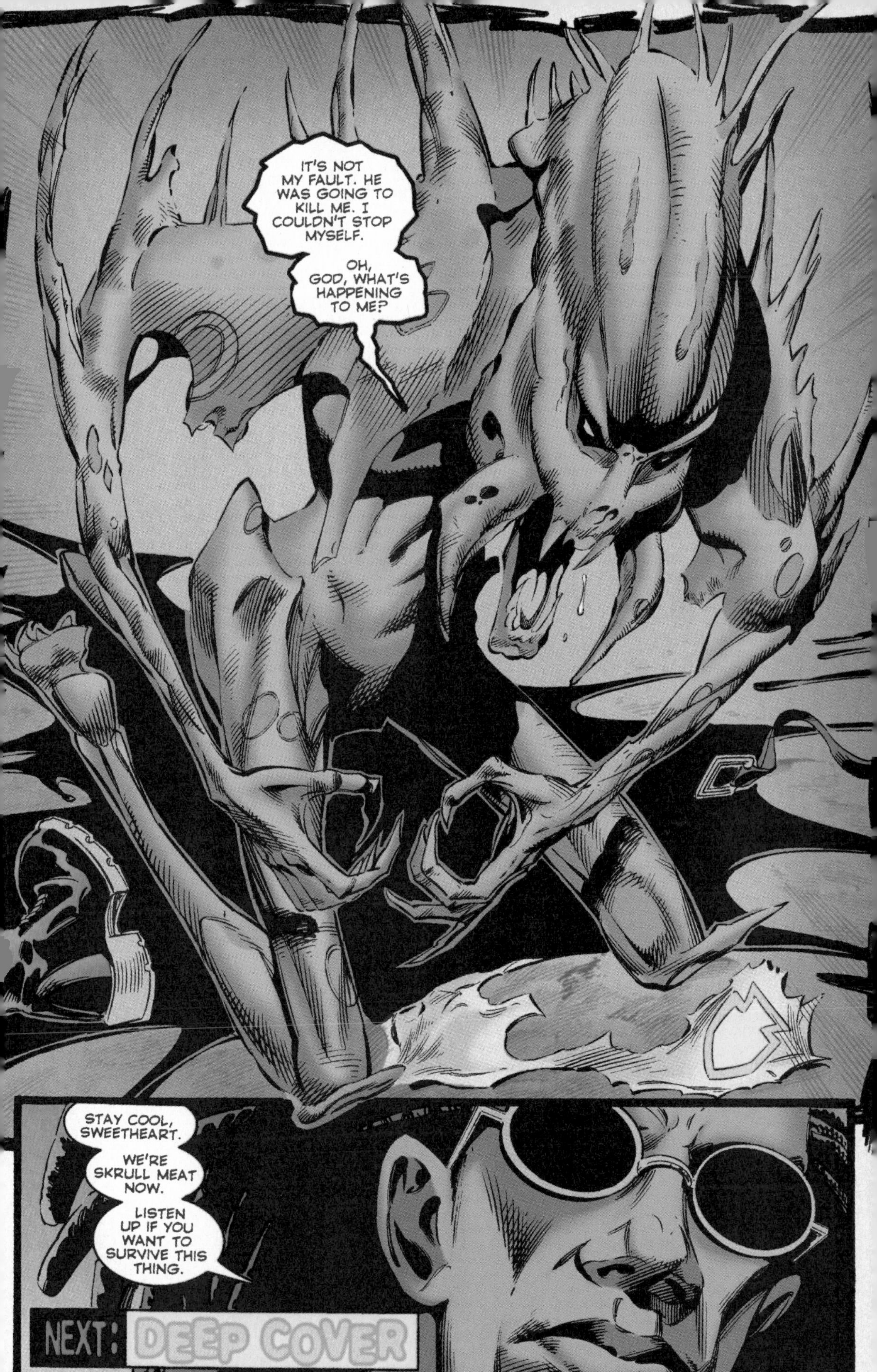
IT'S NOT MY FAULT. HE WAS GOING TO KILL ME. I COULDN'T STOP MYSELF.
OH, GOD, WHAT'S HAPPENING TO ME?
STAY COOL, SWEETHEART.
WE'RE SKRULL MEAT NOW.
LISTEN UP IF YOU WANT TO SURVIVE THIS THING.
NEXT: DEEP COVER

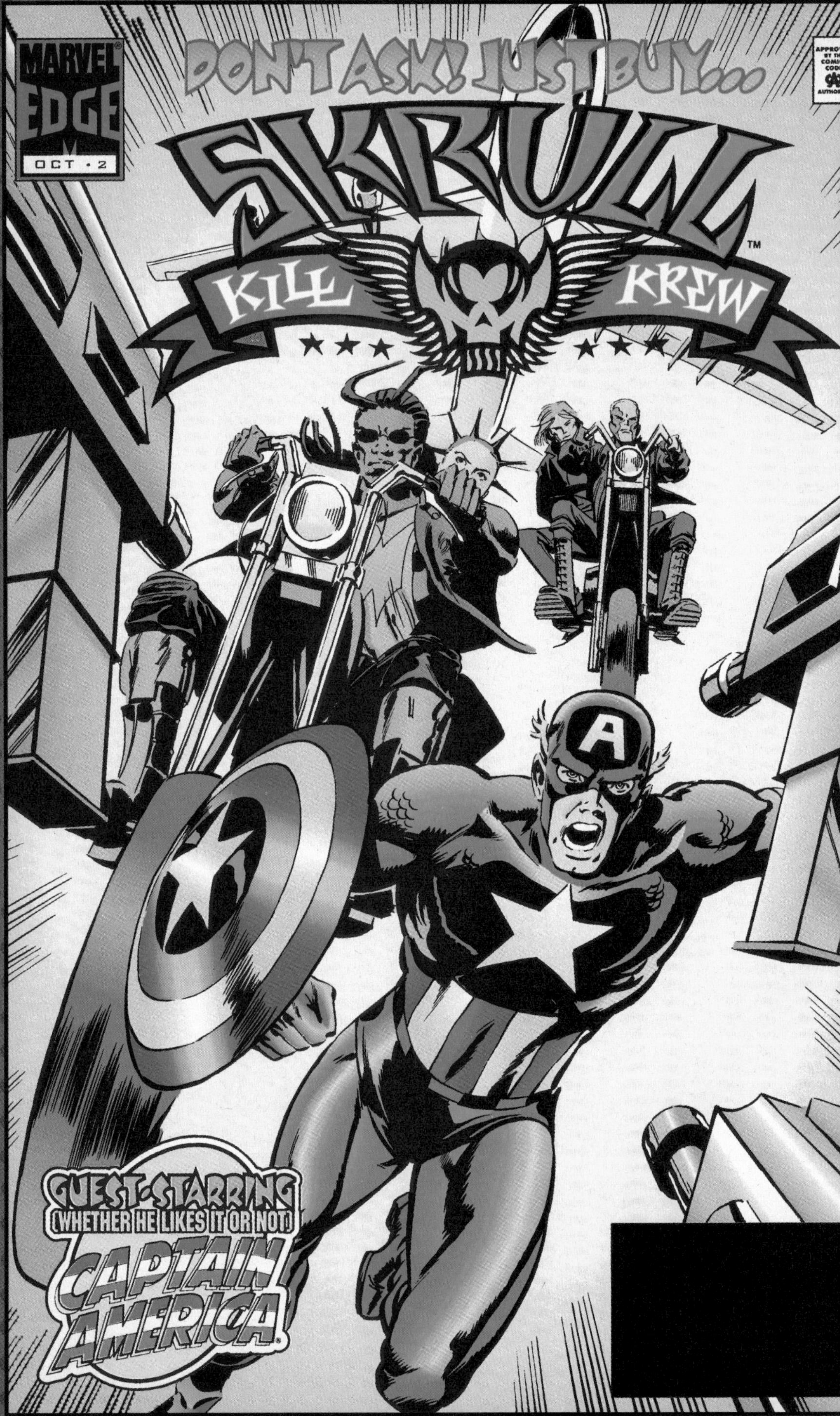
MARVEL EDGE
OCT • 2
APPROVED BY THE COMICS CODE AUTHORITY
DON'T ASK! JUST BUY...
SKRULL™
KILL KREW
GUEST-STARRING
(WHETHER HE LIKES IT OR NOT)
CAPTAIN AMERICA

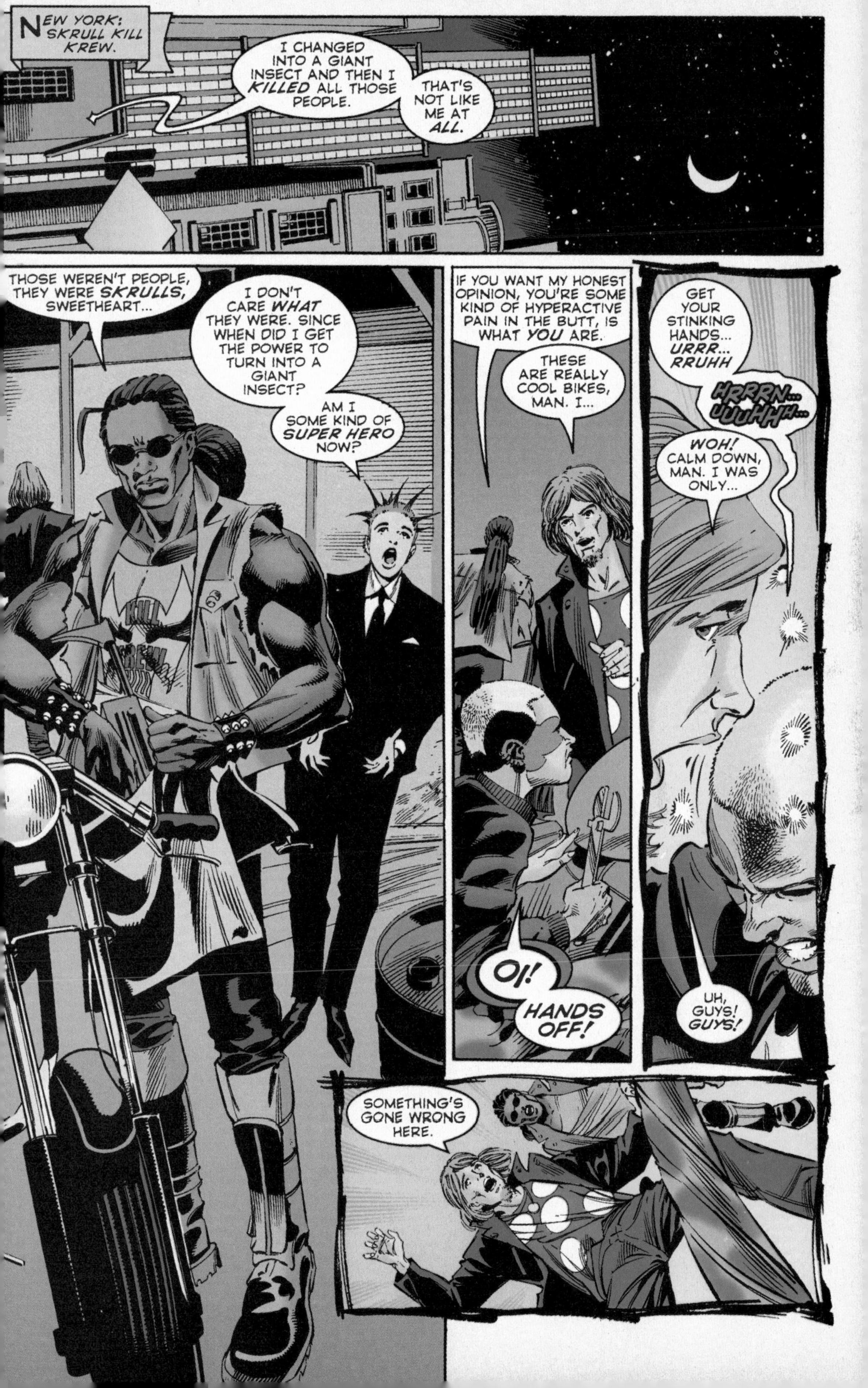
NEW YORK: SKRULL KILL KREW.
I CHANGED INTO A GIANT INSECT AND THEN I KILLED ALL THOSE PEOPLE.
THAT'S NOT LIKE ME AT ALL.
THOSE WEREN'T PEOPLE, THEY WERE SKRULLS, SWEETHEART...
I DON'T CARE WHAT THEY WERE. SINCE WHEN DID I GET THE POWER TO TURN INTO A GIANT INSECT?
AM I SOME KIND OF SUPER HERO NOW?
IF YOU WANT MY HONEST OPINION, YOU'RE SOME KIND OF HYPERACTIVE PAIN IN THE BUTT, IS WHAT YOU ARE.
THESE ARE REALLY COOL BIKES, MAN. I...
OI! HANDS OFF!
GET YOUR STINKING HANDS... URRR... RRUHH
HRRRN... UUUHHH...
WOH! CALM DOWN, MAN. I WAS ONLY...
UH, GUYS! GUYS!
SOMETHING'S GONE WRONG HERE.

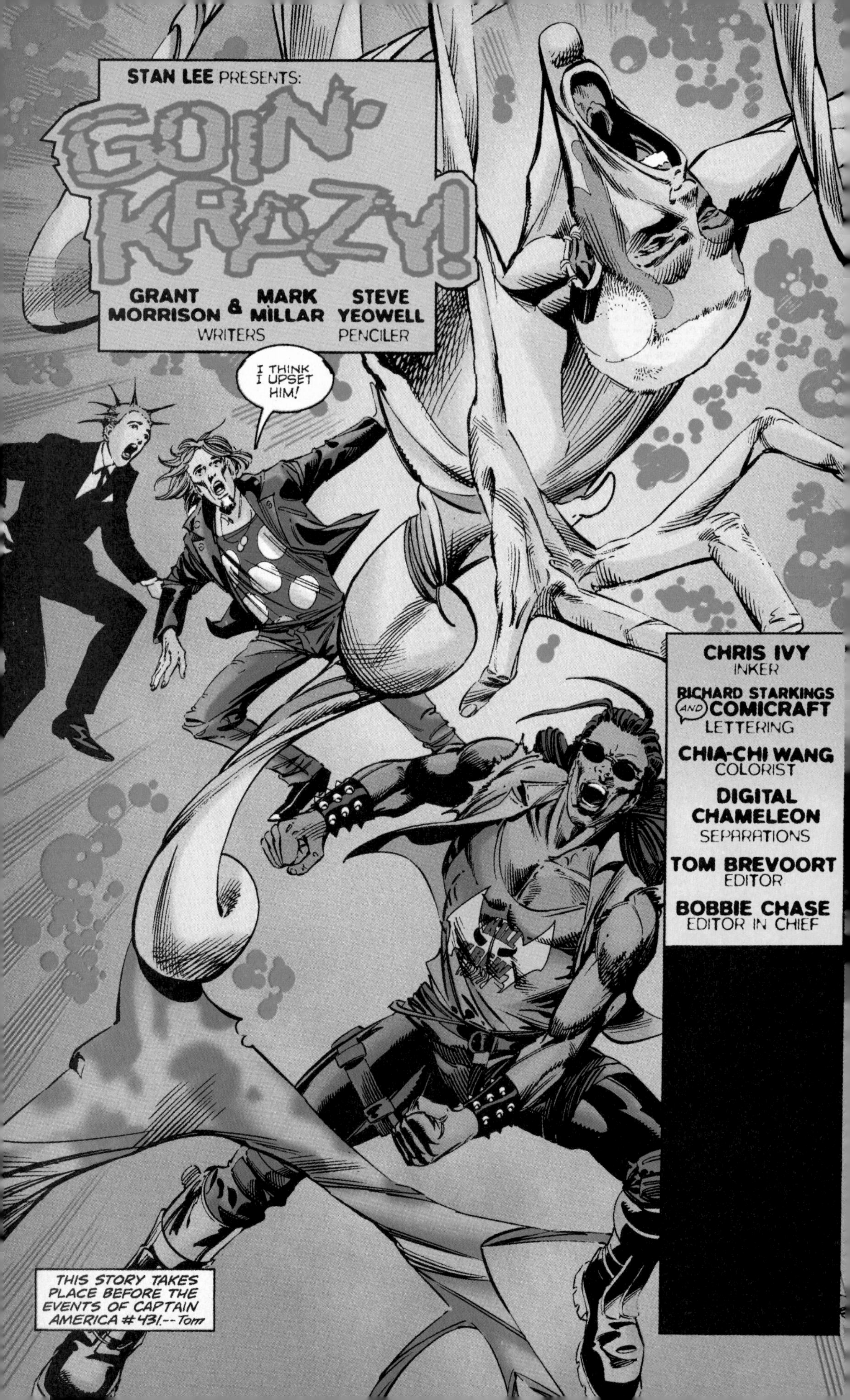
STAN LEE PRESENTS:
GOIN' KRAZY!
GRANT MORRISON & MARK MILLAR WRITERS
STEVE YEOWELL PENCILER
I THINK I UPSET HIM!
CHRIS IVY INKER
RICHARD STARKINGS AND COMICRAFT LETTERING
CHIA-CHI WANG COLORIST
DIGITAL CHAMELEON SEPARATIONS
TOM BREVOORT EDITOR
BOBBIE CHASE EDITOR IN CHIEF
THIS STORY TAKES PLACE BEFORE THE EVENTS OF CAPTAIN AMERICA #431.--Tom

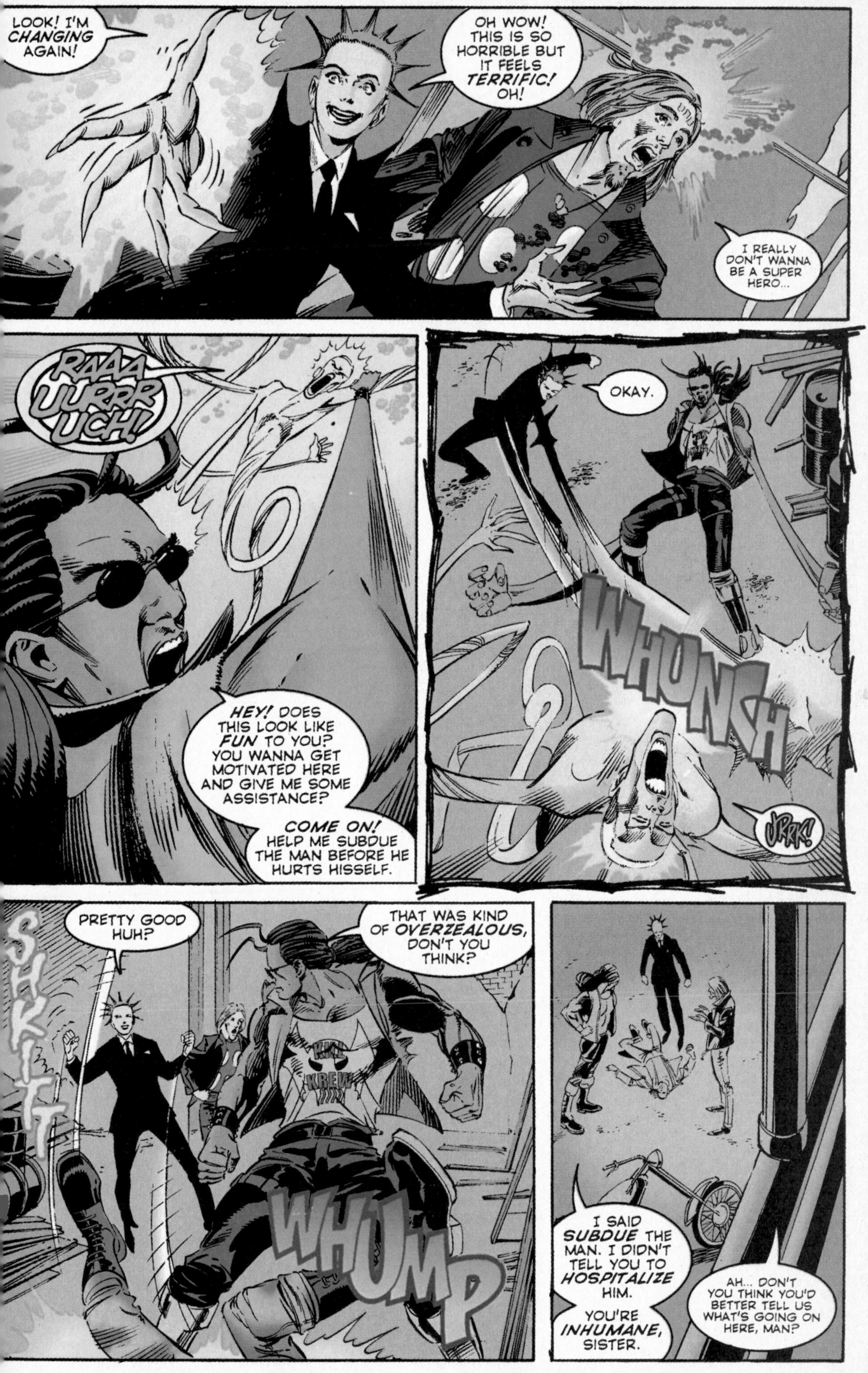
LOOK! I'M CHANGING AGAIN!
OH WOW! THIS IS SO HORRIBLE BUT IT FEELS TERRIFIC! OH!
I REALLY DON'T WANNA BE A SUPER HERO...
RAAAUURRRUCH!
HEY! DOES THIS LOOK LIKE FUN TO YOU? YOU WANNA GET MOTIVATED HERE AND GIVE ME SOME ASSISTANCE?
COME ON! HELP ME SUBDUE THE MAN BEFORE HE HURTS HISSELF.
OKAY.
WHUNCH
URRK!
SHKITT
PRETTY GOOD HUH?
THAT WAS KIND OF OVERZEALOUS, DON'T YOU THINK?
WHUMP
I SAID SUBDUE THE MAN. I DIDN'T TELL YOU TO HOSPITALIZE HIM.
YOU'RE INHUMANE, SISTER.
AH... DON'T YOU THINK YOU'D BETTER TELL US WHAT'S GOING ON HERE, MAN?

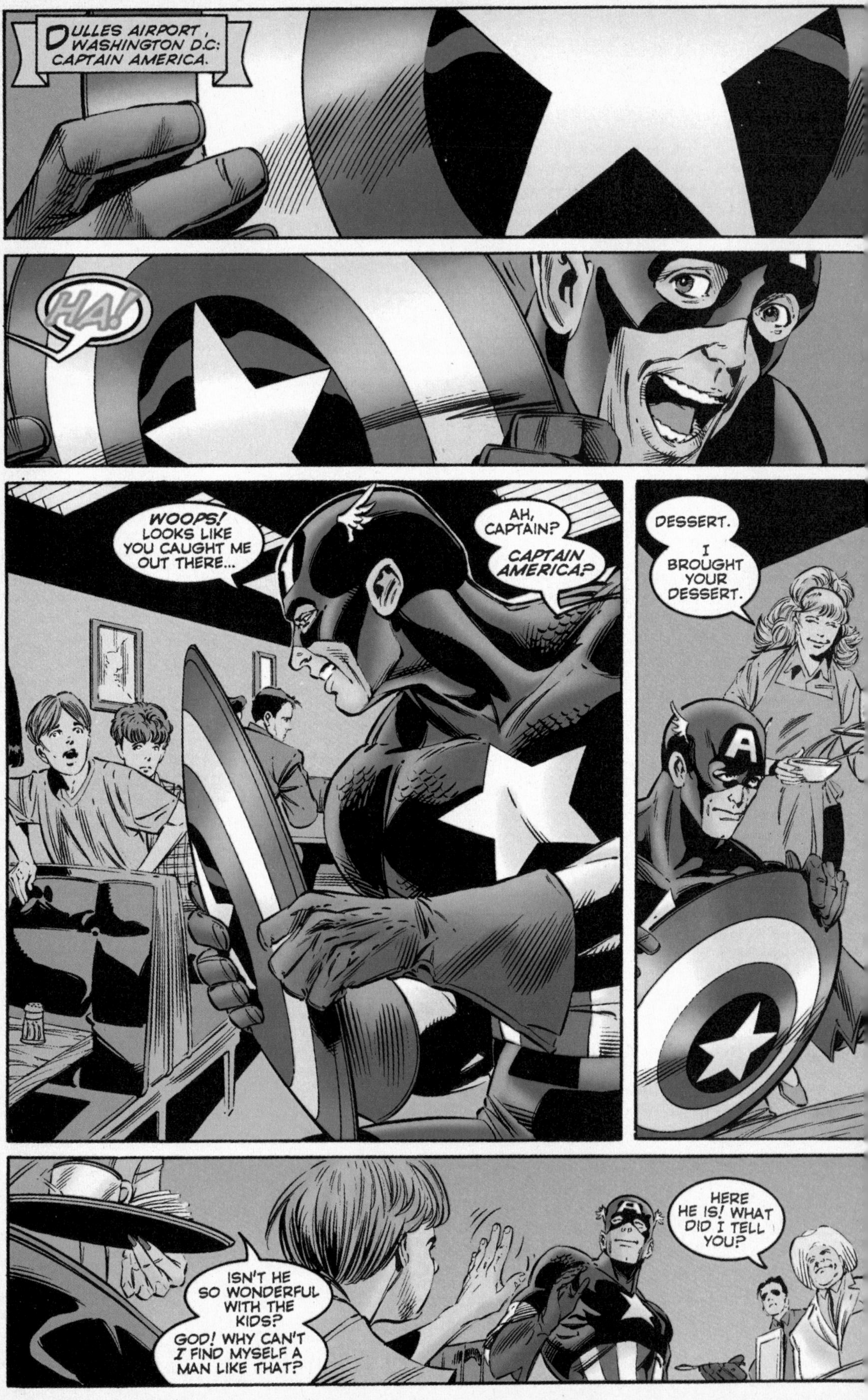
DULLES AIRPORT, WASHINGTON D.C: CAPTAIN AMERICA.
HA!
WOOPS! LOOKS LIKE YOU CAUGHT ME OUT THERE...
AH, CAPTAIN? CAPTAIN AMERICA?
DESSERT.
I BROUGHT YOUR DESSERT.
HERE HE IS! WHAT DID I TELL YOU?
ISN'T HE SO WONDERFUL WITH THE KIDS?
GOD! WHY CAN'T I FIND MYSELF A MAN LIKE THAT?

HERE he is! Sittin' down here just like regular folks. I love this guy.

KUROV'S plane's comin' in, Captain. We better get ourselves out there to the tarmac pretty soon and welcome that ole boy to the USA.

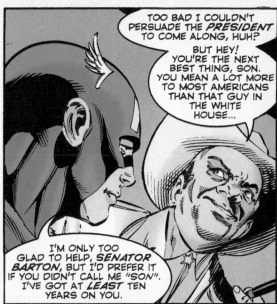

TOO BAD I COULDN'T persuade the PRESIDENT to come along, huh?

BUT HEY! You're the next best thing, SON. You mean a lot more to most Americans than that guy in the WHITE HOUSE...

I'M ONLY TOO glad to help, SENATOR BARTON, but I'd prefer it if you didn't call me "SON". I've got at LEAST ten years on you.

HEY NOW! Are you gentlemen okay here? You've been sitting for HOURS.

HOW ABOUT SOME MORE COFFEE?

AH... YEAH... YEAH. WE'LL... AH... WE'LL HAVE SOME MORE COFFEE.

NO MORE, NO MORE COFFEE I'LL BE SICK.

COME ON, Y'ALL don't wanna get riled, Captain. That's TEXAS for you; we all gotta be bigger 'n' more important 'n' older'n everybody else.

YOU JUST have to smile and shake KUROV'S hand and let him know that BIG BROTHER AMERICA'S looking out for his little Baltic homeland.

I GUESS I can manage that.

SURE YOU CAN!

SAY, WHAT IS THAT? IS that what I think it IS?

SURE. APPLE PIE.

WANT SOME?

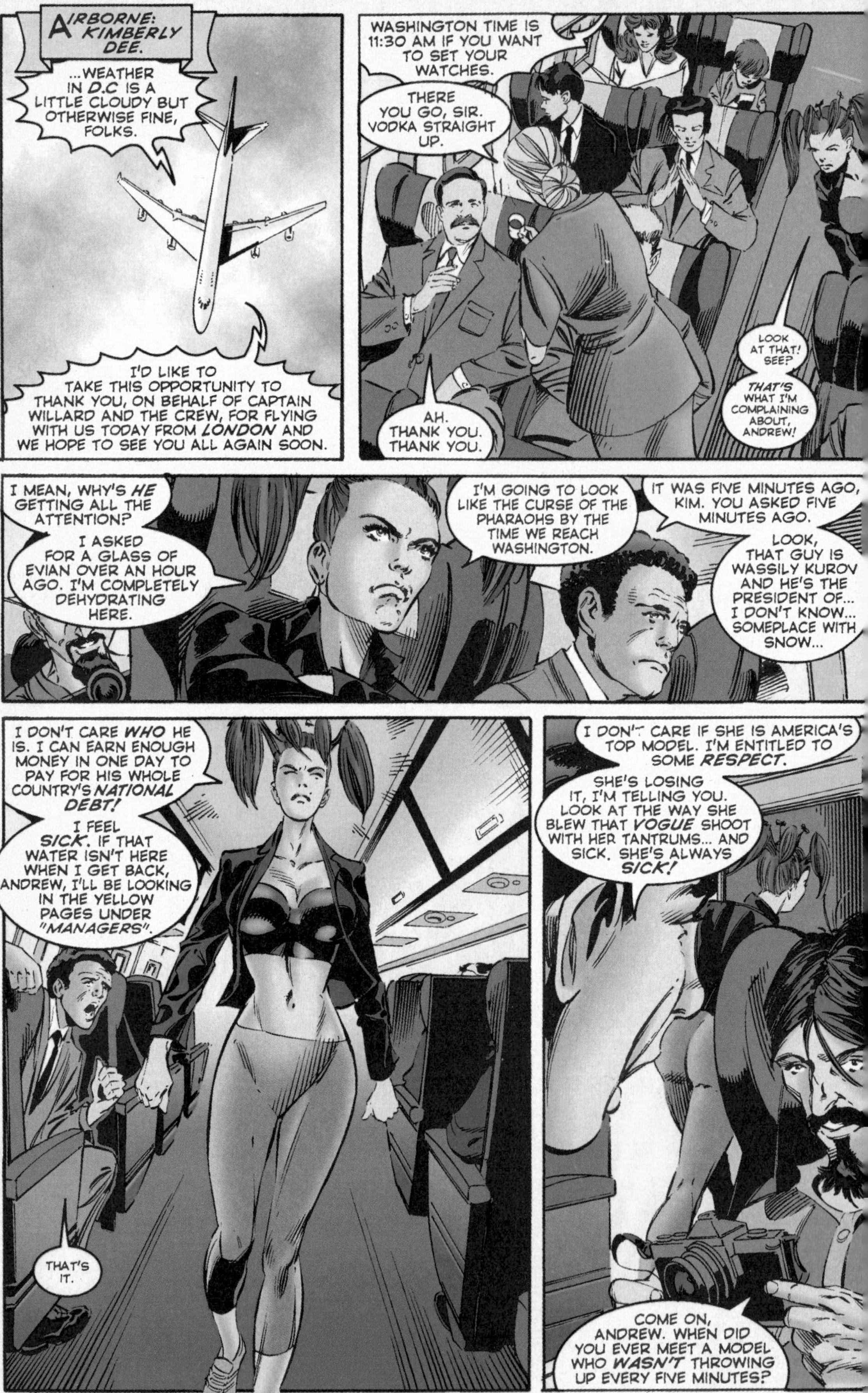
AIRBORNE: KIMBERLY DEE.
...WEATHER IN D.C IS A LITTLE CLOUDY BUT OTHERWISE FINE, FOLKS.
I'D LIKE TO TAKE THIS OPPORTUNITY TO THANK YOU, ON BEHALF OF CAPTAIN WILLARD AND THE CREW, FOR FLYING WITH US TODAY FROM LONDON AND WE HOPE TO SEE YOU ALL AGAIN SOON.
WASHINGTON TIME IS 11:30 AM IF YOU WANT TO SET YOUR WATCHES.
THERE YOU GO, SIR. VODKA STRAIGHT UP.
AH. THANK YOU. THANK YOU.
LOOK AT THAT! SEE?
THAT'S WHAT I'M COMPLAINING ABOUT, ANDREW!
I MEAN, WHY'S HE GETTING ALL THE ATTENTION?
I ASKED FOR A GLASS OF EVIAN OVER AN HOUR AGO. I'M COMPLETELY DEHYDRATING HERE.
I'M GOING TO LOOK LIKE THE CURSE OF THE PHARAOHS BY THE TIME WE REACH WASHINGTON.
IT WAS FIVE MINUTES AGO, KIM. YOU ASKED FIVE MINUTES AGO.
LOOK, THAT GUY IS WASSILY KUROV AND HE'S THE PRESIDENT OF... I DON'T KNOW... SOMEPLACE WITH SNOW...
I DON'T CARE WHO HE IS. I CAN EARN ENOUGH MONEY IN ONE DAY TO PAY FOR HIS WHOLE COUNTRY'S NATIONAL DEBT!
I FEEL SICK. IF THAT WATER ISN'T HERE WHEN I GET BACK, ANDREW, I'LL BE LOOKING IN THE YELLOW PAGES UNDER "MANAGERS".
THAT'S IT.
I DON'T CARE IF SHE IS AMERICA'S TOP MODEL. I'M ENTITLED TO SOME RESPECT.
SHE'S LOSING IT, I'M TELLING YOU. LOOK AT THE WAY SHE BLEW THAT VOGUE SHOOT WITH HER TANTRUMS... AND SICK. SHE'S ALWAYS SICK!
COME ON, ANDREW. WHEN DID YOU EVER MEET A MODEL WHO WASN'T THROWING UP EVERY FIVE MINUTES?

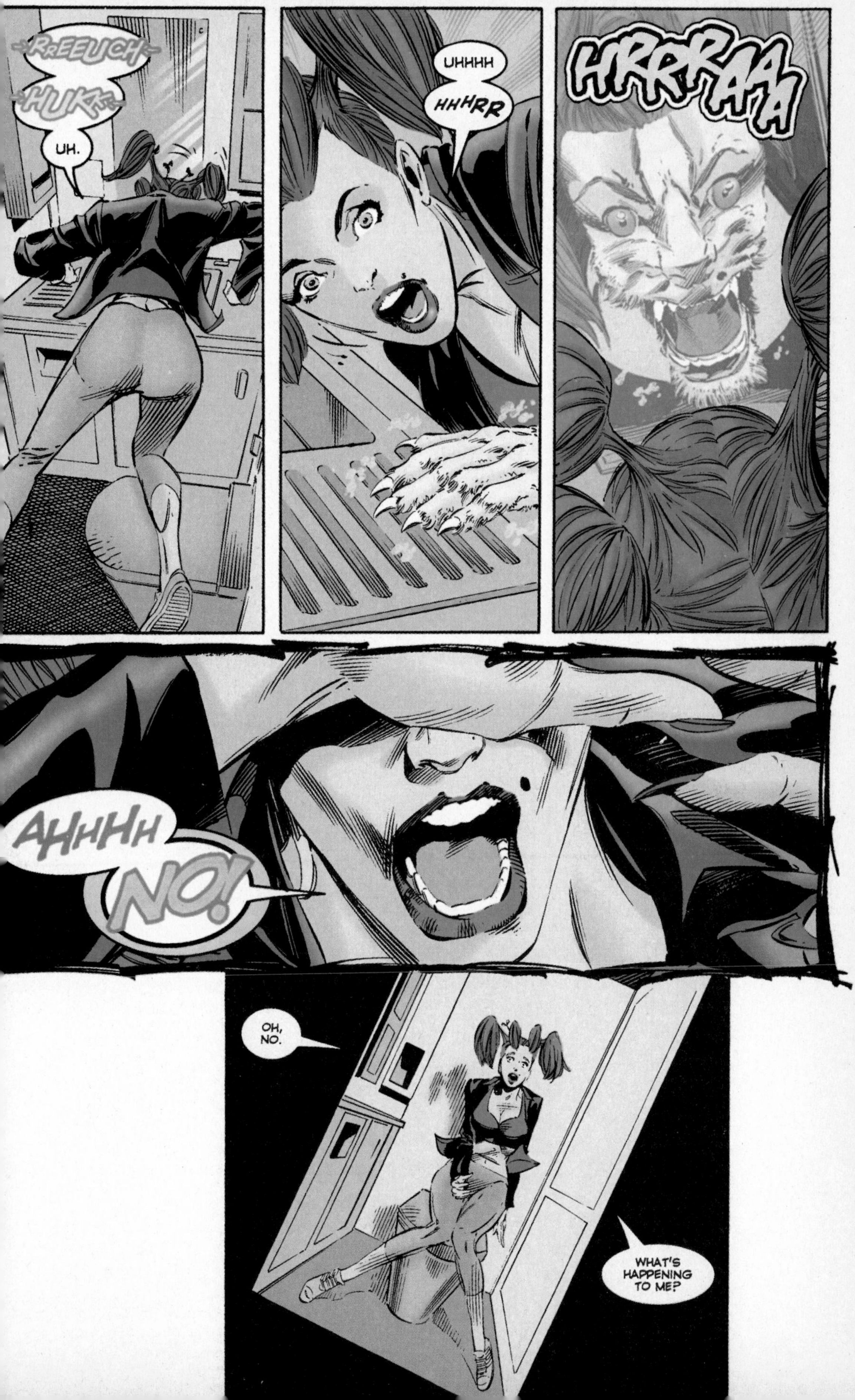
RREEUCH
HUKK
UH.
UHHHH
HHHRR
HRRRAAA
AHHHH NO!
OH, NO.
WHAT'S HAPPENING TO ME?

...SO, MY BOYFRIEND, RIGHT? HE FINDS THIS GUY'S *NUMBER* IN MY PURSE AND IT'S, LIKE, WORLD WAR THREE. I'VE NEVER SEEN HIM SO ANGRY. NOW HE SAYS I HAVE TO FIND ANOTHER JOB.

WHAT AM I GOING TO DO?

SIR? AH... EXCUSE ME, SIR. YOU CAN'T GO UP THERE.

COULD I PLEASE ASK YOU TO RETURN TO YOUR SEAT, SIR? THE PLANE WILL BE LANDING IN...

ARE YOU KIDDING? LISTEN, THERE ARE SO MANY WAYS A SMART GIRL CAN MAKE A LITTLE MONEY FOR HERSELF, BELIEVE ME.

UH!

THE PLANE WILL BE LANDING WHEN *I* SAY SO. UNDERSTAND?

TAKE OVER HERE, AMY.

SORRY ABOUT THIS, SHIRL.

MONEY. SMART GIRL.

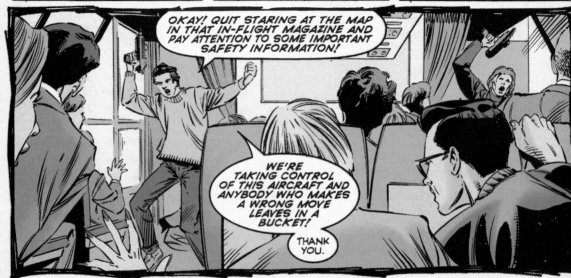

OKAY! QUIT STARING AT THE MAP IN THAT IN-FLIGHT MAGAZINE AND PAY ATTENTION TO SOME IMPORTANT SAFETY INFORMATION!

WE'RE TAKING CONTROL OF THIS AIRCRAFT AND ANYBODY WHO MAKES A WRONG MOVE LEAVES IN A BUCKET!

THANK YOU.

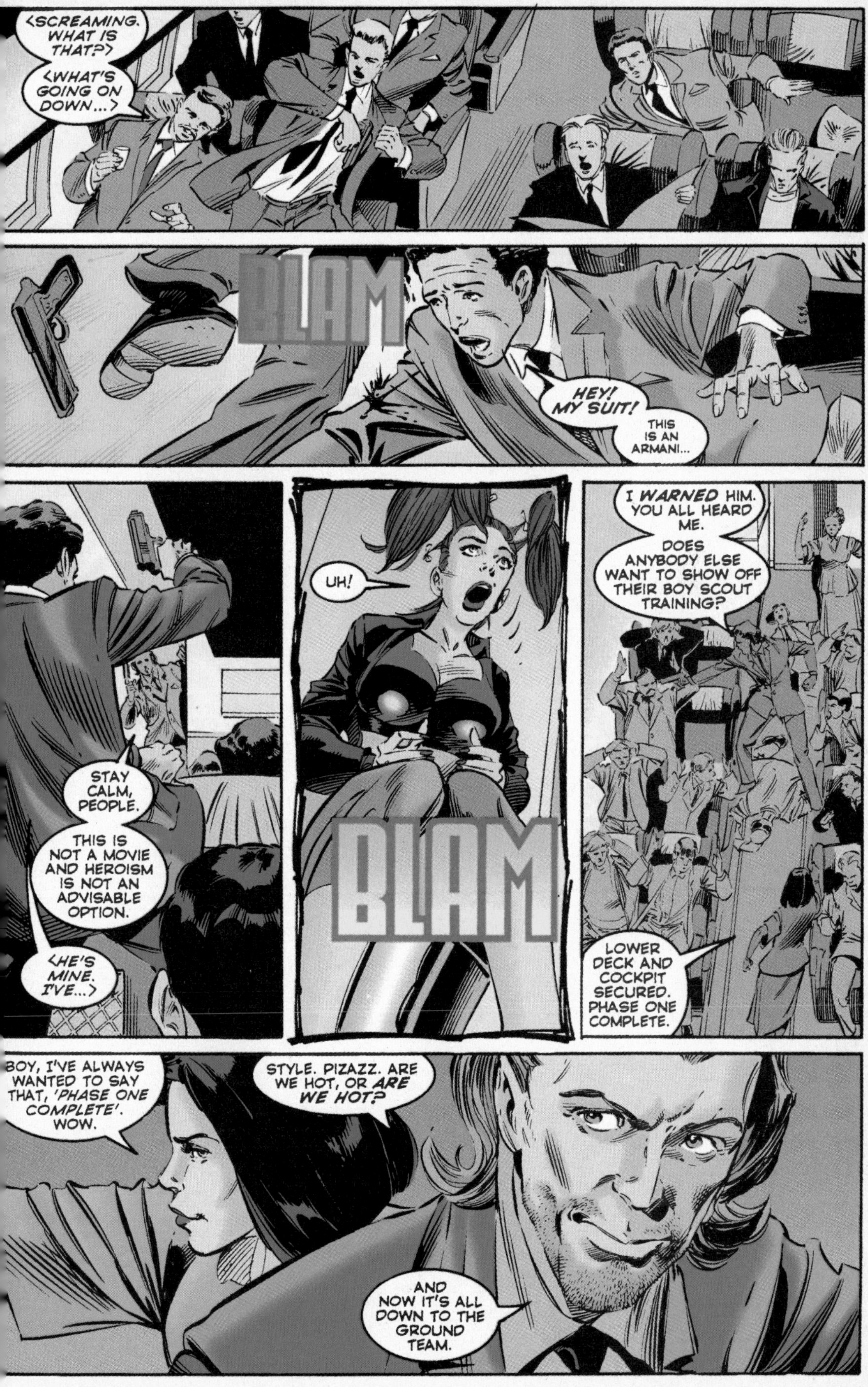
<SCREAMING. WHAT IS THAT?>
<WHAT'S GOING ON DOWN...>
BLAM
HEY! MY SUIT!
THIS IS AN ARMANI...
STAY CALM, PEOPLE.
THIS IS NOT A MOVIE AND HEROISM IS NOT AN ADVISABLE OPTION.
<HE'S MINE. I'VE...>
UH!
BLAM
I WARNED HIM. YOU ALL HEARD ME.
DOES ANYBODY ELSE WANT TO SHOW OFF THEIR BOY SCOUT TRAINING?
LOWER DECK AND COCKPIT SECURED. PHASE ONE COMPLETE.
BOY, I'VE ALWAYS WANTED TO SAY THAT, 'PHASE ONE COMPLETE'. WOW.
STYLE. PIZAZZ. ARE WE HOT, OR ARE WE HOT?
AND NOW IT'S ALL DOWN TO THE GROUND TEAM.

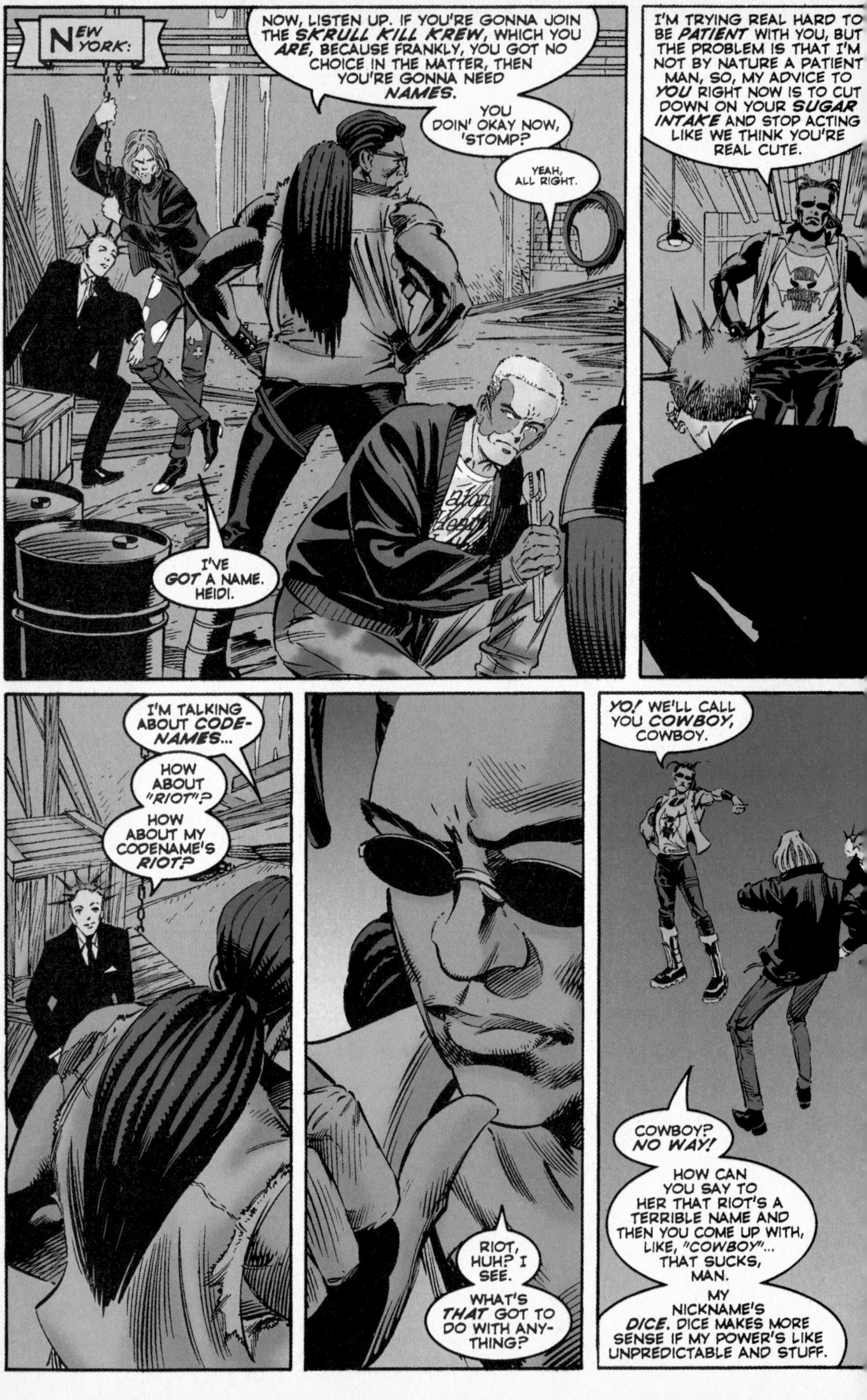
NEW YORK:
NOW, LISTEN UP. IF YOU'RE GONNA JOIN THE SKRULL KILL KREW, WHICH YOU ARE, BECAUSE FRANKLY, YOU GOT NO CHOICE IN THE MATTER, THEN YOU'RE GONNA NEED NAMES.
YOU DOIN' OKAY NOW, 'STOMP?
YEAH, ALL RIGHT.
I'VE GOT A NAME. HEIDI.
I'M TRYING REAL HARD TO BE PATIENT WITH YOU, BUT THE PROBLEM IS THAT I'M NOT BY NATURE A PATIENT MAN, SO, MY ADVICE TO YOU RIGHT NOW IS TO CUT DOWN ON YOUR SUGAR INTAKE AND STOP ACTING LIKE WE THINK YOU'RE REAL CUTE.
I'M TALKING ABOUT CODE-NAMES...
HOW ABOUT "RIOT"?
HOW ABOUT MY CODENAME'S RIOT?
RIOT, HUH? I SEE.
WHAT'S THAT GOT TO DO WITH ANY-THING?
YO! WE'LL CALL YOU COWBOY, COWBOY.
COWBOY? NO WAY!
HOW CAN YOU SAY TO HER THAT RIOT'S A TERRIBLE NAME AND THEN YOU COME UP WITH, LIKE, "COWBOY"... THAT SUCKS, MAN.
MY NICKNAME'S DICE. DICE MAKES MORE SENSE IF MY POWER'S LIKE UNPREDICTABLE AND STUFF.

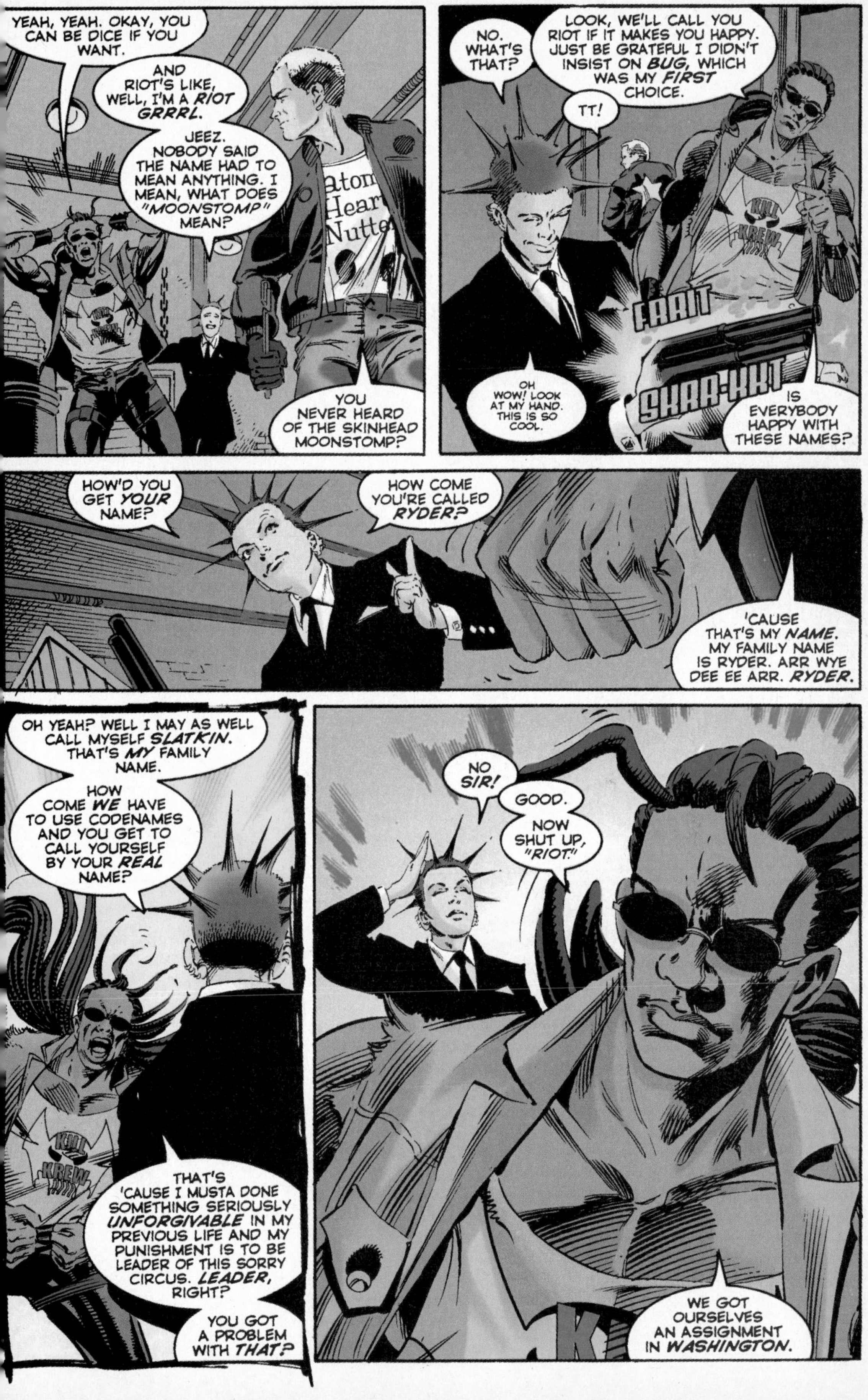
YEAH, YEAH. OKAY, YOU CAN BE DICE IF YOU WANT.
AND RIOT'S LIKE, WELL, I'M A *RIOT GRRRL.*
JEEZ. NOBODY SAID THE NAME HAD TO MEAN ANYTHING. I MEAN, WHAT DOES *"MOONSTOMP"* MEAN?
YOU NEVER HEARD OF THE SKINHEAD MOONSTOMP?
NO. WHAT'S THAT?
LOOK, WE'LL CALL YOU RIOT IF IT MAKES YOU HAPPY. JUST BE GRATEFUL I DIDN'T INSIST ON *BUG,* WHICH WAS MY *FIRST* CHOICE.
TT!
KILL KREW
FRRIT
OH WOW! LOOK AT MY HAND. THIS IS SO COOL.
SKRR-KKT
IS EVERYBODY HAPPY WITH THESE NAMES?
HOW'D YOU GET *YOUR* NAME?
HOW COME YOU'RE CALLED *RYDER?*
'CAUSE THAT'S MY *NAME.* MY FAMILY NAME IS RYDER. ARR WYE DEE EE ARR. *RYDER.*
OH YEAH? WELL I MAY AS WELL CALL MYSELF *SLATKIN.* THAT'S *MY* FAMILY NAME.
HOW COME *WE* HAVE TO USE CODENAMES AND YOU GET TO CALL YOURSELF BY YOUR *REAL* NAME?
KILL KREW
THAT'S 'CAUSE I MUSTA DONE SOMETHING SERIOUSLY *UNFORGIVABLE* IN MY PREVIOUS LIFE AND MY PUNISHMENT IS TO BE LEADER OF THIS SORRY CIRCUS. *LEADER,* RIGHT?
YOU GOT A PROBLEM WITH *THAT?*
NO *SIR!*
GOOD.
NOW SHUT UP, *"RIOT."*
WE GOT OURSELVES AN ASSIGNMENT IN *WASHINGTON.*

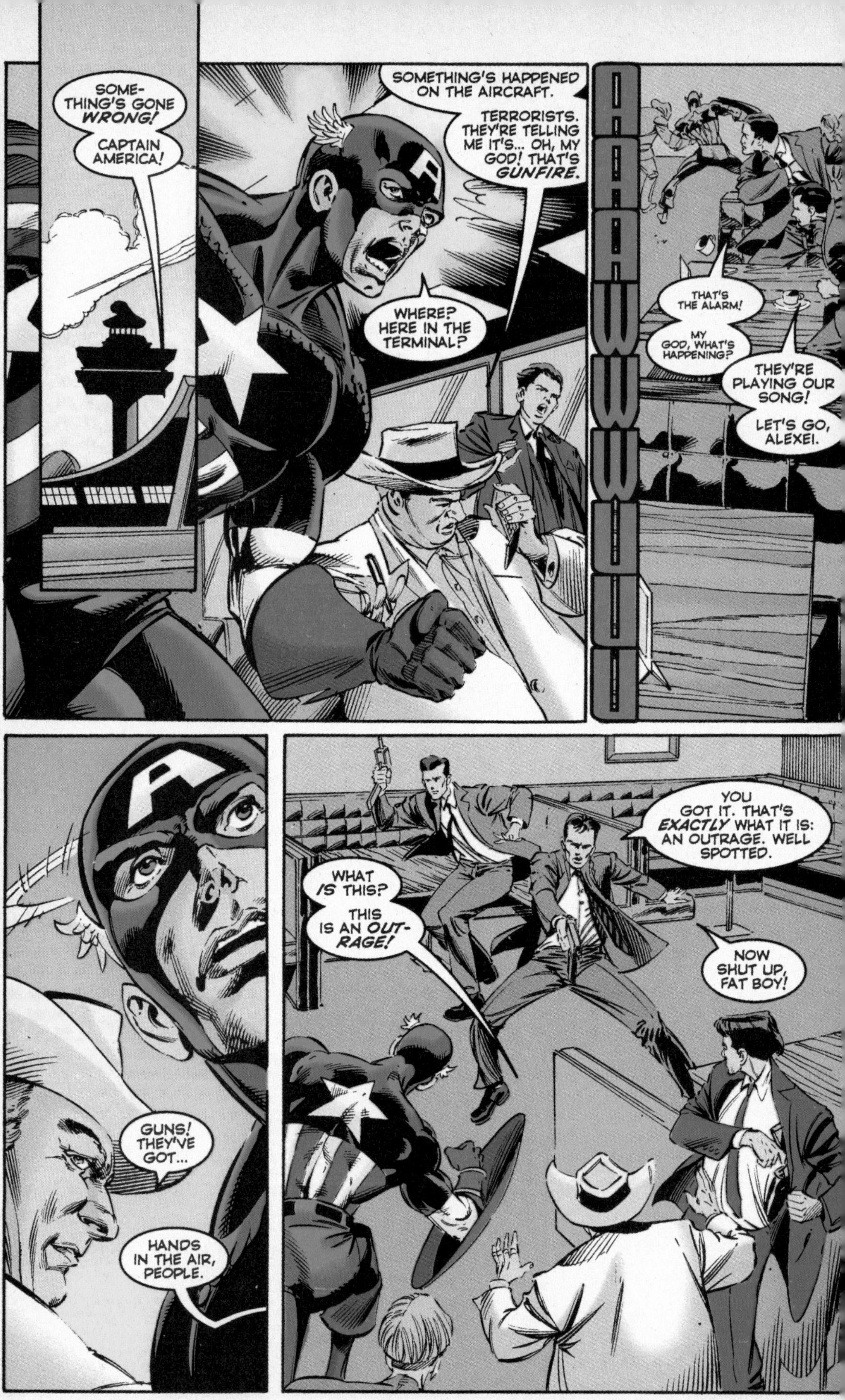

SOME-THING'S GONE WRONG!
CAPTAIN AMERICA!
SOMETHING'S HAPPENED ON THE AIRCRAFT.
TERRORISTS. THEY'RE TELLING ME IT'S... OH, MY GOD! THAT'S GUNFIRE.
WHERE? HERE IN THE TERMINAL?
AAAAAWWWWUUUU
THAT'S THE ALARM!
MY GOD, WHAT'S HAPPENING?
THEY'RE PLAYING OUR SONG!
LET'S GO, ALEXEI.
GUNS! THEY'VE GOT...
HANDS IN THE AIR, PEOPLE.
WHAT IS THIS?
THIS IS AN OUT-RAGE!
YOU GOT IT. THAT'S EXACTLY WHAT IT IS: AN OUTRAGE. WELL SPOTTED.
NOW SHUT UP, FAT BOY!

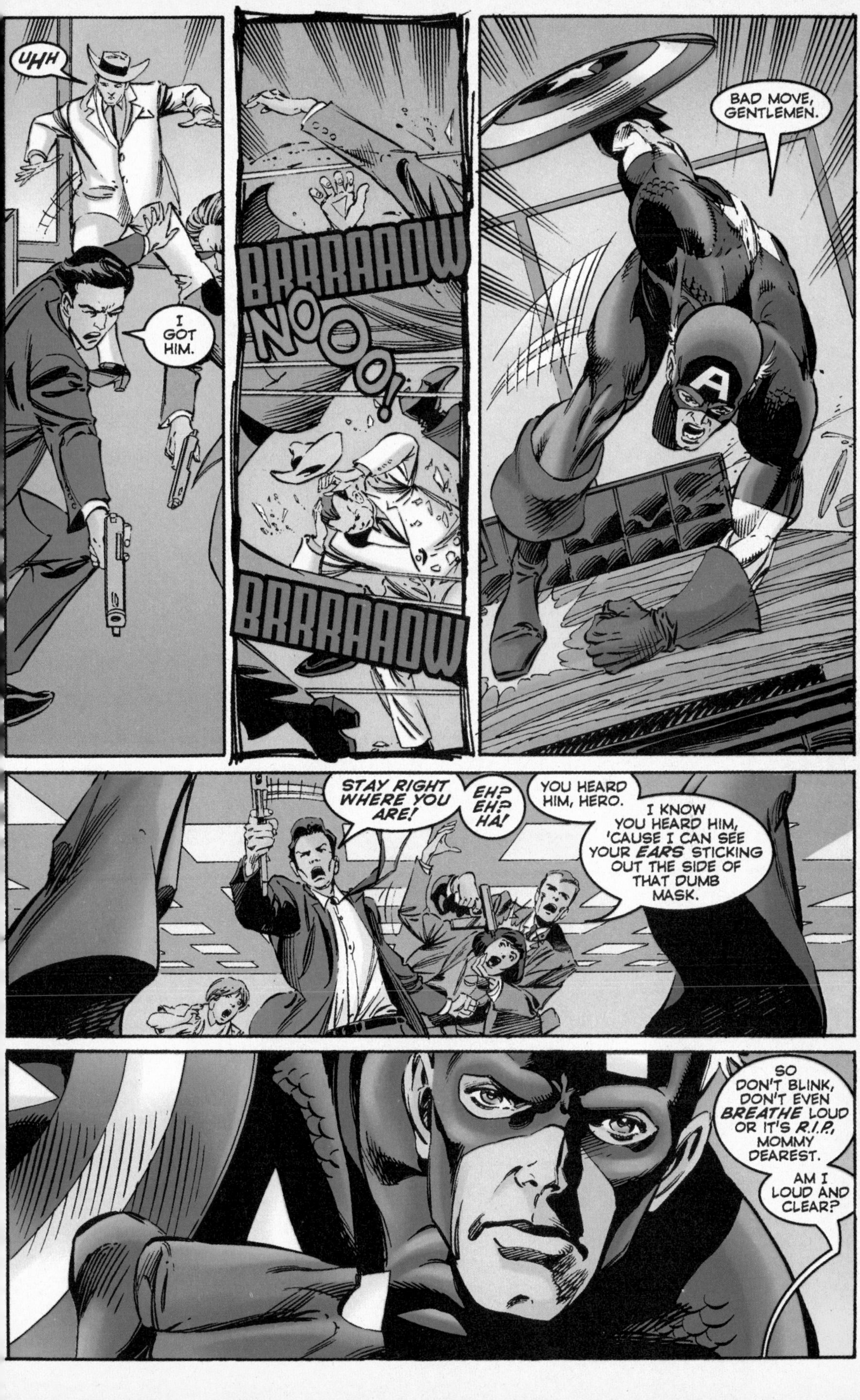
UHH
I GOT HIM.
BRRRAAOW
NOOOO!
BRRRAAOW
BAD MOVE, GENTLEMEN.
STAY RIGHT WHERE YOU ARE!
EH? EH? HA!
YOU HEARD HIM, HERO.
I KNOW YOU HEARD HIM, 'CAUSE I CAN SEE YOUR EARS STICKING OUT THE SIDE OF THAT DUMB MASK.
SO DON'T BLINK, DON'T EVEN BREATHE LOUD OR IT'S R.I.P., MOMMY DEAREST.
AM I LOUD AND CLEAR?

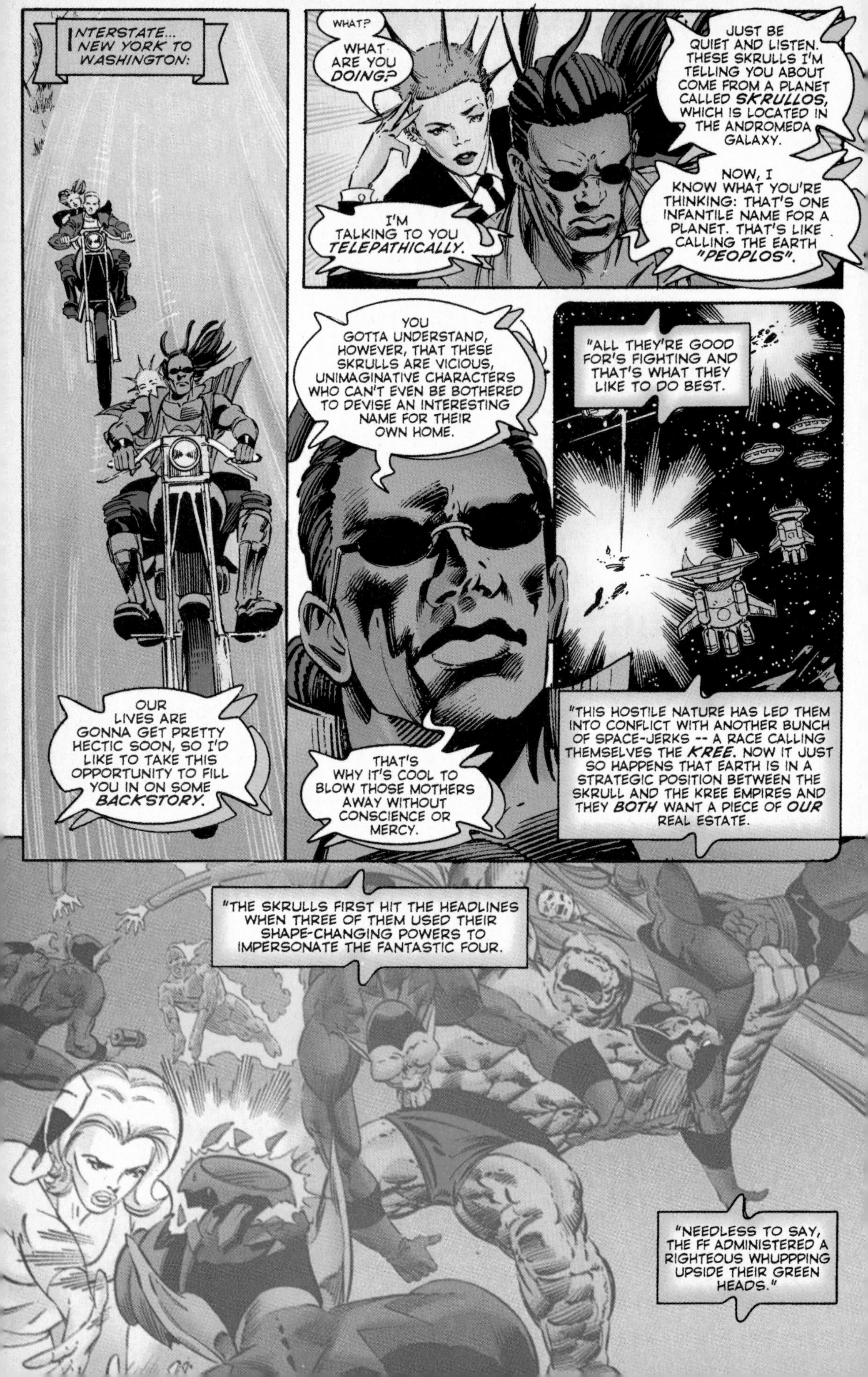
INTERSTATE... NEW YORK TO WASHINGTON:
WHAT?
WHAT ARE YOU DOING?
JUST BE QUIET AND LISTEN. THESE SKRULLS I'M TELLING YOU ABOUT COME FROM A PLANET CALLED SKRULLOS, WHICH IS LOCATED IN THE ANDROMEDA GALAXY.
I'M TALKING TO YOU TELEPATHICALLY.
NOW, I KNOW WHAT YOU'RE THINKING: THAT'S ONE INFANTILE NAME FOR A PLANET. THAT'S LIKE CALLING THE EARTH "PEOPLOS".
YOU GOTTA UNDERSTAND, HOWEVER, THAT THESE SKRULLS ARE VICIOUS, UNIMAGINATIVE CHARACTERS WHO CAN'T EVEN BE BOTHERED TO DEVISE AN INTERESTING NAME FOR THEIR OWN HOME.
"ALL THEY'RE GOOD FOR'S FIGHTING AND THAT'S WHAT THEY LIKE TO DO BEST.
OUR LIVES ARE GONNA GET PRETTY HECTIC SOON, SO I'D LIKE TO TAKE THIS OPPORTUNITY TO FILL YOU IN ON SOME BACKSTORY.
THAT'S WHY IT'S COOL TO BLOW THOSE MOTHERS AWAY WITHOUT CONSCIENCE OR MERCY.
"THIS HOSTILE NATURE HAS LED THEM INTO CONFLICT WITH ANOTHER BUNCH OF SPACE-JERKS -- A RACE CALLING THEMSELVES THE KREE. NOW IT JUST SO HAPPENS THAT EARTH IS IN A STRATEGIC POSITION BETWEEN THE SKRULL AND THE KREE EMPIRES AND THEY BOTH WANT A PIECE OF OUR REAL ESTATE.
"THE SKRULLS FIRST HIT THE HEADLINES WHEN THREE OF THEM USED THEIR SHAPE-CHANGING POWERS TO IMPERSONATE THE FANTASTIC FOUR.
"NEEDLESS TO SAY, THE FF ADMINISTERED A RIGHTEOUS WHUPPPING UPSIDE THEIR GREEN HEADS."

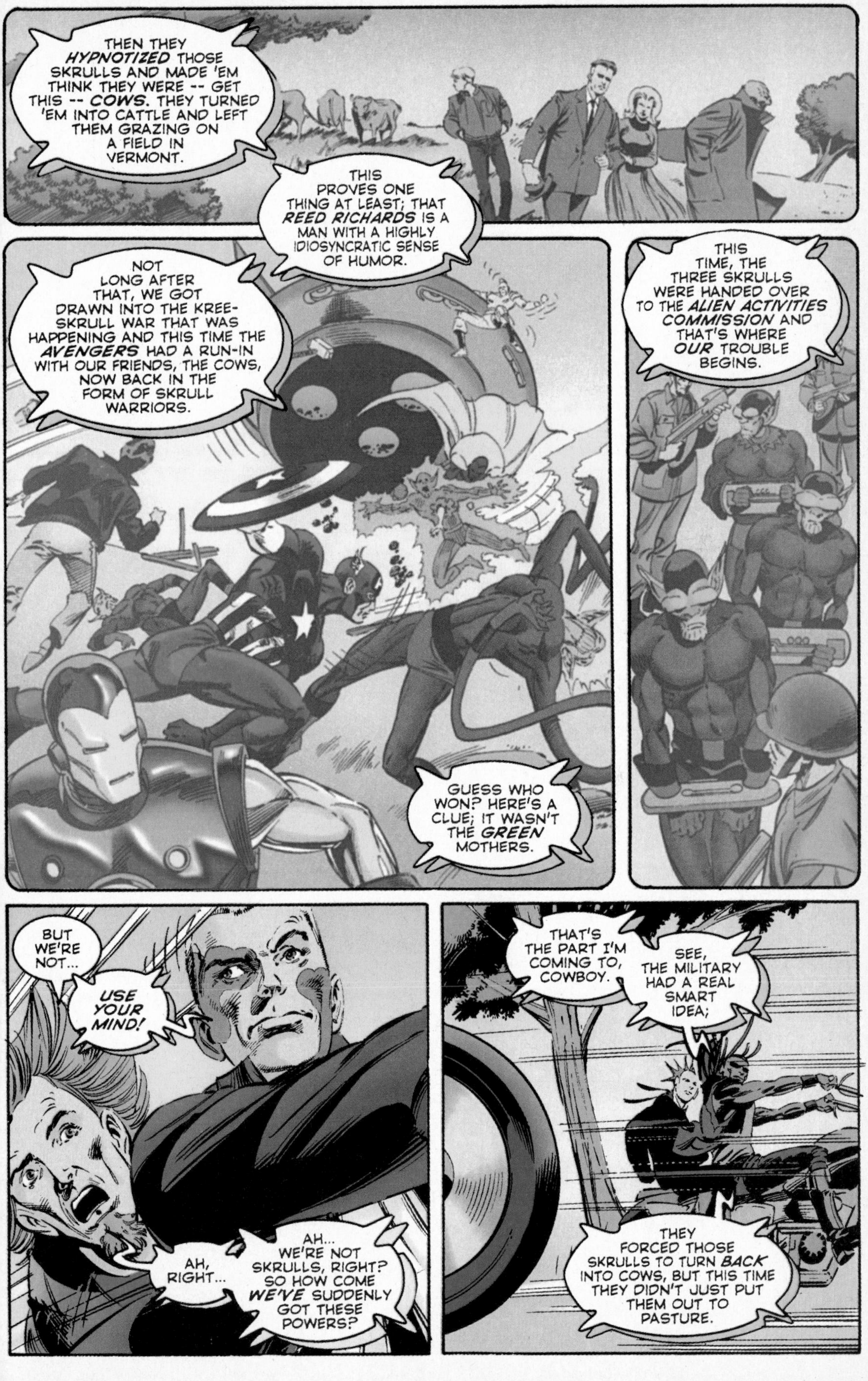
THEN THEY HYPNOTIZED THOSE SKRULLS AND MADE 'EM THINK THEY WERE -- GET THIS -- COWS. THEY TURNED 'EM INTO CATTLE AND LEFT THEM GRAZING ON A FIELD IN VERMONT.
THIS PROVES ONE THING AT LEAST; THAT REED RICHARDS IS A MAN WITH A HIGHLY IDIOSYNCRATIC SENSE OF HUMOR.
NOT LONG AFTER THAT, WE GOT DRAWN INTO THE KREE-SKRULL WAR THAT WAS HAPPENING AND THIS TIME THE AVENGERS HAD A RUN-IN WITH OUR FRIENDS, THE COWS, NOW BACK IN THE FORM OF SKRULL WARRIORS.
GUESS WHO WON? HERE'S A CLUE; IT WASN'T THE GREEN MOTHERS.
THIS TIME, THE THREE SKRULLS WERE HANDED OVER TO THE ALIEN ACTIVITIES COMMISSION AND THAT'S WHERE OUR TROUBLE BEGINS.
BUT WE'RE NOT...
USE YOUR MIND!
AH, RIGHT...
AH... WE'RE NOT SKRULLS, RIGHT? SO HOW COME WE'VE SUDDENLY GOT THESE POWERS?
THAT'S THE PART I'M COMING TO, COWBOY.
SEE, THE MILITARY HAD A REAL SMART IDEA;
THEY FORCED THOSE SKRULLS TO TURN BACK INTO COWS, BUT THIS TIME THEY DIDN'T JUST PUT THEM OUT TO PASTURE.

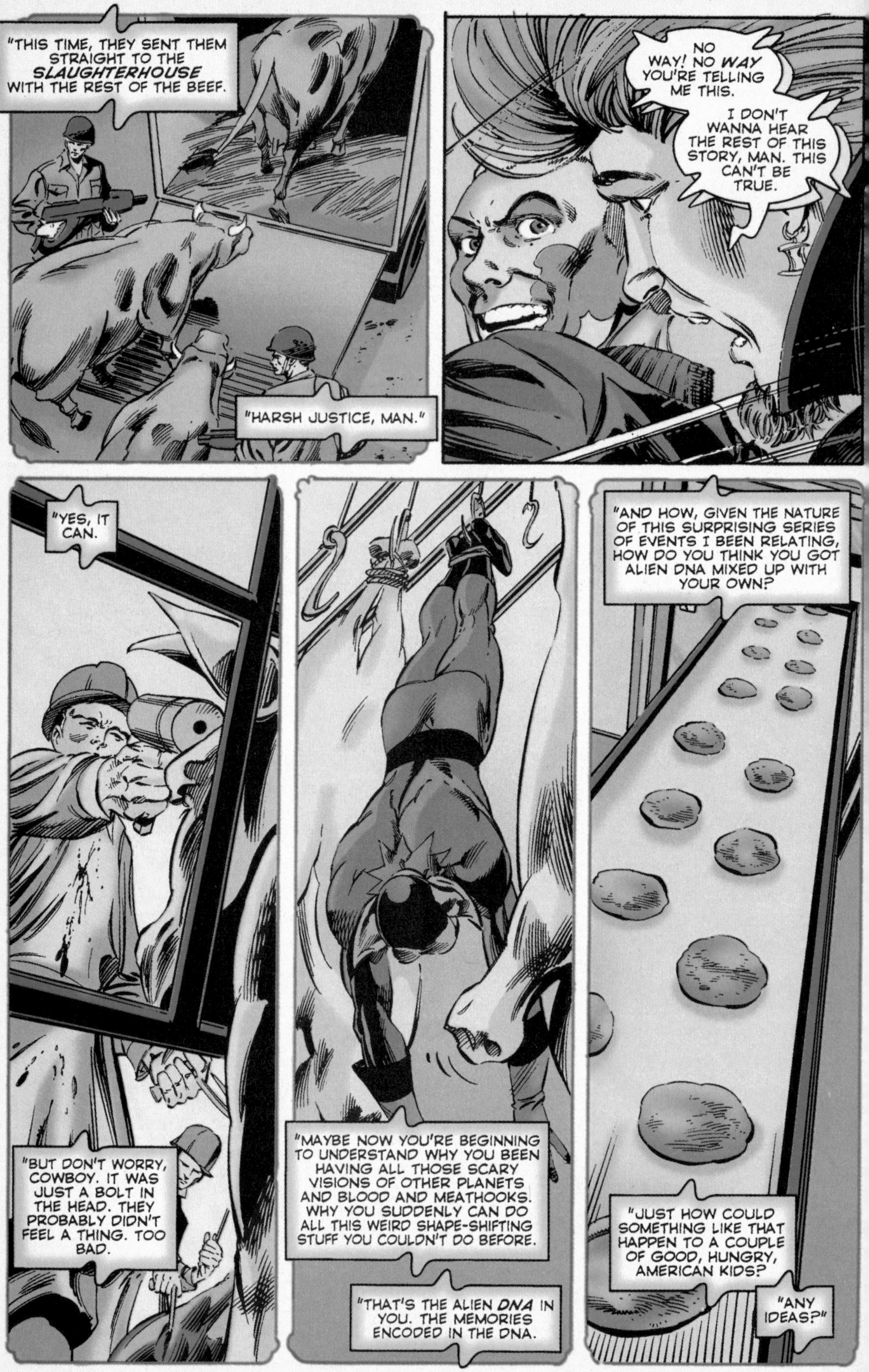
"THIS TIME, THEY SENT THEM STRAIGHT TO THE SLAUGHTERHOUSE WITH THE REST OF THE BEEF.
"HARSH JUSTICE, MAN."
NO WAY! NO WAY YOU'RE TELLING ME THIS.
I DON'T WANNA HEAR THE REST OF THIS STORY, MAN. THIS CAN'T BE TRUE.
"YES, IT CAN.
"BUT DON'T WORRY, COWBOY. IT WAS JUST A BOLT IN THE HEAD. THEY PROBABLY DIDN'T FEEL A THING. TOO BAD.
"MAYBE NOW YOU'RE BEGINNING TO UNDERSTAND WHY YOU BEEN HAVING ALL THOSE SCARY VISIONS OF OTHER PLANETS AND BLOOD AND MEATHOOKS. WHY YOU SUDDENLY CAN DO ALL THIS WEIRD SHAPE-SHIFTING STUFF YOU COULDN'T DO BEFORE.
"THAT'S THE ALIEN DNA IN YOU. THE MEMORIES ENCODED IN THE DNA.
"AND HOW, GIVEN THE NATURE OF THIS SURPRISING SERIES OF EVENTS I BEEN RELATING, HOW DO YOU THINK YOU GOT ALIEN DNA MIXED UP WITH YOUR OWN?
"JUST HOW COULD SOMETHING LIKE THAT HAPPEN TO A COUPLE OF GOOD, HUNGRY, AMERICAN KIDS?
"ANY IDEAS?"

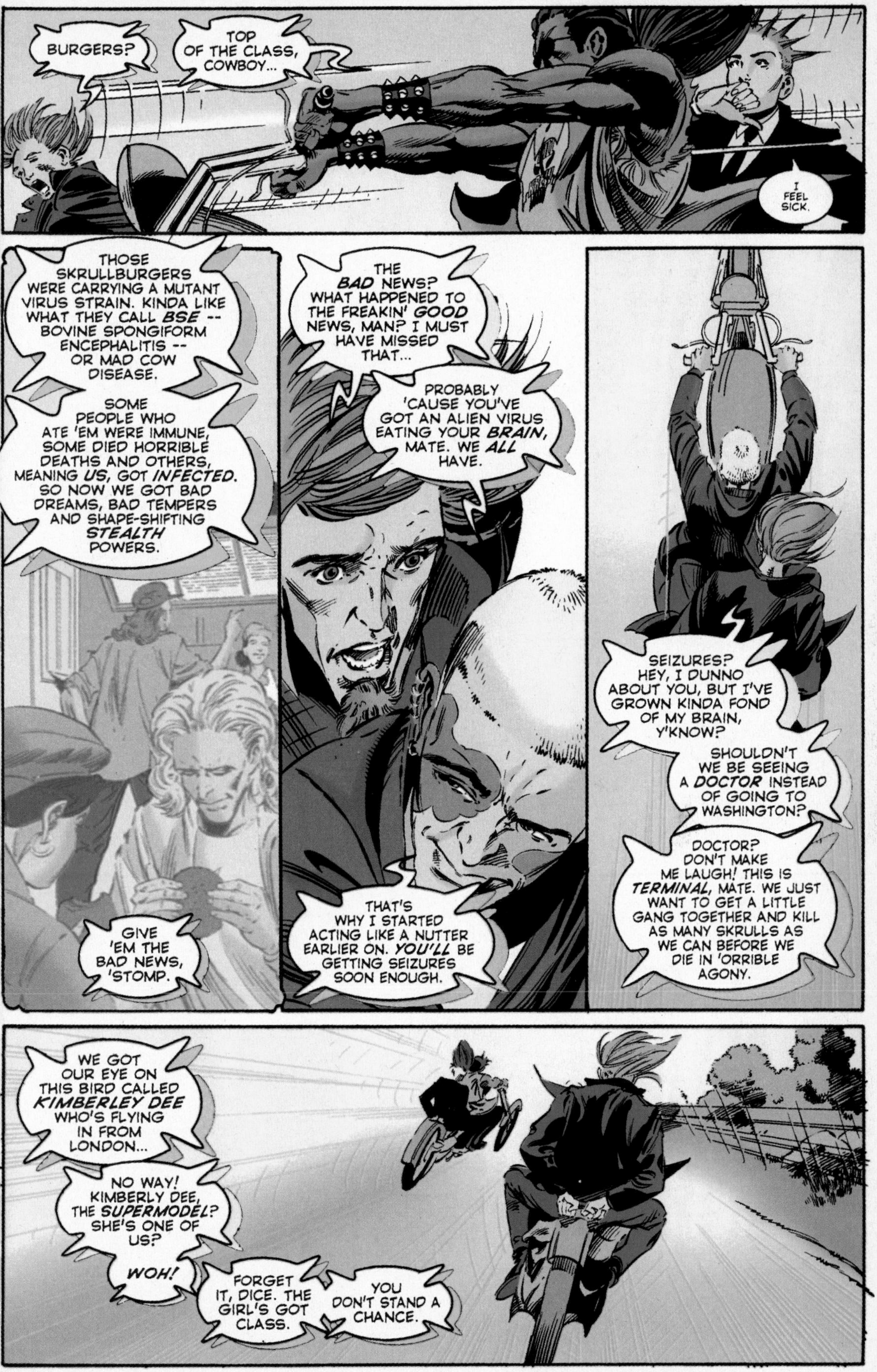
BURGERS?
TOP OF THE CLASS, COWBOY...
I FEEL SICK.
THOSE SKRULLBURGERS WERE CARRYING A MUTANT VIRUS STRAIN. KINDA LIKE WHAT THEY CALL BSE -- BOVINE SPONGIFORM ENCEPHALITIS -- OR MAD COW DISEASE.
SOME PEOPLE WHO ATE 'EM WERE IMMUNE, SOME DIED HORRIBLE DEATHS AND OTHERS, MEANING US, GOT INFECTED. SO NOW WE GOT BAD DREAMS, BAD TEMPERS AND SHAPE-SHIFTING STEALTH POWERS.
GIVE 'EM THE BAD NEWS, 'STOMP.
THE BAD NEWS? WHAT HAPPENED TO THE FREAKIN' GOOD NEWS, MAN? I MUST HAVE MISSED THAT...
PROBABLY 'CAUSE YOU'VE GOT AN ALIEN VIRUS EATING YOUR BRAIN, MATE. WE ALL HAVE.
THAT'S WHY I STARTED ACTING LIKE A NUTTER EARLIER ON. YOU'LL BE GETTING SEIZURES SOON ENOUGH.
SEIZURES? HEY, I DUNNO ABOUT YOU, BUT I'VE GROWN KINDA FOND OF MY BRAIN, Y'KNOW?
SHOULDN'T WE BE SEEING A DOCTOR INSTEAD OF GOING TO WASHINGTON?
DOCTOR? DON'T MAKE ME LAUGH! THIS IS TERMINAL, MATE. WE JUST WANT TO GET A LITTLE GANG TOGETHER AND KILL AS MANY SKRULLS AS WE CAN BEFORE WE DIE IN 'ORRIBLE AGONY.
WE GOT OUR EYE ON THIS BIRD CALLED KIMBERLEY DEE WHO'S FLYING IN FROM LONDON...
NO WAY! KIMBERLY DEE, THE SUPERMODEL? SHE'S ONE OF US?
WOH!
FORGET IT, DICE. THE GIRL'S GOT CLASS.
YOU DON'T STAND A CHANCE.

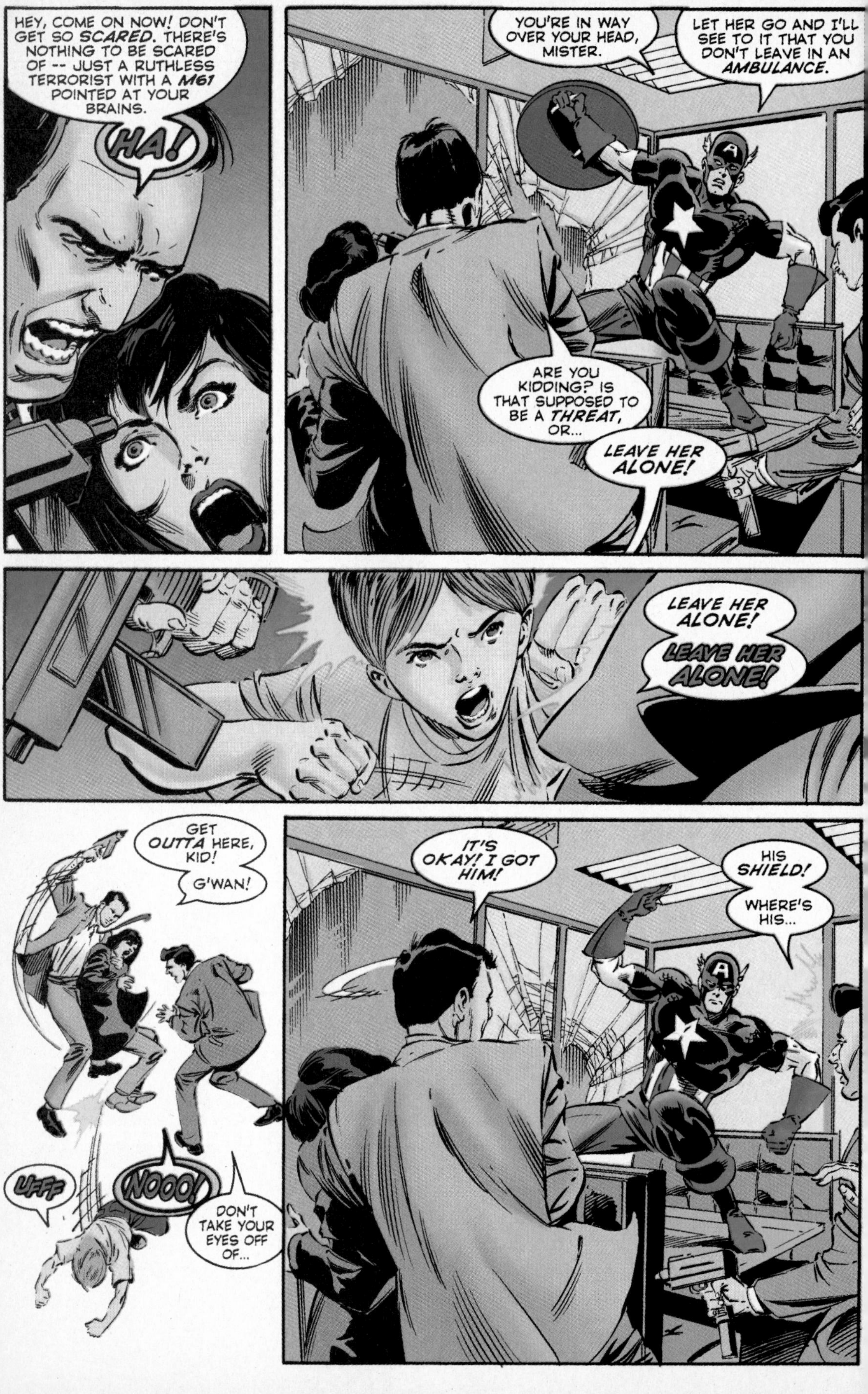
HEY, COME ON NOW! DON'T GET SO SCARED. THERE'S NOTHING TO BE SCARED OF -- JUST A RUTHLESS TERRORIST WITH A M61 POINTED AT YOUR BRAINS.
HA!
YOU'RE IN WAY OVER YOUR HEAD, MISTER.
LET HER GO AND I'LL SEE TO IT THAT YOU DON'T LEAVE IN AN AMBULANCE.
ARE YOU KIDDING? IS THAT SUPPOSED TO BE A THREAT, OR...
LEAVE HER ALONE!
LEAVE HER ALONE!
LEAVE HER ALONE!
GET OUTTA HERE, KID!
G'WAN!
UFFF
NOOO!
DON'T TAKE YOUR EYES OFF OF...
IT'S OKAY! I GOT HIM!
HIS SHIELD!
WHERE'S HIS...

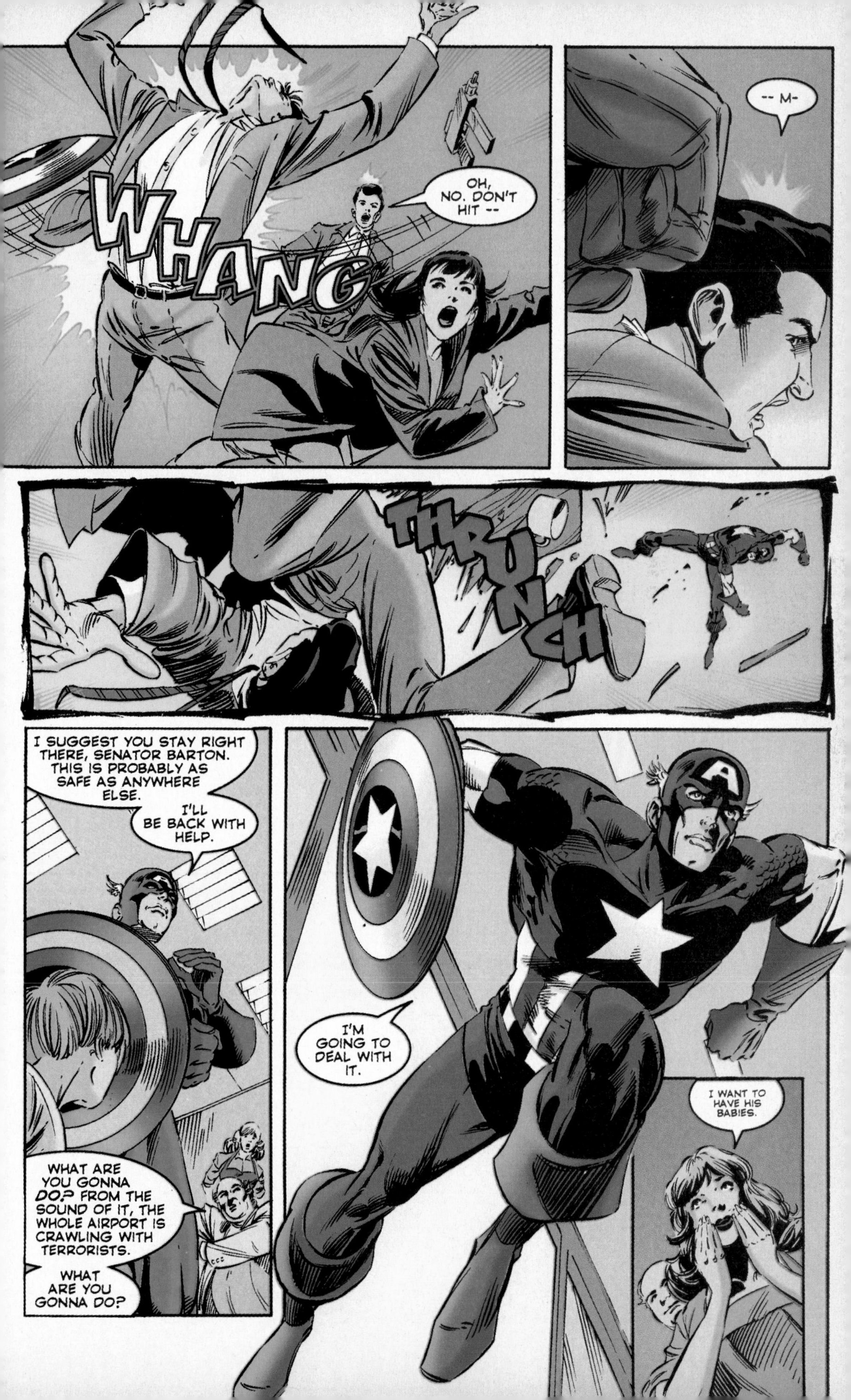
WHANG
OH, NO. DON'T HIT --
-- M-
THRUNCH
I SUGGEST YOU STAY RIGHT THERE, SENATOR BARTON. THIS IS PROBABLY AS SAFE AS ANYWHERE ELSE.
I'LL BE BACK WITH HELP.
WHAT ARE YOU GONNA *DO?* FROM THE SOUND OF IT, THE WHOLE AIRPORT IS CRAWLING WITH TERRORISTS.
WHAT ARE YOU GONNA DO?
I'M GOING TO DEAL WITH IT.
I WANT TO HAVE HIS BABIES.

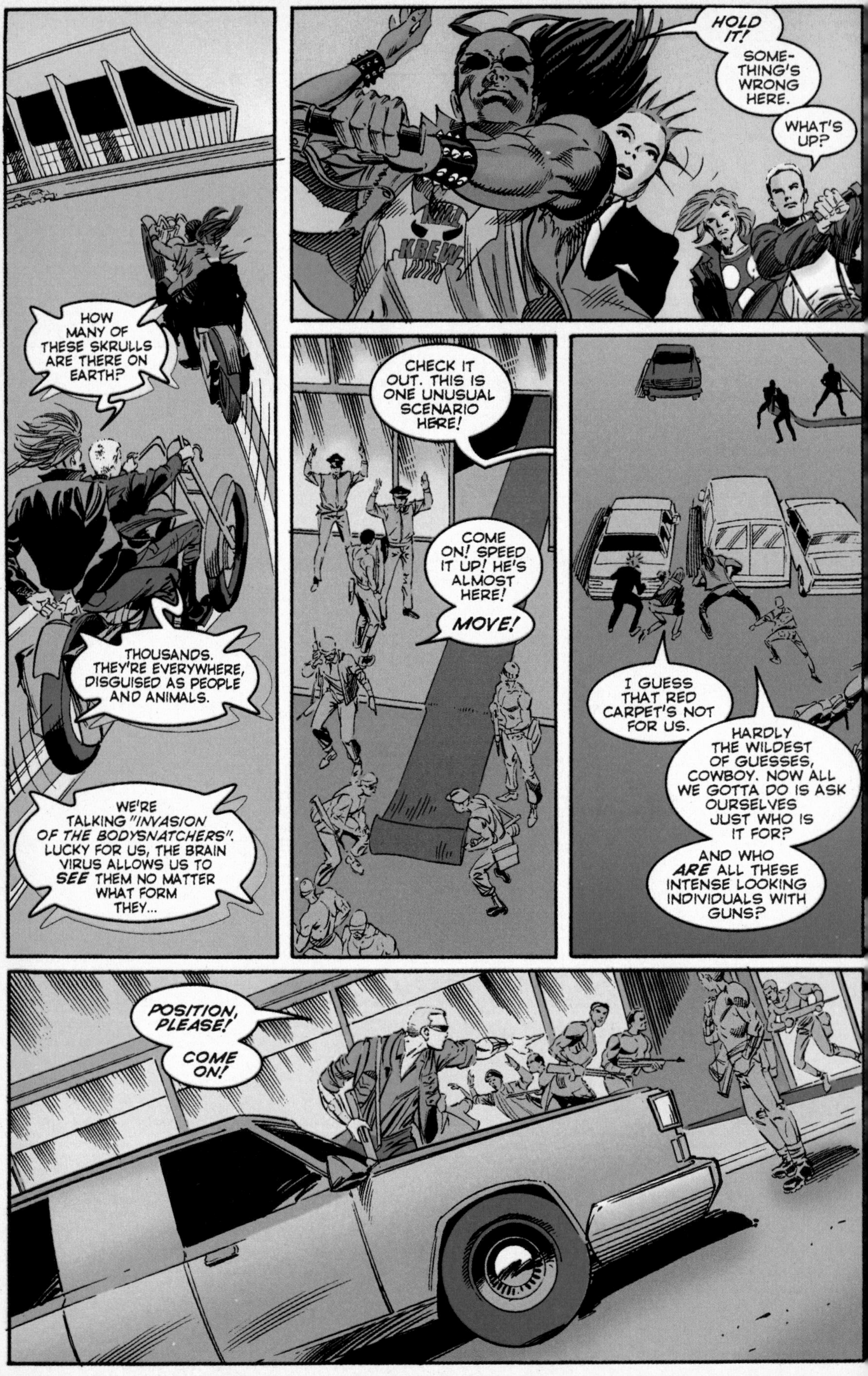
HOW MANY OF THESE SKRULLS ARE THERE ON EARTH?
THOUSANDS. THEY'RE EVERYWHERE, DISGUISED AS PEOPLE AND ANIMALS.
WE'RE TALKING "INVASION OF THE BODYSNATCHERS". LUCKY FOR US, THE BRAIN VIRUS ALLOWS US TO SEE THEM NO MATTER WHAT FORM THEY...
HOLD IT! SOMETHING'S WRONG HERE.
WHAT'S UP?
KREW
CHECK IT OUT. THIS IS ONE UNUSUAL SCENARIO HERE!
COME ON! SPEED IT UP! HE'S ALMOST HERE! MOVE!
I GUESS THAT RED CARPET'S NOT FOR US.
HARDLY THE WILDEST OF GUESSES, COWBOY. NOW ALL WE GOTTA DO IS ASK OURSELVES JUST WHO IS IT FOR?
AND WHO ARE ALL THESE INTENSE LOOKING INDIVIDUALS WITH GUNS?
POSITION, PLEASE!
COME ON!

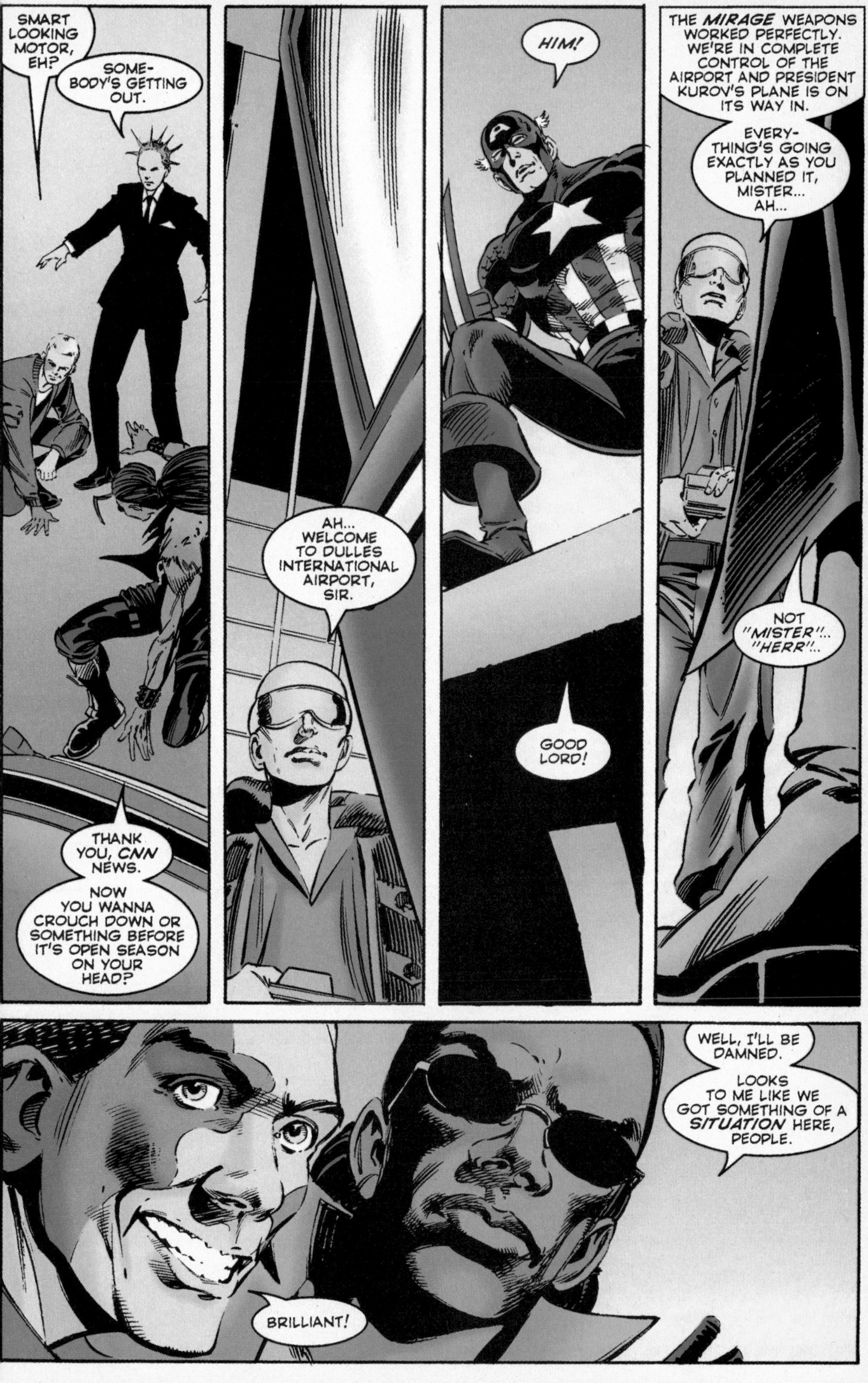
SMART LOOKING MOTOR, EH?
SOME-BODY'S GETTING OUT.
THANK YOU, *CNN* NEWS.
NOW YOU WANNA CROUCH DOWN OR SOMETHING BEFORE IT'S OPEN SEASON ON YOUR HEAD?
AH... WELCOME TO DULLES INTERNATIONAL AIRPORT, SIR.
*HIM!*
GOOD LORD!
THE *MIRAGE* WEAPONS WORKED PERFECTLY. WE'RE IN COMPLETE CONTROL OF THE AIRPORT AND PRESIDENT KUROV'S PLANE IS ON ITS WAY IN.
EVERY-THING'S GOING EXACTLY AS YOU PLANNED IT, MISTER... AH...
NOT *"MISTER"*... *"HERR"*...
WELL, I'LL BE DAMNED.
LOOKS TO ME LIKE WE GOT SOMETHING OF A *SITUATION* HERE, PEOPLE.
BRILLIANT!

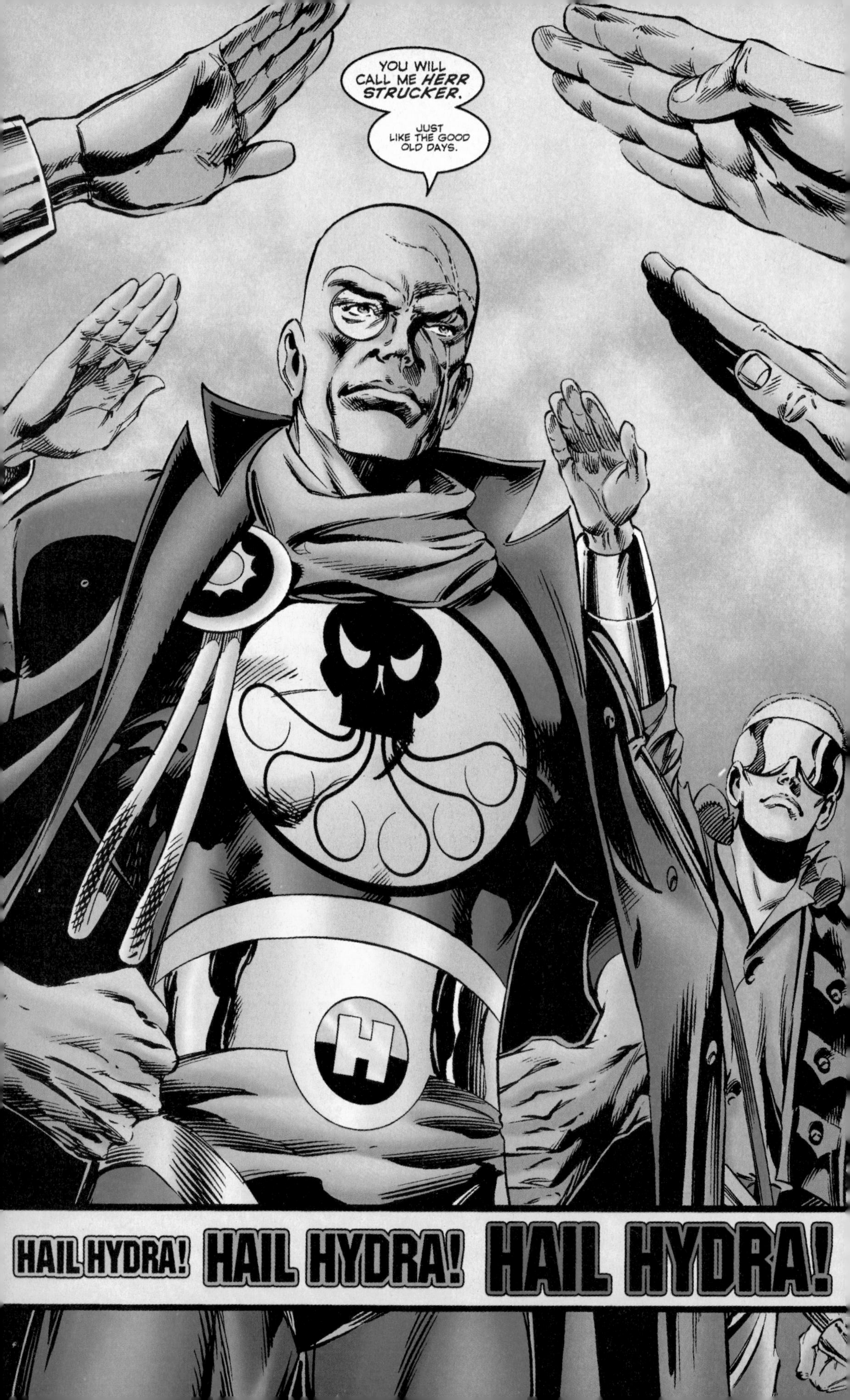
YOU WILL CALL ME HERR STRUCKER.
JUST LIKE THE GOOD OLD DAYS.
HAIL HYDRA! HAIL HYDRA! HAIL HYDRA!

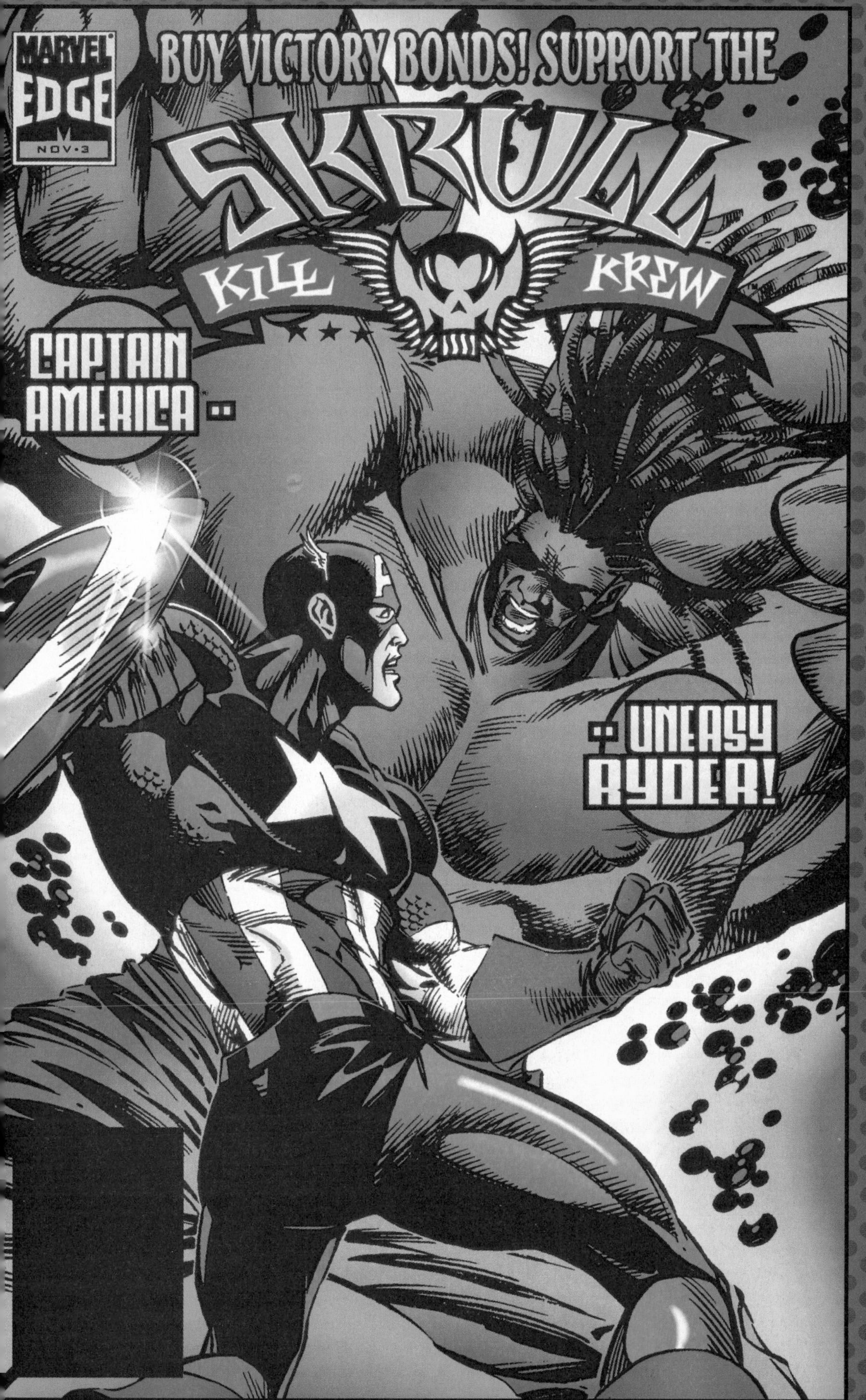
MARVEL EDGE
NOV·3
BUY VICTORY BONDS! SUPPORT THE
SKRULL
KILL KREW
CAPTAIN AMERICA
UNEASY RYDER!

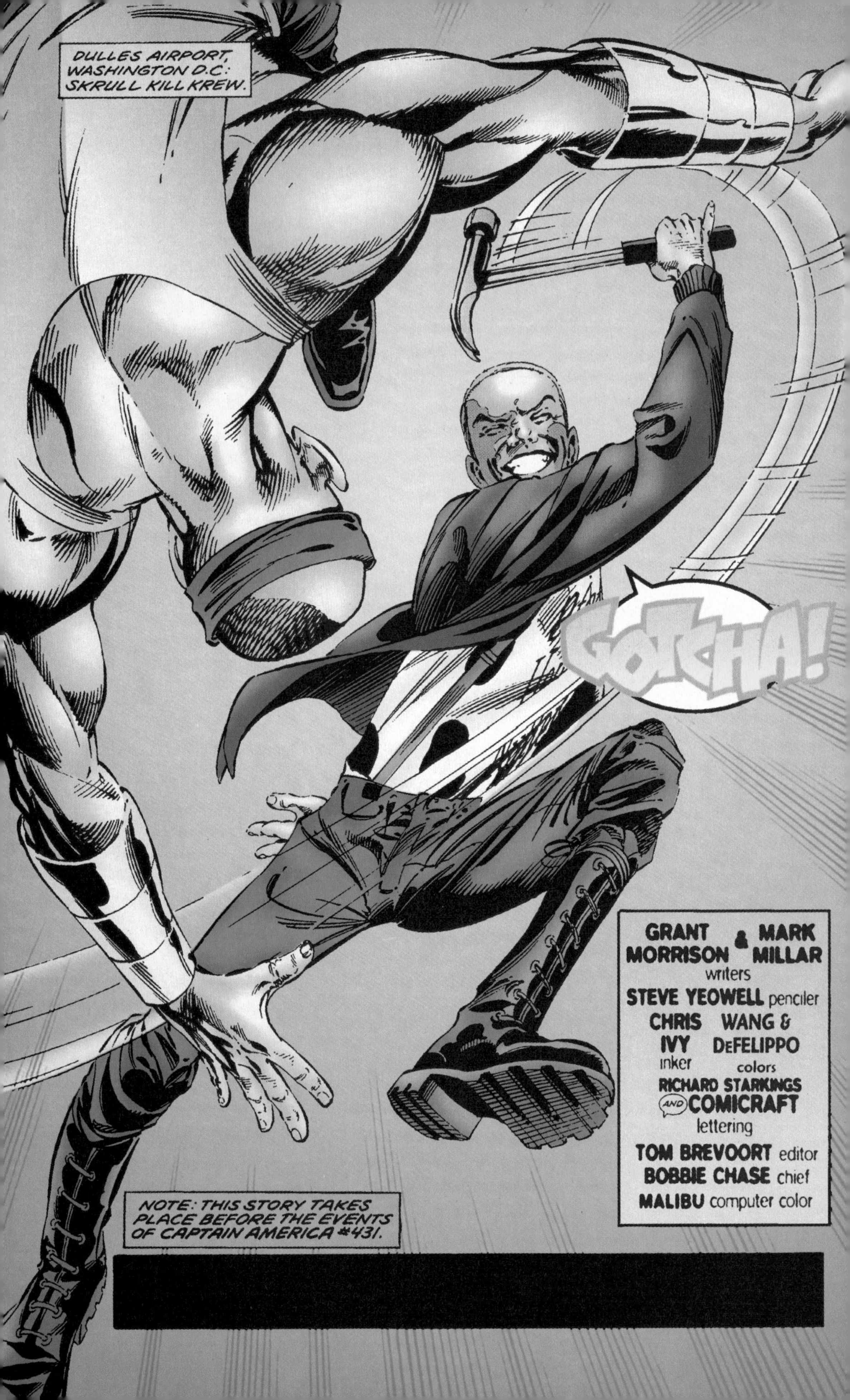
DULLES AIRPORT, WASHINGTON D.C: SKRULL KILL KREW.
GOTCHA!
GRANT MORRISON & MARK MILLAR writers
STEVE YEOWELL penciler
CHRIS IVY inker
WANG & DeFELIPPO colors
RICHARD STARKINGS AND COMICRAFT lettering
TOM BREVOORT editor
BOBBIE CHASE chief
MALIBU computer color
NOTE: THIS STORY TAKES PLACE BEFORE THE EVENTS OF CAPTAIN AMERICA #431.

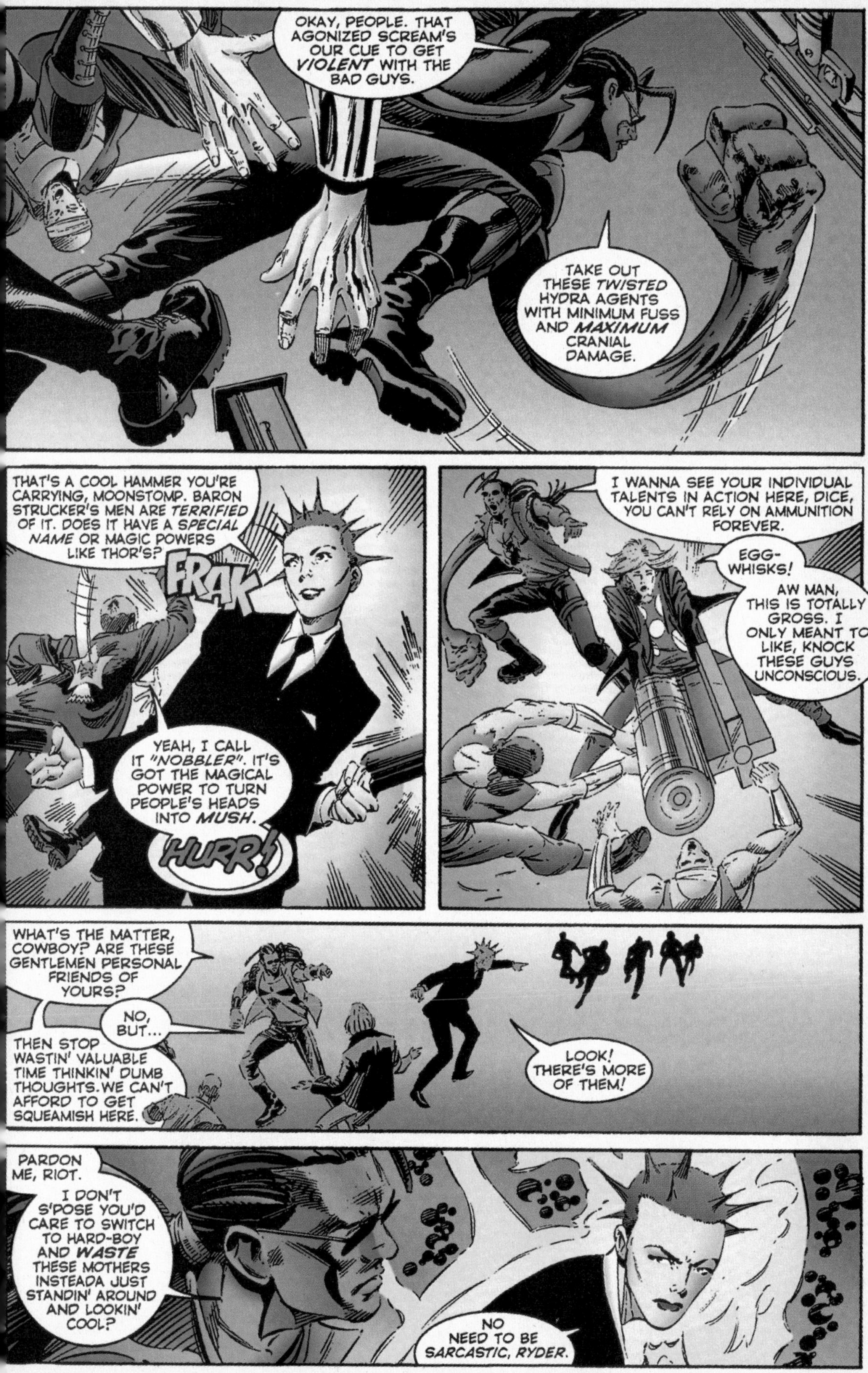
OKAY, PEOPLE. THAT AGONIZED SCREAM'S OUR CUE TO GET VIOLENT WITH THE BAD GUYS.
TAKE OUT THESE TWISTED HYDRA AGENTS WITH MINIMUM FUSS AND MAXIMUM CRANIAL DAMAGE.
THAT'S A COOL HAMMER YOU'RE CARRYING, MOONSTOMP. BARON STRUCKER'S MEN ARE TERRIFIED OF IT. DOES IT HAVE A SPECIAL NAME OR MAGIC POWERS LIKE THOR'S?
FRAK
YEAH, I CALL IT "NOBBLER". IT'S GOT THE MAGICAL POWER TO TURN PEOPLE'S HEADS INTO MUSH.
HURR!
I WANNA SEE YOUR INDIVIDUAL TALENTS IN ACTION HERE, DICE, YOU CAN'T RELY ON AMMUNITION FOREVER.
EGG-WHISKS!
AW MAN, THIS IS TOTALLY GROSS. I ONLY MEANT TO LIKE, KNOCK THESE GUYS UNCONSCIOUS.
WHAT'S THE MATTER, COWBOY? ARE THESE GENTLEMEN PERSONAL FRIENDS OF YOURS?
NO, BUT...
THEN STOP WASTIN' VALUABLE TIME THINKIN' DUMB THOUGHTS. WE CAN'T AFFORD TO GET SQUEAMISH HERE.
LOOK! THERE'S MORE OF THEM!
PARDON ME, RIOT.
I DON'T S'POSE YOU'D CARE TO SWITCH TO HARD-BOY AND WASTE THESE MOTHERS INSTEADA JUST STANDIN' AROUND AND LOOKIN' COOL?
NO NEED TO BE SARCASTIC, RYDER.

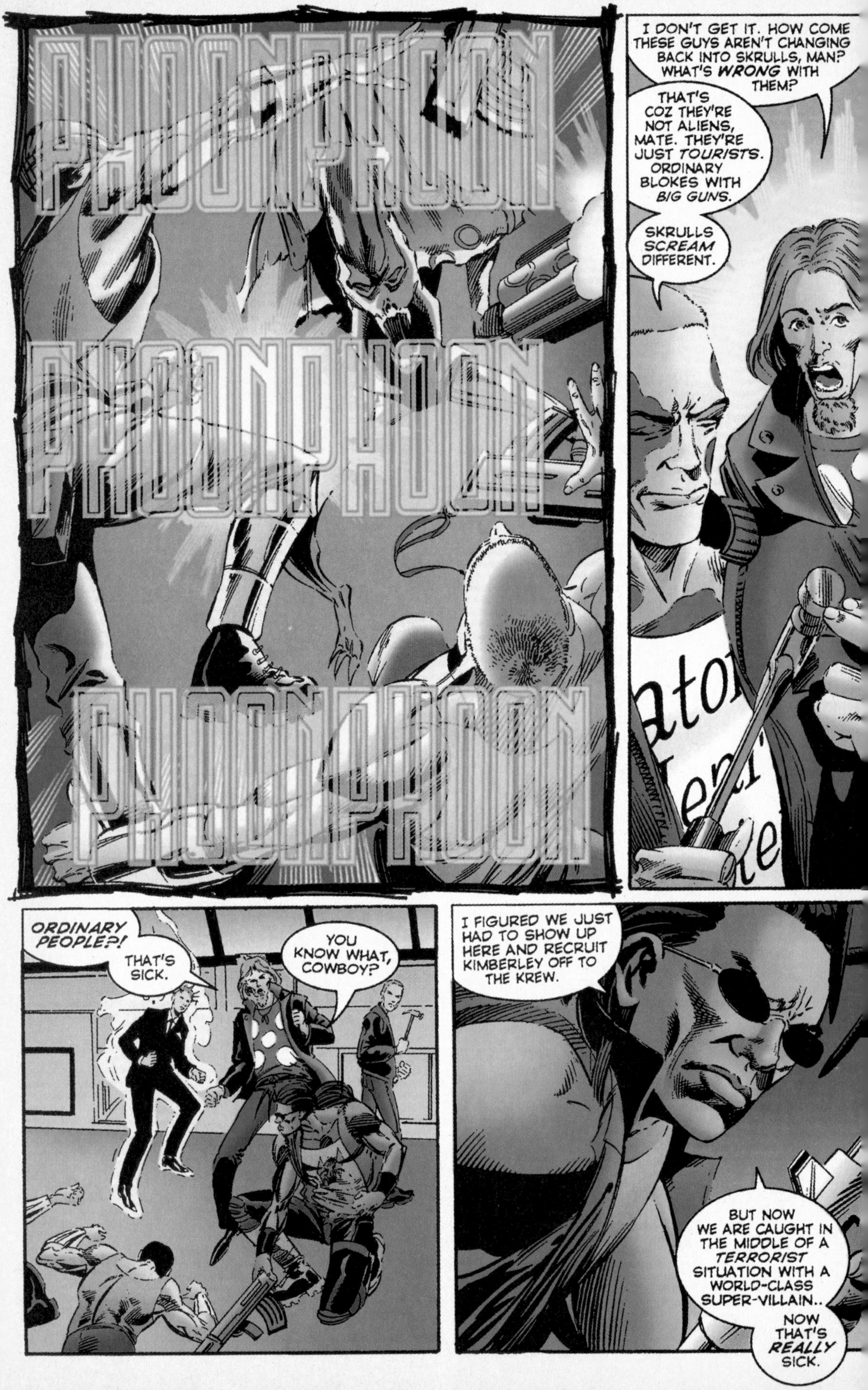
PHOONPHOON
PHOONPHOON
PHOONPHOON
I DON'T GET IT. HOW COME THESE GUYS AREN'T CHANGING BACK INTO SKRULLS, MAN? WHAT'S *WRONG* WITH THEM?
THAT'S COZ THEY'RE NOT ALIENS, MATE. THEY'RE JUST *TOURISTS*. ORDINARY BLOKES WITH *BIG GUNS*.
SKRULLS *SCREAM* DIFFERENT.
*ORDINARY PEOPLE?!*
THAT'S SICK.
YOU KNOW WHAT, COWBOY?
I FIGURED WE JUST HAD TO SHOW UP HERE AND RECRUIT KIMBERLEY OFF TO THE KREW.
BUT NOW WE ARE CAUGHT IN THE MIDDLE OF A *TERRORIST* SITUATION WITH A WORLD-CLASS SUPER-VILLAIN..
NOW THAT'S *REALLY* SICK.

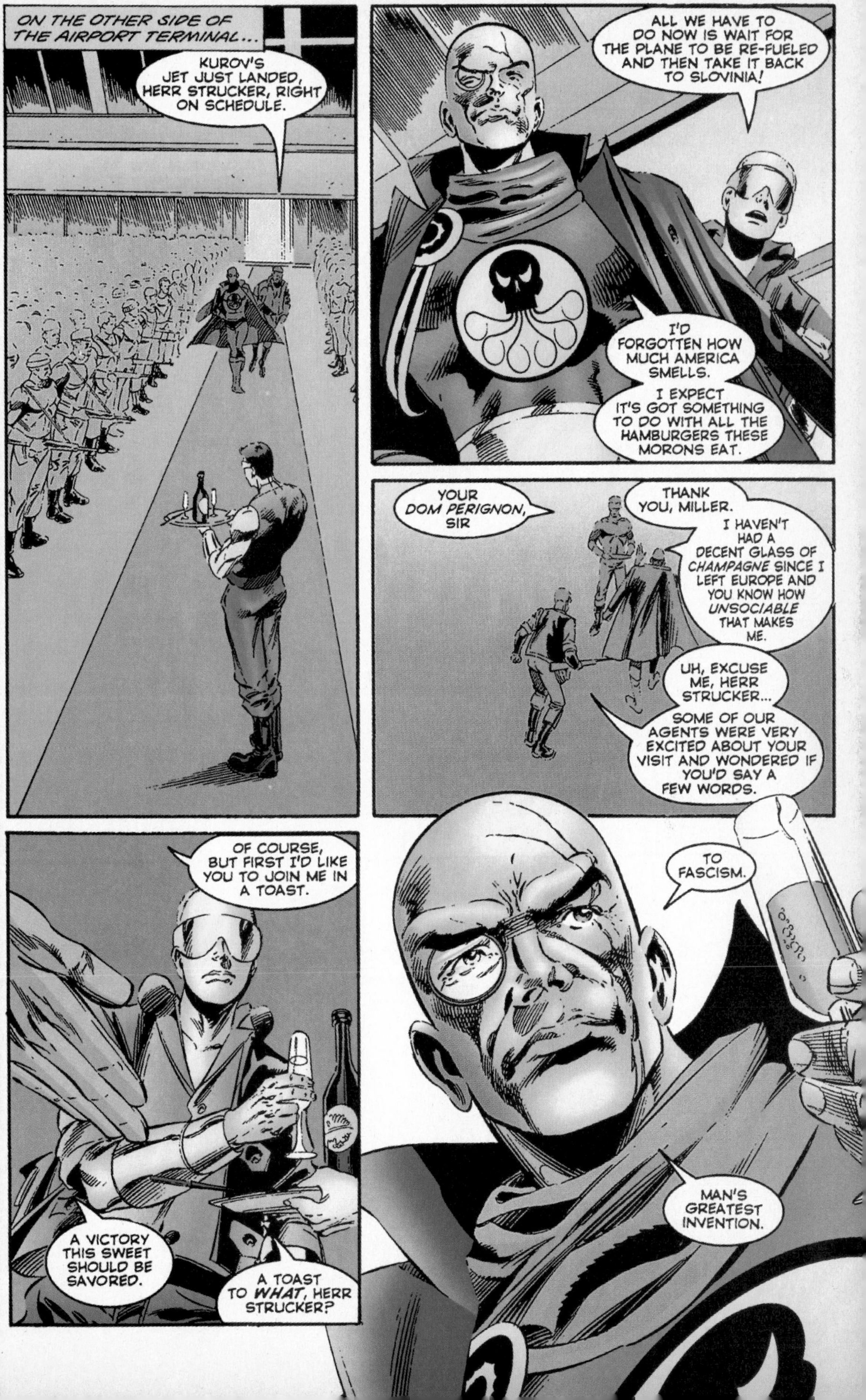
ON THE OTHER SIDE OF THE AIRPORT TERMINAL...
KUROV'S JET JUST LANDED, HERR STRUCKER, RIGHT ON SCHEDULE.
ALL WE HAVE TO DO NOW IS WAIT FOR THE PLANE TO BE RE-FUELED AND THEN TAKE IT BACK TO SLOVINIA!
I'D FORGOTTEN HOW MUCH AMERICA SMELLS.
I EXPECT IT'S GOT SOMETHING TO DO WITH ALL THE HAMBURGERS THESE MORONS EAT.
YOUR DOM PERIGNON, SIR
THANK YOU, MILLER.
I HAVEN'T HAD A DECENT GLASS OF CHAMPAGNE SINCE I LEFT EUROPE AND YOU KNOW HOW UNSOCIABLE THAT MAKES ME.
UH, EXCUSE ME, HERR STRUCKER...
SOME OF OUR AGENTS WERE VERY EXCITED ABOUT YOUR VISIT AND WONDERED IF YOU'D SAY A FEW WORDS.
OF COURSE, BUT FIRST I'D LIKE YOU TO JOIN ME IN A TOAST.
A VICTORY THIS SWEET SHOULD BE SAVORED.
A TOAST TO WHAT, HERR STRUCKER?
TO FASCISM.
MAN'S GREATEST INVENTION.

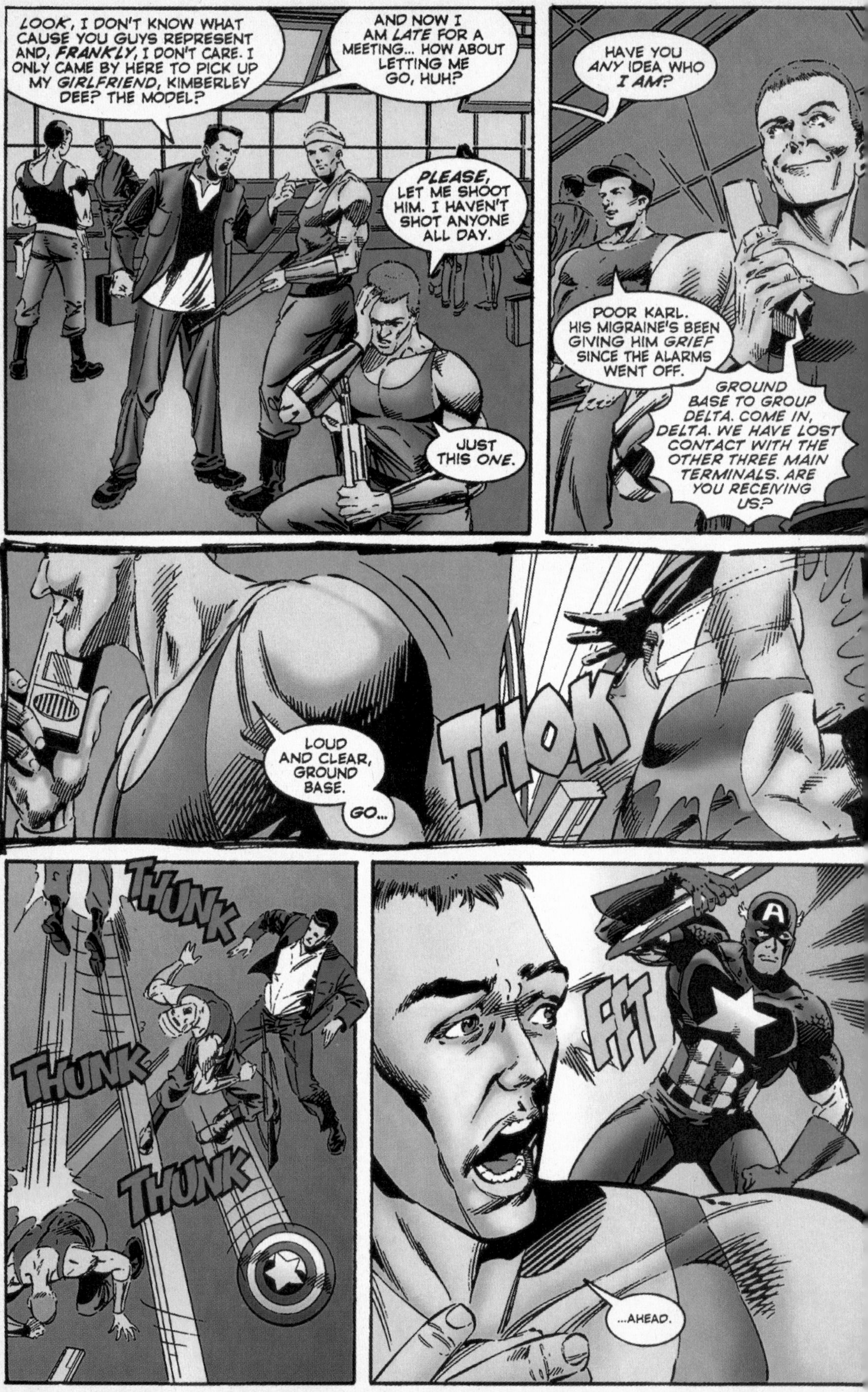
LOOK, I DON'T KNOW WHAT CAUSE YOU GUYS REPRESENT AND, FRANKLY, I DON'T CARE. I ONLY CAME BY HERE TO PICK UP MY GIRLFRIEND, KIMBERLEY DEE? THE MODEL?
AND NOW I AM LATE FOR A MEETING... HOW ABOUT LETTING ME GO, HUH?
PLEASE, LET ME SHOOT HIM. I HAVEN'T SHOT ANYONE ALL DAY.
JUST THIS ONE.
HAVE YOU ANY IDEA WHO I AM?
POOR KARL. HIS MIGRAINE'S BEEN GIVING HIM GRIEF SINCE THE ALARMS WENT OFF.
GROUND BASE TO GROUP DELTA. COME IN, DELTA. WE HAVE LOST CONTACT WITH THE OTHER THREE MAIN TERMINALS. ARE YOU RECEIVING US?
LOUD AND CLEAR, GROUND BASE.
GO...
THOK
THUNK
THUNK
THUNK
FFT
...AHEAD.

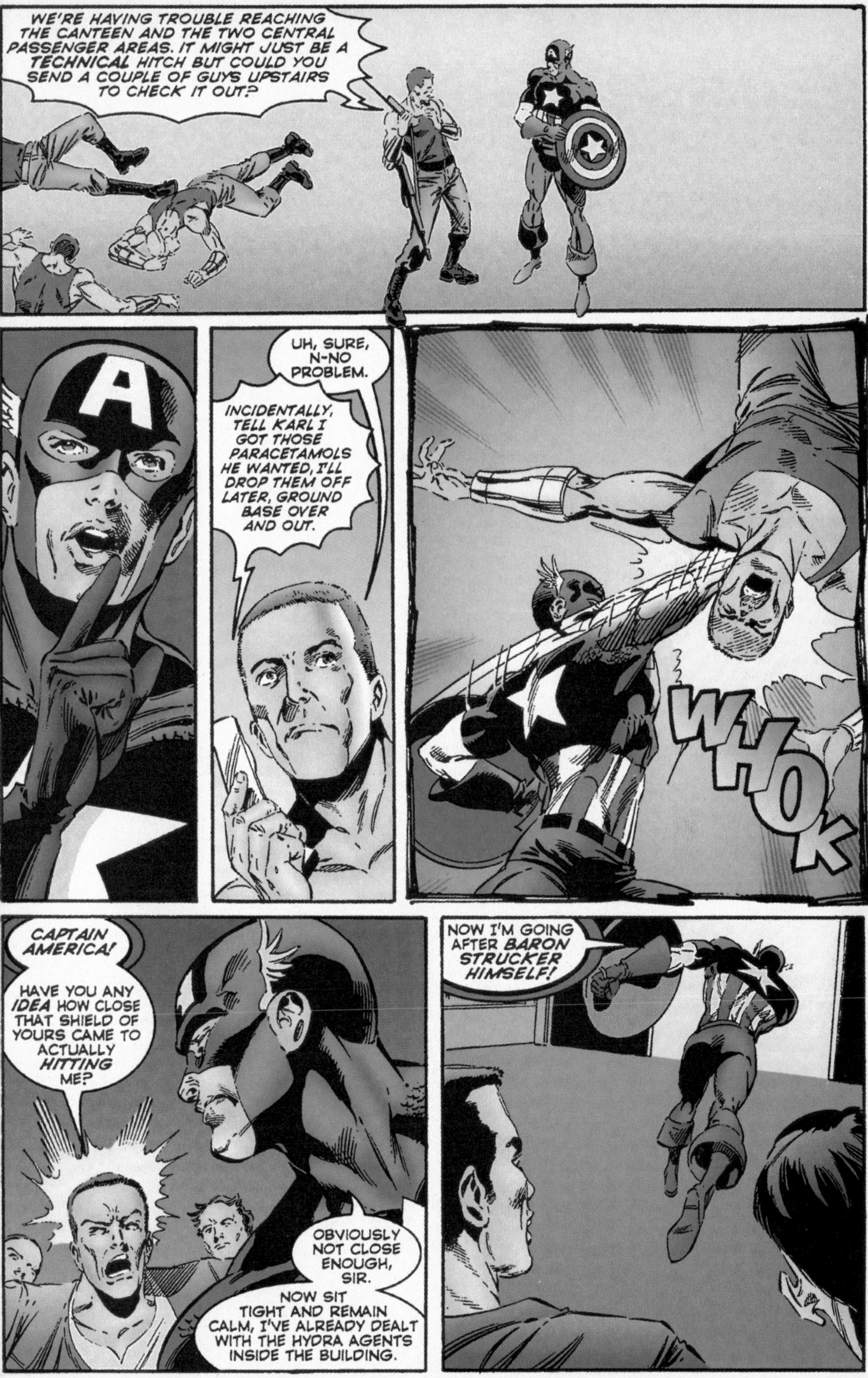
WE'RE HAVING TROUBLE REACHING THE CANTEEN AND THE TWO CENTRAL PASSENGER AREAS. IT MIGHT JUST BE A TECHNICAL HITCH BUT COULD YOU SEND A COUPLE OF GUYS UPSTAIRS TO CHECK IT OUT?
UH, SURE, N-NO PROBLEM.
INCIDENTALLY, TELL KARL I GOT THOSE PARACETAMOLS HE WANTED, I'LL DROP THEM OFF LATER, GROUND BASE OVER AND OUT.
WHOK
CAPTAIN AMERICA!
HAVE YOU ANY IDEA HOW CLOSE THAT SHIELD OF YOURS CAME TO ACTUALLY HITTING ME?
OBVIOUSLY NOT CLOSE ENOUGH, SIR.
NOW SIT TIGHT AND REMAIN CALM, I'VE ALREADY DEALT WITH THE HYDRA AGENTS INSIDE THE BUILDING.
NOW I'M GOING AFTER BARON STRUCKER HIMSELF!

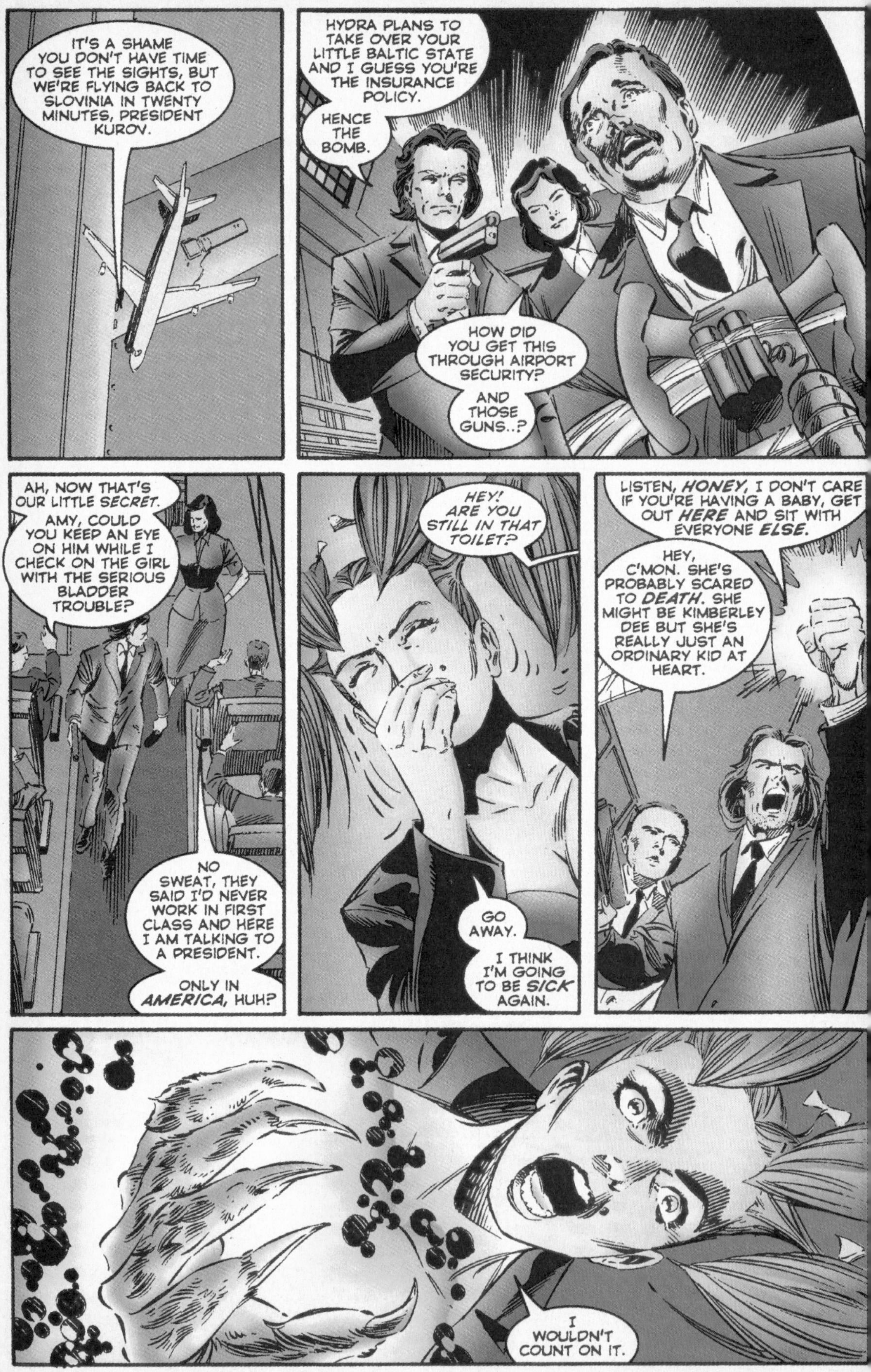
IT'S A SHAME YOU DON'T HAVE TIME TO SEE THE SIGHTS, BUT WE'RE FLYING BACK TO SLOVINIA IN TWENTY MINUTES, PRESIDENT KUROV.
HYDRA PLANS TO TAKE OVER YOUR LITTLE BALTIC STATE AND I GUESS YOU'RE THE INSURANCE POLICY.
HENCE THE BOMB.
HOW DID YOU GET THIS THROUGH AIRPORT SECURITY?
AND THOSE GUNS..?
AH, NOW THAT'S OUR LITTLE SECRET.
AMY, COULD YOU KEEP AN EYE ON HIM WHILE I CHECK ON THE GIRL WITH THE SERIOUS BLADDER TROUBLE?
NO SWEAT, THEY SAID I'D NEVER WORK IN FIRST CLASS AND HERE I AM TALKING TO A PRESIDENT.
ONLY IN AMERICA, HUH?
HEY! ARE YOU STILL IN THAT TOILET?
GO AWAY.
I THINK I'M GOING TO BE SICK AGAIN.
LISTEN, HONEY, I DON'T CARE IF YOU'RE HAVING A BABY, GET OUT HERE AND SIT WITH EVERYONE ELSE.
HEY, C'MON. SHE'S PROBABLY SCARED TO DEATH. SHE MIGHT BE KIMBERLEY DEE BUT SHE'S REALLY JUST AN ORDINARY KID AT HEART.
I WOULDN'T COUNT ON IT.

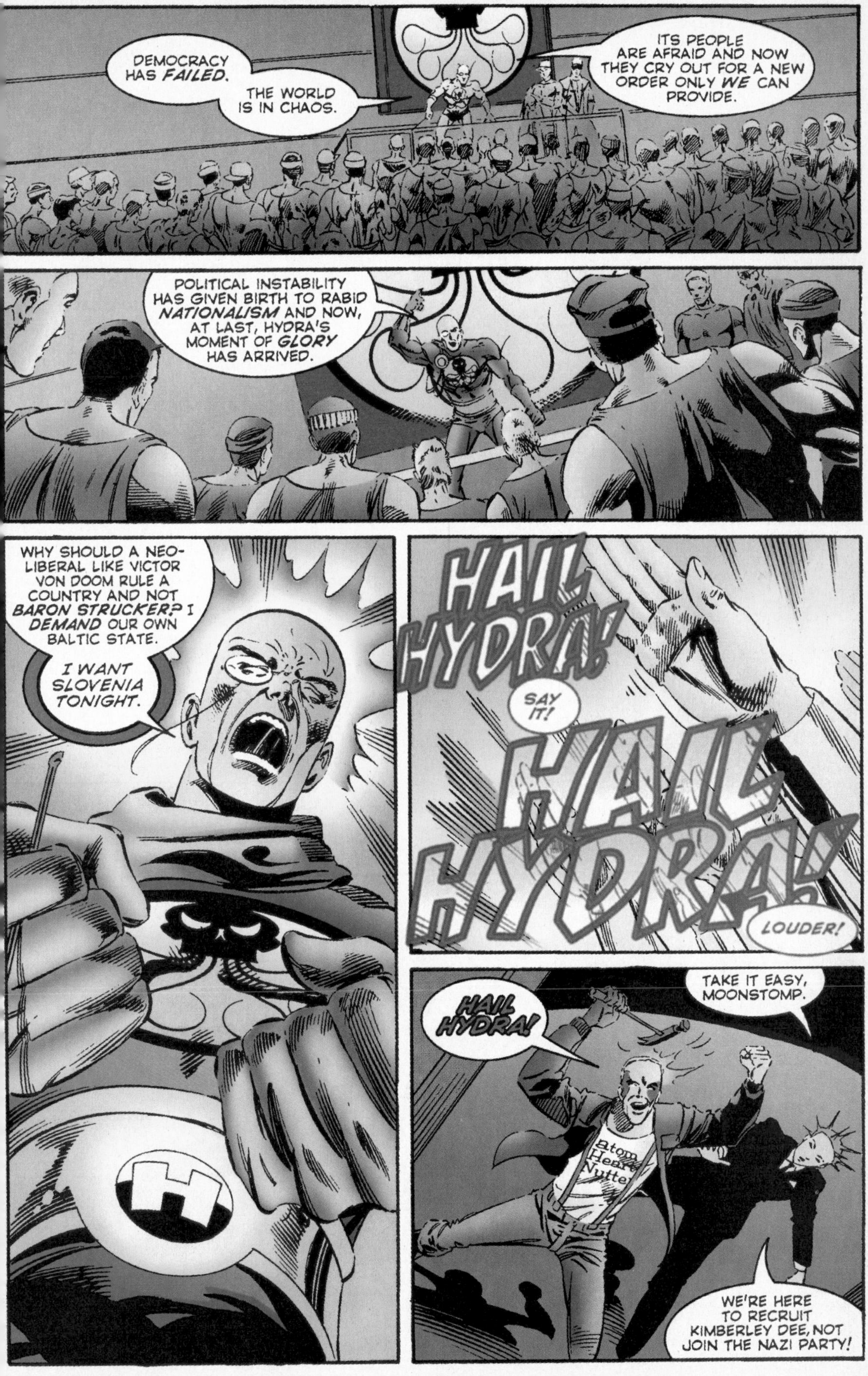
DEMOCRACY HAS FAILED.
THE WORLD IS IN CHAOS.
ITS PEOPLE ARE AFRAID AND NOW THEY CRY OUT FOR A NEW ORDER ONLY WE CAN PROVIDE.
POLITICAL INSTABILITY HAS GIVEN BIRTH TO RABID NATIONALISM AND NOW, AT LAST, HYDRA'S MOMENT OF GLORY HAS ARRIVED.
WHY SHOULD A NEO-LIBERAL LIKE VICTOR VON DOOM RULE A COUNTRY AND NOT BARON STRUCKER? I DEMAND OUR OWN BALTIC STATE.
I WANT SLOVENIA TONIGHT.
HAIL HYDRA!
SAY IT!
HAIL HYDRA!
LOUDER!
HAIL HYDRA!
TAKE IT EASY, MOONSTOMP.
WE'RE HERE TO RECRUIT KIMBERLEY DEE, NOT JOIN THE NAZI PARTY!

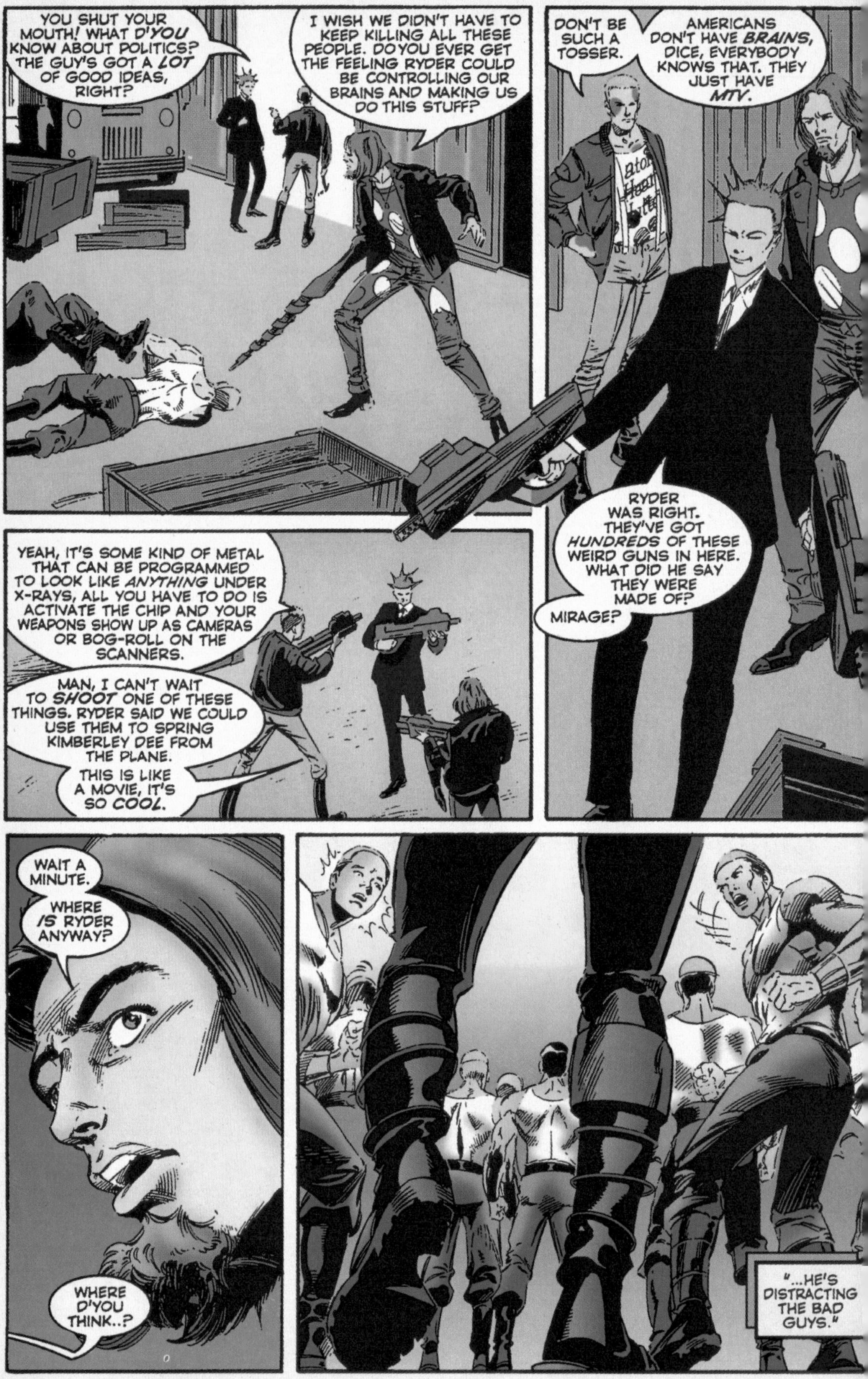
YOU SHUT YOUR MOUTH! WHAT D'YOU KNOW ABOUT POLITICS? THE GUY'S GOT A LOT OF GOOD IDEAS, RIGHT?
I WISH WE DIDN'T HAVE TO KEEP KILLING ALL THESE PEOPLE. DO YOU EVER GET THE FEELING RYDER COULD BE CONTROLLING OUR BRAINS AND MAKING US DO THIS STUFF?
DON'T BE SUCH A TOSSER.
AMERICANS DON'T HAVE BRAINS, DICE, EVERYBODY KNOWS THAT. THEY JUST HAVE MTV.
RYDER WAS RIGHT. THEY'VE GOT HUNDREDS OF THESE WEIRD GUNS IN HERE. WHAT DID HE SAY THEY WERE MADE OF?
MIRAGE?
YEAH, IT'S SOME KIND OF METAL THAT CAN BE PROGRAMMED TO LOOK LIKE ANYTHING UNDER X-RAYS, ALL YOU HAVE TO DO IS ACTIVATE THE CHIP AND YOUR WEAPONS SHOW UP AS CAMERAS OR BOG-ROLL ON THE SCANNERS.
MAN, I CAN'T WAIT TO SHOOT ONE OF THESE THINGS. RYDER SAID WE COULD USE THEM TO SPRING KIMBERLEY DEE FROM THE PLANE.
THIS IS LIKE A MOVIE, IT'S SO COOL.
WAIT A MINUTE.
WHERE IS RYDER ANYWAY?
WHERE D'YOU THINK..?
"...HE'S DISTRACTING THE BAD GUYS."

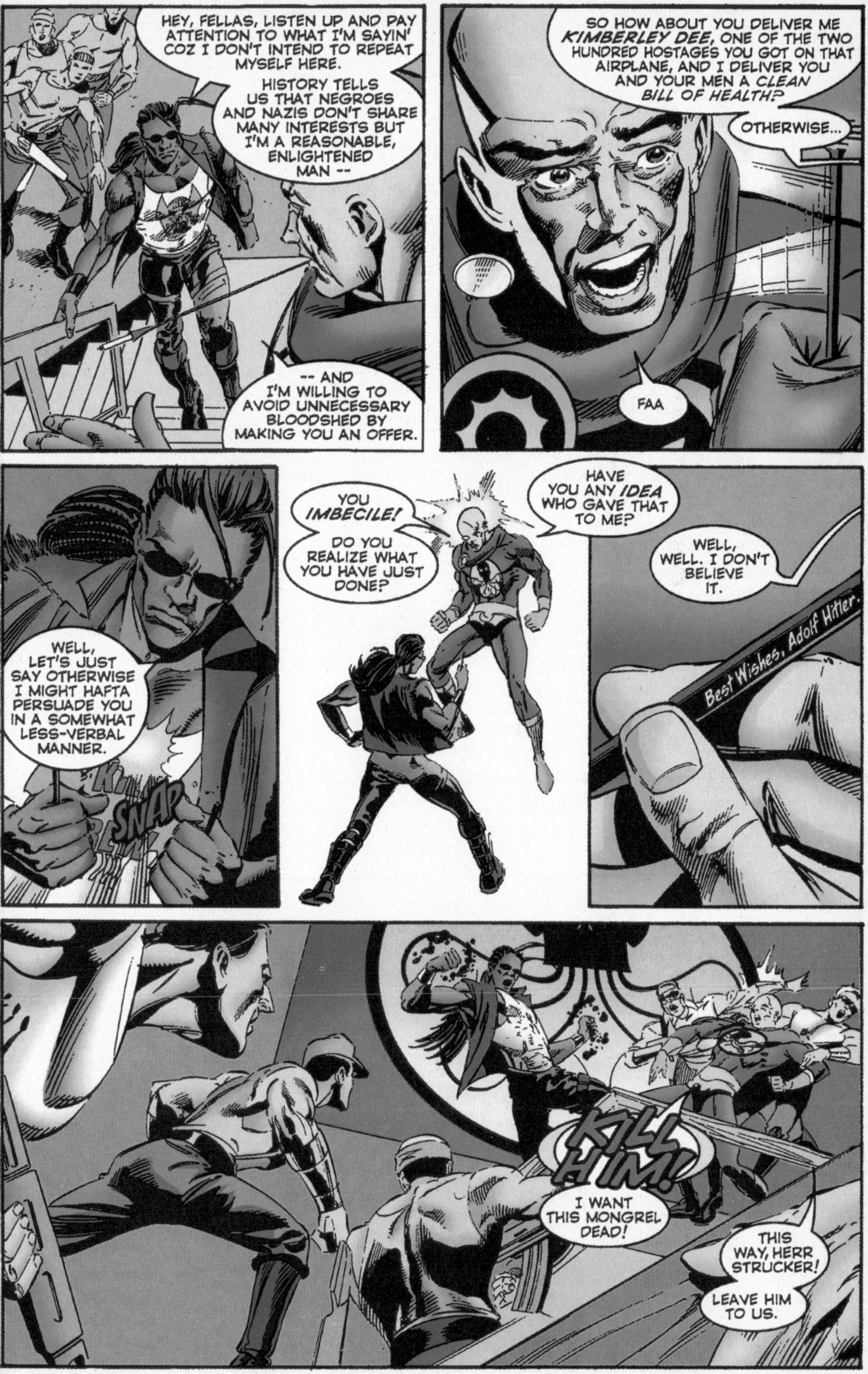
HEY, FELLAS, LISTEN UP AND PAY ATTENTION TO WHAT I'M SAYIN' COZ I DON'T INTEND TO REPEAT MYSELF HERE.
HISTORY TELLS US THAT NEGROES AND NAZIS DON'T SHARE MANY INTERESTS BUT I'M A REASONABLE, ENLIGHTENED MAN --
-- AND I'M WILLING TO AVOID UNNECESSARY BLOODSHED BY MAKING YOU AN OFFER.
SO HOW ABOUT YOU DELIVER ME KIMBERLEY DEE, ONE OF THE TWO HUNDRED HOSTAGES YOU GOT ON THAT AIRPLANE, AND I DELIVER YOU AND YOUR MEN A CLEAN BILL OF HEALTH?
OTHERWISE...
FAA
WELL, LET'S JUST SAY OTHERWISE I MIGHT HAFTA PERSUADE YOU IN A SOMEWHAT LESS-VERBAL MANNER.
SNAP
YOU IMBECILE!
DO YOU REALIZE WHAT YOU HAVE JUST DONE?
HAVE YOU ANY IDEA WHO GAVE THAT TO ME?
WELL, WELL. I DON'T BELIEVE IT.
Best Wishes, Adolf Hitler.
KILL HIM!
I WANT THIS MONGREL DEAD!
THIS WAY, HERR STRUCKER!
LEAVE HIM TO US.

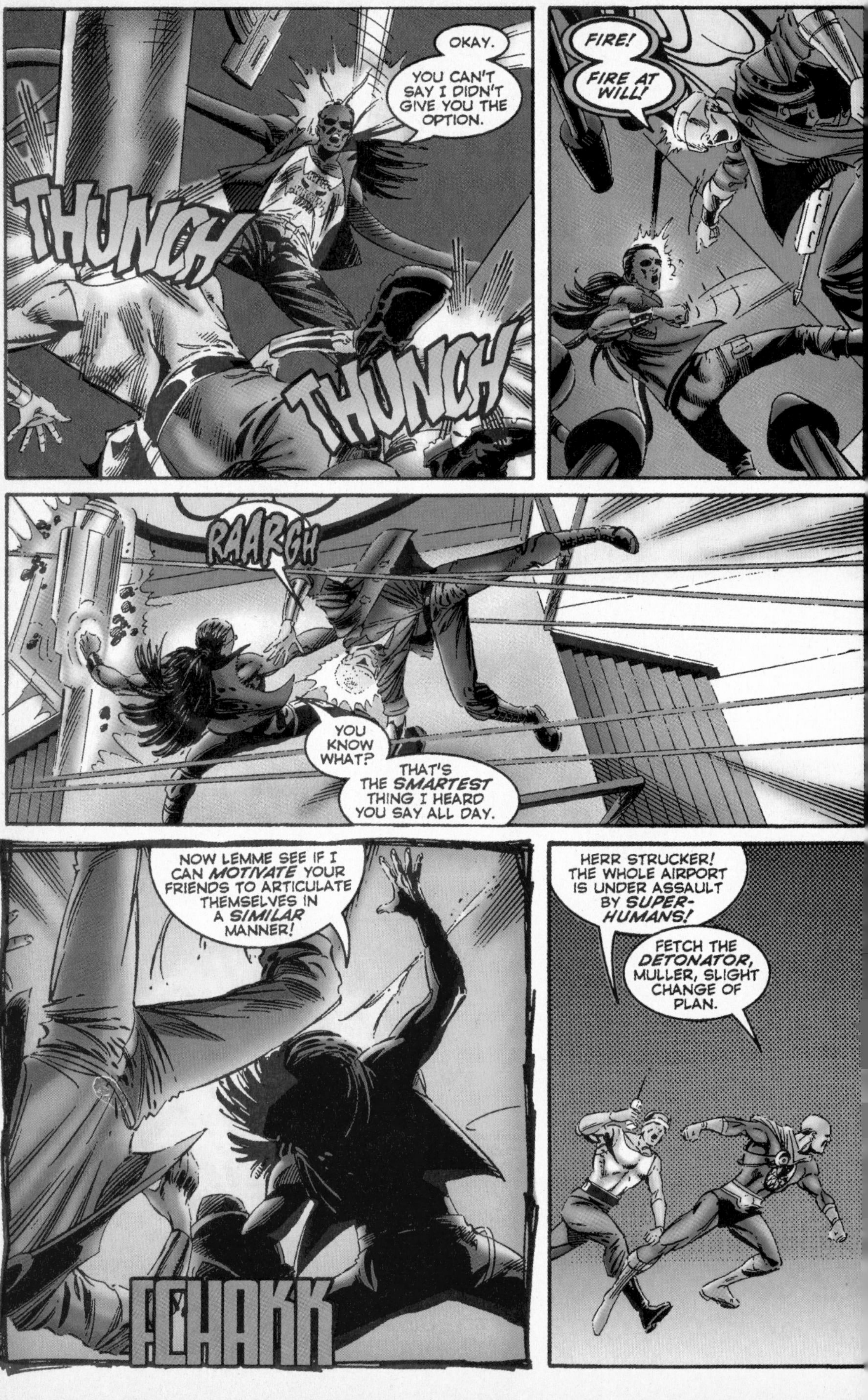
OKAY.
YOU CAN'T SAY I DIDN'T GIVE YOU THE OPTION.
THUNCH
THUNCH
FIRE!
FIRE AT WILL!
RAARGH
YOU KNOW WHAT?
THAT'S THE SMARTEST THING I HEARD YOU SAY ALL DAY.
NOW LEMME SEE IF I CAN MOTIVATE YOUR FRIENDS TO ARTICULATE THEMSELVES IN A SIMILAR MANNER!
FCHAKK
HERR STRUCKER! THE WHOLE AIRPORT IS UNDER ASSAULT BY SUPER-HUMANS!
FETCH THE DETONATOR, MULLER, SLIGHT CHANGE OF PLAN.

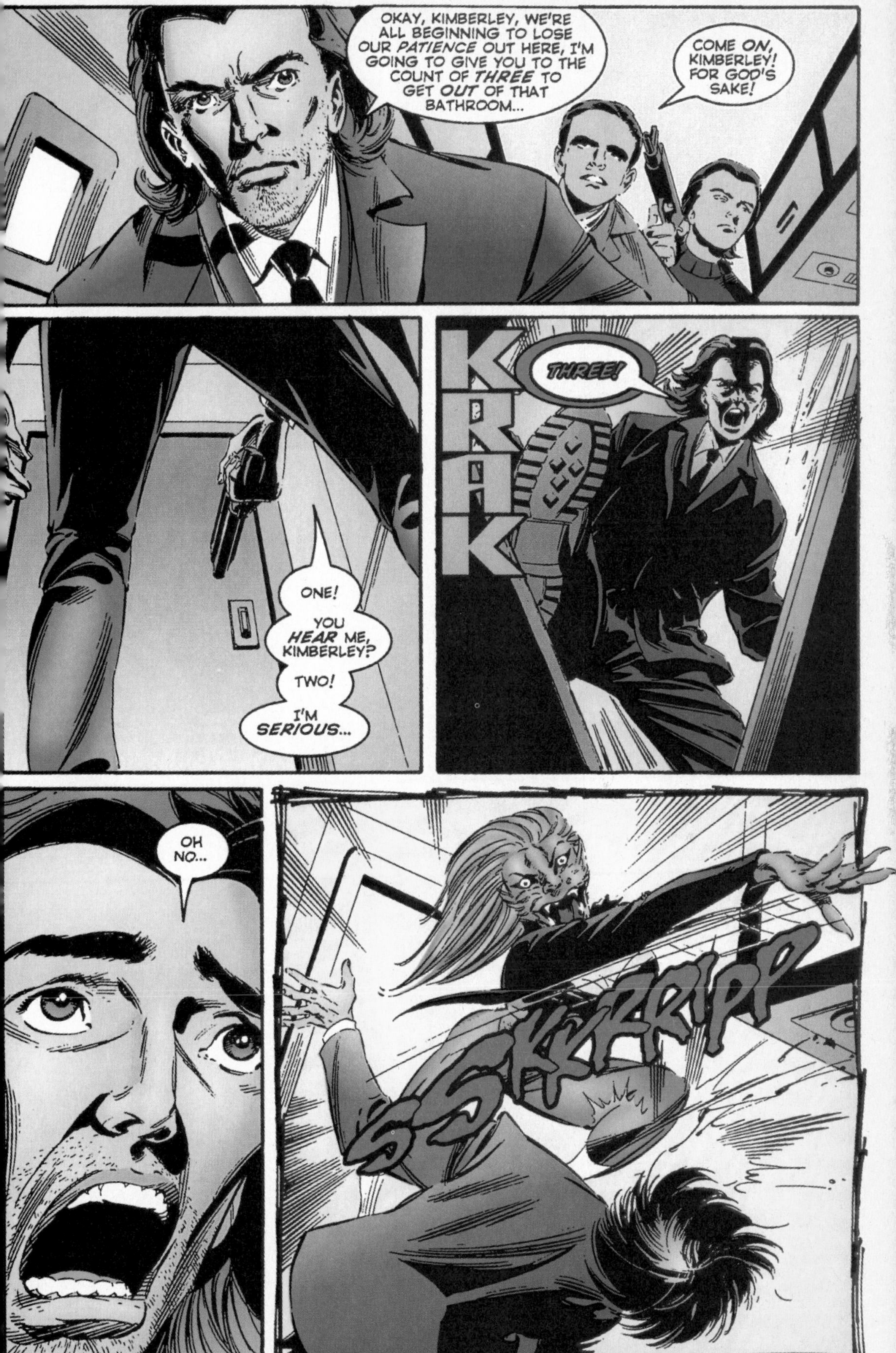
OKAY, KIMBERLEY, WE'RE ALL BEGINNING TO LOSE OUR PATIENCE OUT HERE, I'M GOING TO GIVE YOU TO THE COUNT OF THREE TO GET OUT OF THAT BATHROOM...
COME ON, KIMBERLEY! FOR GOD'S SAKE!
ONE!
YOU HEAR ME, KIMBERLEY?
TWO!
I'M SERIOUS...
KRAK
THREE!
OH NO...
SSKKRRIPP

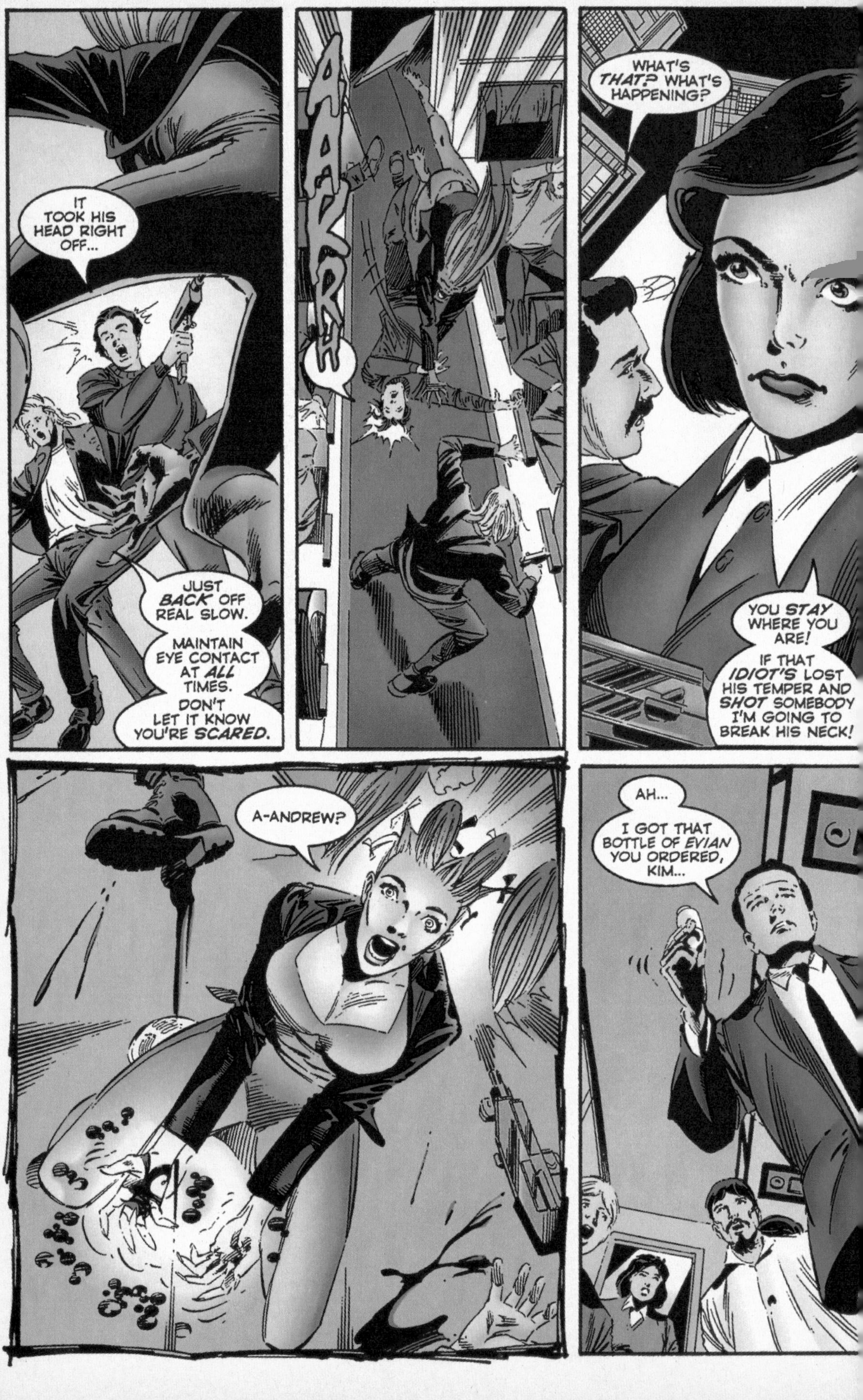
IT TOOK HIS HEAD RIGHT OFF...
JUST BACK OFF REAL SLOW.
MAINTAIN EYE CONTACT AT ALL TIMES.
DON'T LET IT KNOW YOU'RE SCARED.
AAAKRH
WHAT'S THAT? WHAT'S HAPPENING?
YOU STAY WHERE YOU ARE!
IF THAT IDIOT'S LOST HIS TEMPER AND SHOT SOMEBODY I'M GOING TO BREAK HIS NECK!
A-ANDREW?
AH...
I GOT THAT BOTTLE OF EVIAN YOU ORDERED, KIM...

THE BOMB! I THOUGHT I TOLD YOU NOT TO TOUCH ANYTHING!

IT WASN'T ME! SOMEONE MUST HAVE DETONATED IT!

OH GOD...

THAT MEANS THE PLANE'S GOING TO BLOW UP IN FIVE MINUTES.

KIMBERLEY! DO SOMETHING!

WHAT D'YOU MEAN? I HAVEN'T EVEN WORKED OUT HOW I DID THIS YET!

IT'S NO USE! THE DOOR'S LOCKED!

THERE'S NO WAY OUT!

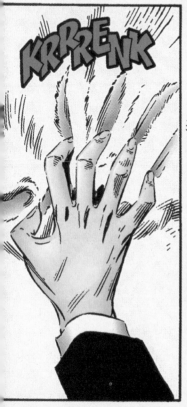

KRRRENK

CHANG

BRITIS

HEY, EVERYBODY! THE CAVALRY'S ARRIVED.

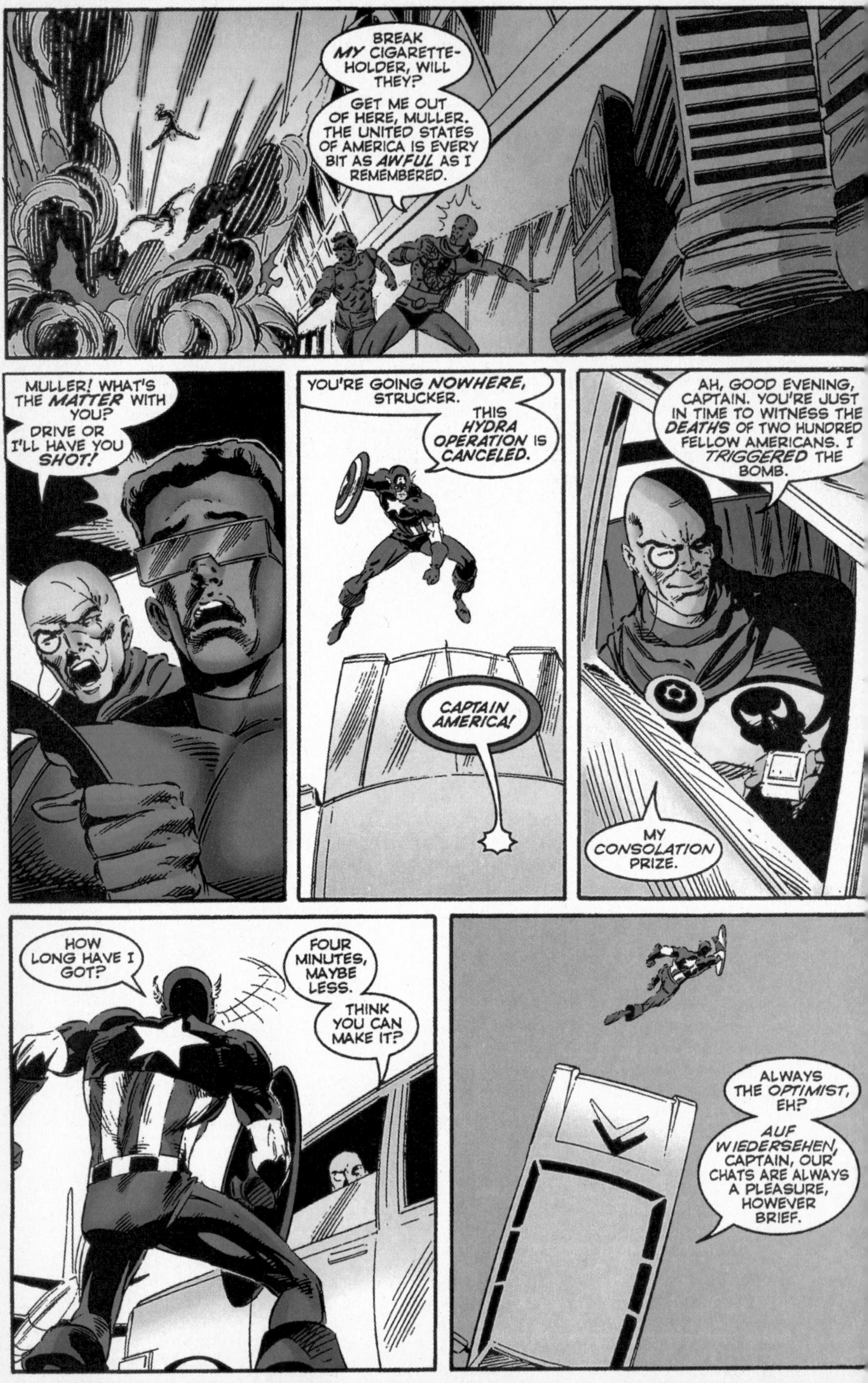
BREAK MY CIGARETTE-HOLDER, WILL THEY?
GET ME OUT OF HERE, MULLER. THE UNITED STATES OF AMERICA IS EVERY BIT AS AWFUL AS I REMEMBERED.
MULLER! WHAT'S THE MATTER WITH YOU?
DRIVE OR I'LL HAVE YOU SHOT!
YOU'RE GOING NOWHERE, STRUCKER.
THIS HYDRA OPERATION IS CANCELED.
CAPTAIN AMERICA!
AH, GOOD EVENING, CAPTAIN. YOU'RE JUST IN TIME TO WITNESS THE DEATHS OF TWO HUNDRED FELLOW AMERICANS. I TRIGGERED THE BOMB.
MY CONSOLATION PRIZE.
HOW LONG HAVE I GOT?
FOUR MINUTES, MAYBE LESS.
THINK YOU CAN MAKE IT?
ALWAYS THE OPTIMIST, EH?
AUF WIEDERSEHEN, CAPTAIN, OUR CHATS ARE ALWAYS A PLEASURE, HOWEVER BRIEF.

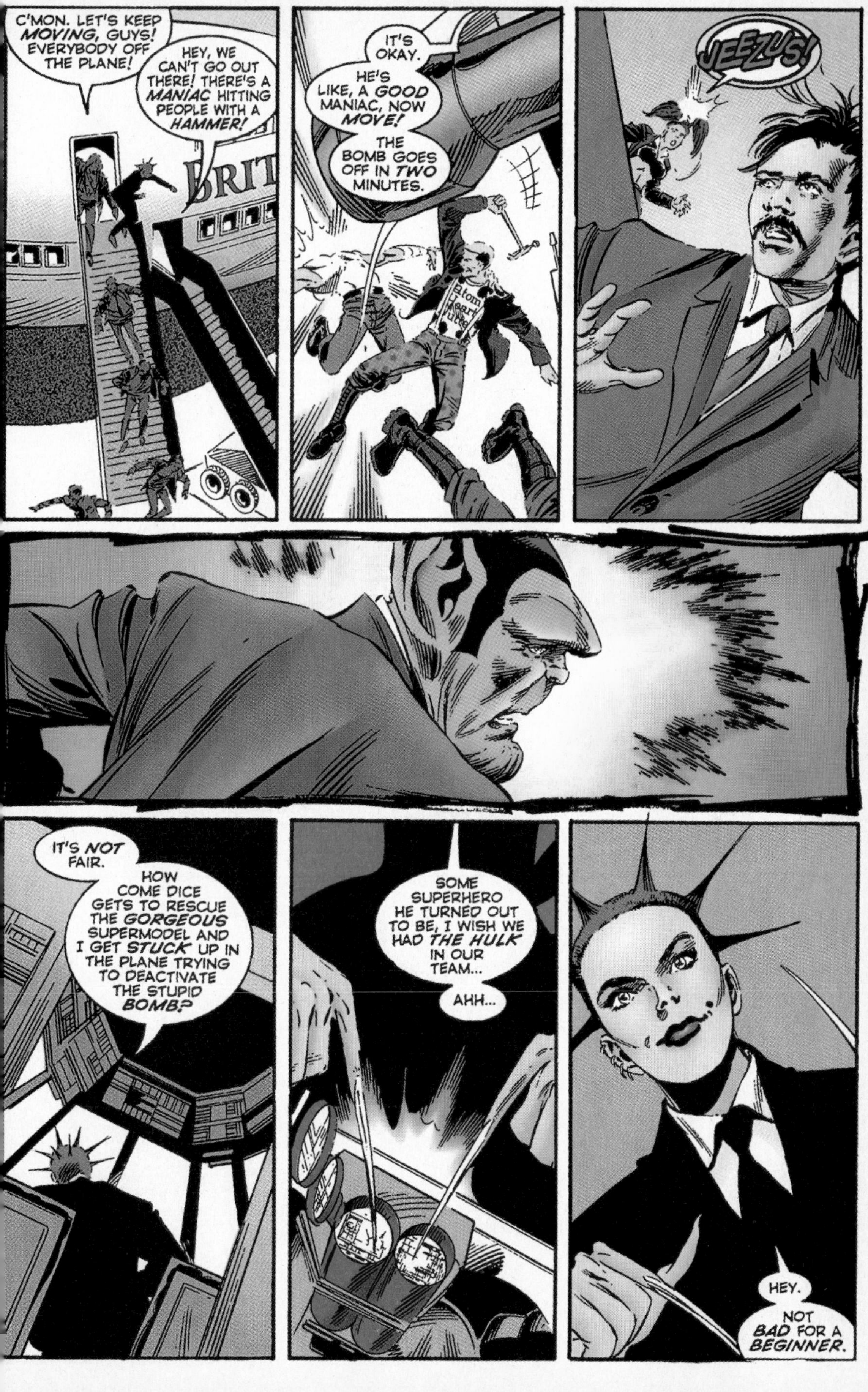
C'MON. LET'S KEEP MOVING, GUYS! EVERYBODY OFF THE PLANE!
HEY, WE CAN'T GO OUT THERE! THERE'S A MANIAC HITTING PEOPLE WITH A HAMMER!
BRIT
IT'S OKAY.
HE'S LIKE, A GOOD MANIAC, NOW MOVE!
THE BOMB GOES OFF IN TWO MINUTES.
JEEZUS!
IT'S NOT FAIR.
HOW COME DICE GETS TO RESCUE THE GORGEOUS SUPERMODEL AND I GET STUCK UP IN THE PLANE TRYING TO DEACTIVATE THE STUPID BOMB?
SOME SUPERHERO HE TURNED OUT TO BE, I WISH WE HAD THE HULK IN OUR TEAM...
AHH...
HEY.
NOT BAD FOR A BEGINNER.

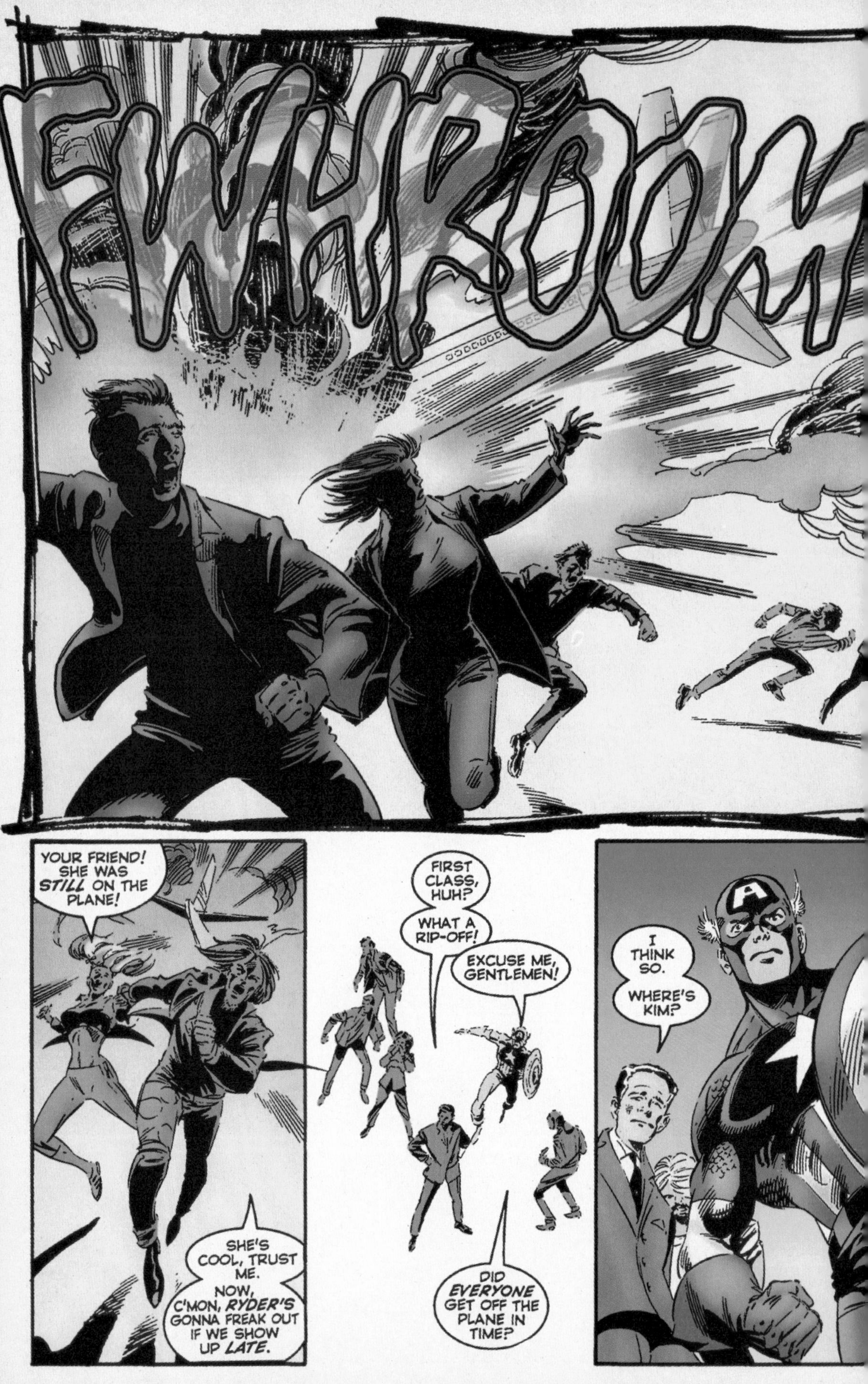
FWHOOM
YOUR FRIEND! SHE WAS STILL ON THE PLANE!
SHE'S COOL, TRUST ME. NOW, C'MON, RYDER'S GONNA FREAK OUT IF WE SHOW UP LATE.
FIRST CLASS, HUH?
WHAT A RIP-OFF!
EXCUSE ME, GENTLEMEN!
DID EVERYONE GET OFF THE PLANE IN TIME?
I THINK SO.
WHERE'S KIM?

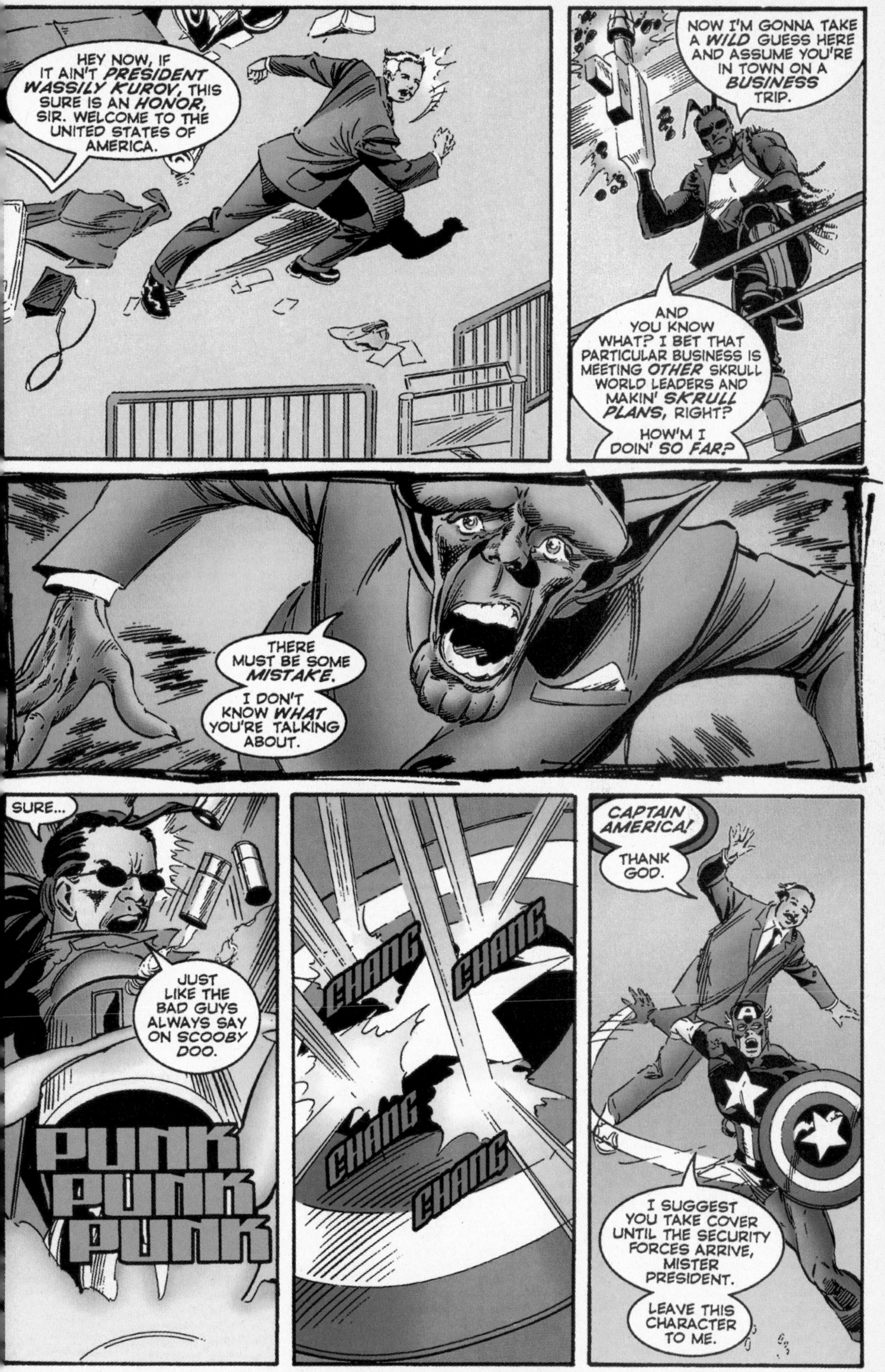
HEY NOW, IF IT AIN'T PRESIDENT WASSILY KUROV, THIS SURE IS AN HONOR, SIR. WELCOME TO THE UNITED STATES OF AMERICA.
NOW I'M GONNA TAKE A WILD GUESS HERE AND ASSUME YOU'RE IN TOWN ON A BUSINESS TRIP.
AND YOU KNOW WHAT? I BET THAT PARTICULAR BUSINESS IS MEETING OTHER SKRULL WORLD LEADERS AND MAKIN' SKRULL PLANS, RIGHT?
HOW'M I DOIN' SO FAR?
THERE MUST BE SOME MISTAKE.
I DON'T KNOW WHAT YOU'RE TALKING ABOUT.
SURE...
JUST LIKE THE BAD GUYS ALWAYS SAY ON SCOOBY DOO.
PUNK PUNK PUNK
CHANG CHANG
CHANG
CHANG
CHANG
CAPTAIN AMERICA!
THANK GOD.
I SUGGEST YOU TAKE COVER UNTIL THE SECURITY FORCES ARRIVE, MISTER PRESIDENT.
LEAVE THIS CHARACTER TO ME.

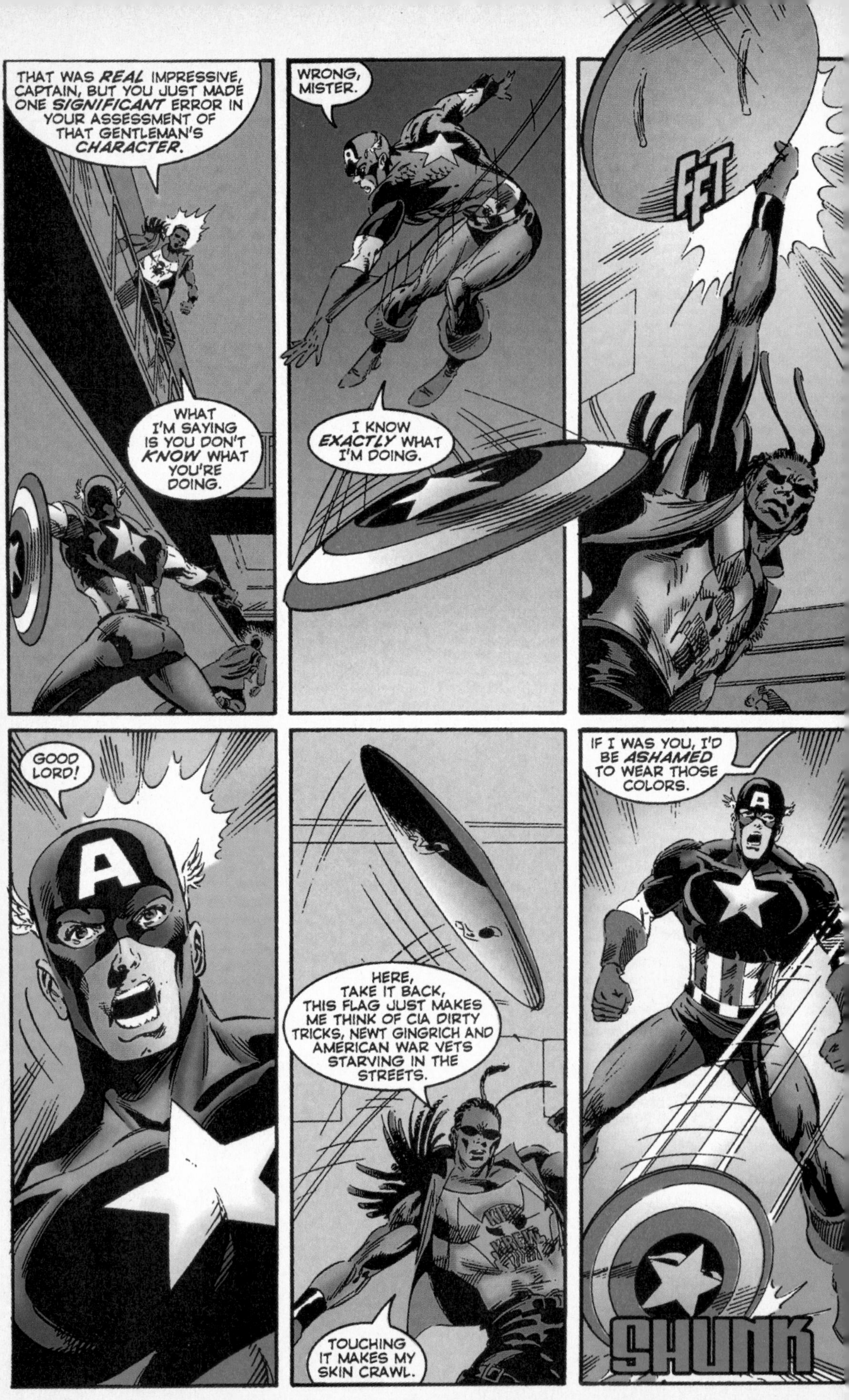
THAT WAS REAL IMPRESSIVE, CAPTAIN, BUT YOU JUST MADE ONE SIGNIFICANT ERROR IN YOUR ASSESSMENT OF THAT GENTLEMAN'S CHARACTER.
WHAT I'M SAYING IS YOU DON'T KNOW WHAT YOU'RE DOING.
WRONG, MISTER.
I KNOW EXACTLY WHAT I'M DOING.
FFT
GOOD LORD!
HERE, TAKE IT BACK, THIS FLAG JUST MAKES ME THINK OF CIA DIRTY TRICKS, NEWT GINGRICH AND AMERICAN WAR VETS STARVING IN THE STREETS.
TOUCHING IT MAKES MY SKIN CRAWL.
IF I WAS YOU, I'D BE ASHAMED TO WEAR THOSE COLORS.
SHUNK

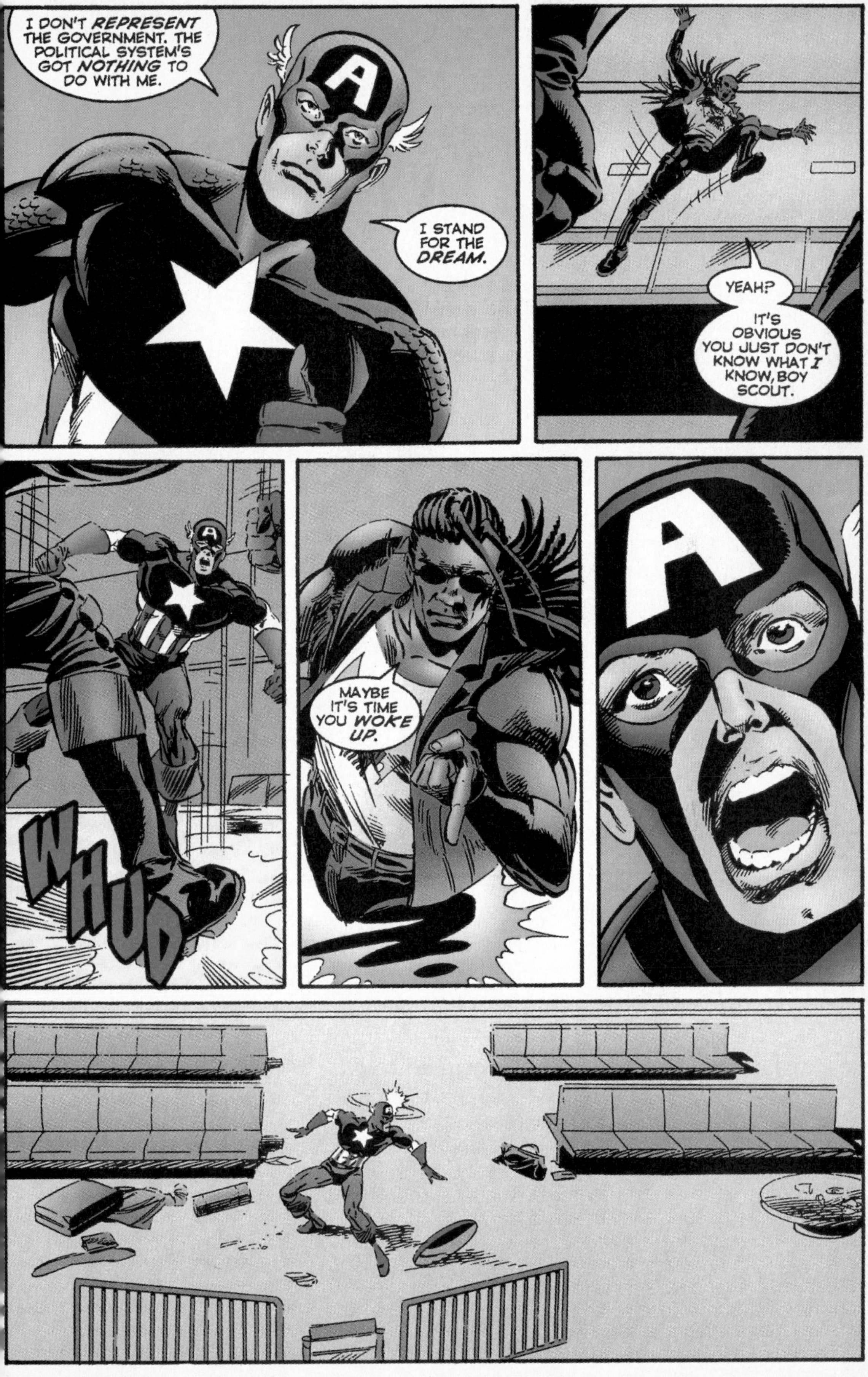
I DON'T REPRESENT THE GOVERNMENT. THE POLITICAL SYSTEM'S GOT NOTHING TO DO WITH ME.
I STAND FOR THE DREAM.
YEAH?
IT'S OBVIOUS YOU JUST DON'T KNOW WHAT I KNOW, BOY SCOUT.
WHUD
MAYBE IT'S TIME YOU WOKE UP.

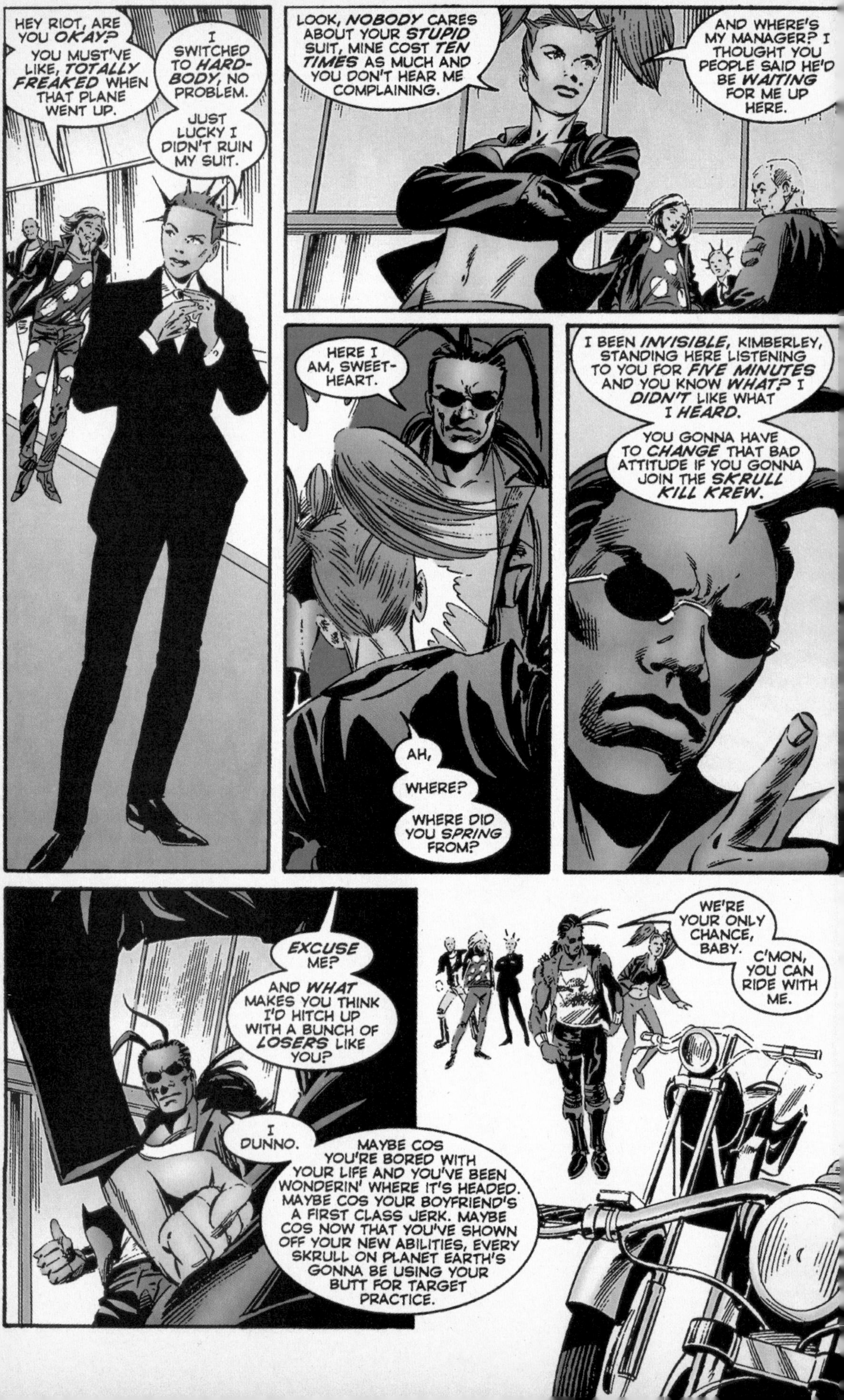
HEY RIOT, ARE YOU OKAY? YOU MUST'VE LIKE, TOTALLY FREAKED WHEN THAT PLANE WENT UP.
I SWITCHED TO HARD-BODY, NO PROBLEM.
JUST LUCKY I DIDN'T RUIN MY SUIT.
LOOK, NOBODY CARES ABOUT YOUR STUPID SUIT, MINE COST TEN TIMES AS MUCH AND YOU DON'T HEAR ME COMPLAINING.
AND WHERE'S MY MANAGER? I THOUGHT YOU PEOPLE SAID HE'D BE WAITING FOR ME UP HERE.
HERE I AM, SWEET-HEART.
AH,
WHERE?
WHERE DID YOU SPRING FROM?
I BEEN INVISIBLE, KIMBERLEY, STANDING HERE LISTENING TO YOU FOR FIVE MINUTES AND YOU KNOW WHAT? I DIDN'T LIKE WHAT I HEARD.
YOU GONNA HAVE TO CHANGE THAT BAD ATTITUDE IF YOU GONNA JOIN THE SKRULL KILL KREW.
EXCUSE ME?
AND WHAT MAKES YOU THINK I'D HITCH UP WITH A BUNCH OF LOSERS LIKE YOU?
I DUNNO.
MAYBE COS YOU'RE BORED WITH YOUR LIFE AND YOU'VE BEEN WONDERIN' WHERE IT'S HEADED. MAYBE COS YOUR BOYFRIEND'S A FIRST CLASS JERK. MAYBE COS NOW THAT YOU'VE SHOWN OFF YOUR NEW ABILITIES, EVERY SKRULL ON PLANET EARTH'S GONNA BE USING YOUR BUTT FOR TARGET PRACTICE.
WE'RE YOUR ONLY CHANCE, BABY.
C'MON, YOU CAN RIDE WITH ME.

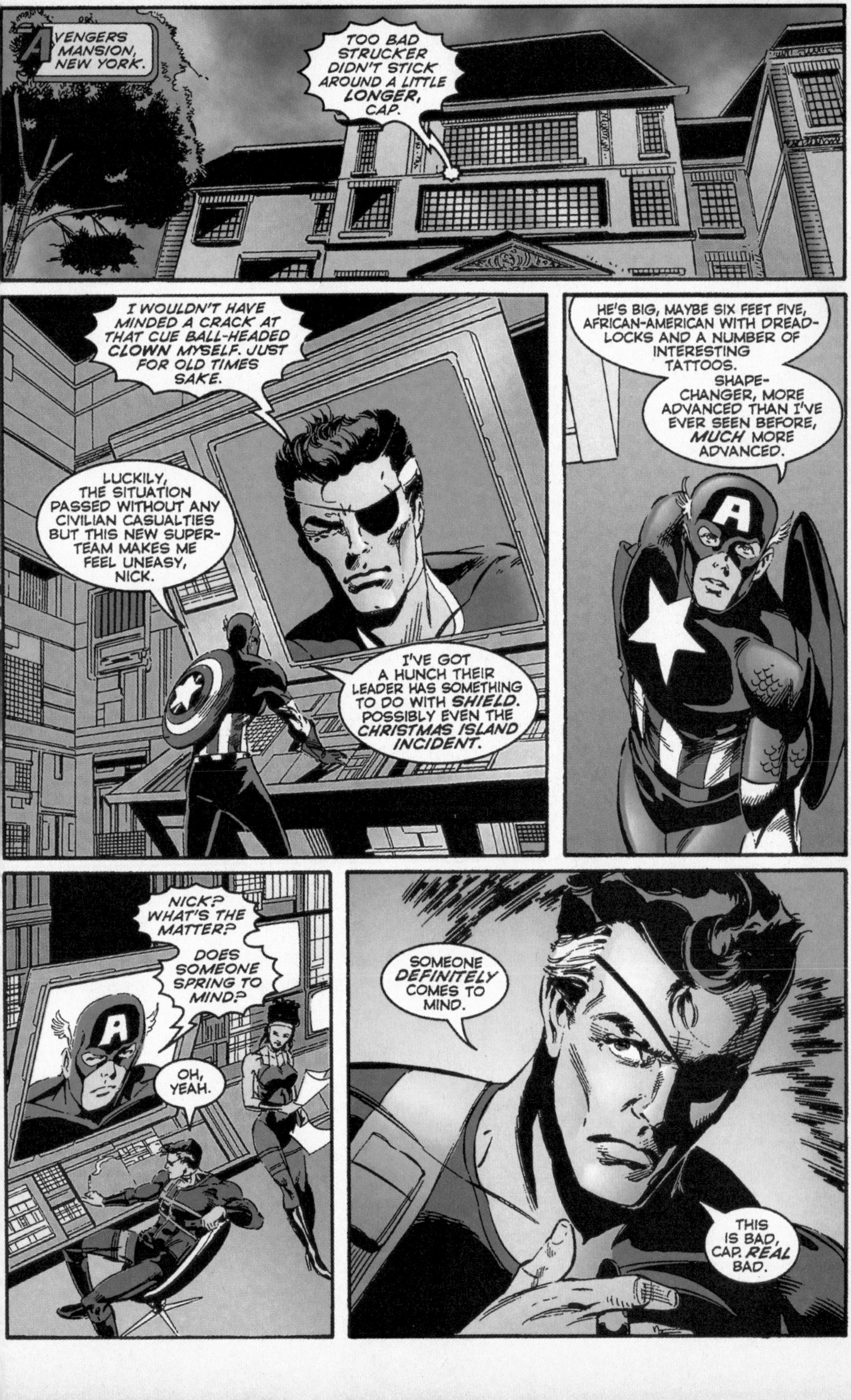
AVENGERS MANSION, NEW YORK.
TOO BAD STRUCKER DIDN'T STICK AROUND A LITTLE LONGER, CAP.
I WOULDN'T HAVE MINDED A CRACK AT THAT CUE BALL-HEADED CLOWN MYSELF. JUST FOR OLD TIMES SAKE.
LUCKILY, THE SITUATION PASSED WITHOUT ANY CIVILIAN CASUALTIES BUT THIS NEW SUPER-TEAM MAKES ME FEEL UNEASY, NICK.
I'VE GOT A HUNCH THEIR LEADER HAS SOMETHING TO DO WITH SHIELD. POSSIBLY EVEN THE CHRISTMAS ISLAND INCIDENT.
HE'S BIG, MAYBE SIX FEET FIVE, AFRICAN-AMERICAN WITH DREAD-LOCKS AND A NUMBER OF INTERESTING TATTOOS.
SHAPE-CHANGER, MORE ADVANCED THAN I'VE EVER SEEN BEFORE, MUCH MORE ADVANCED.
NICK? WHAT'S THE MATTER?
DOES SOMEONE SPRING TO MIND?
OH, YEAH.
SOMEONE DEFINITELY COMES TO MIND.
THIS IS BAD, CAP. REAL BAD.

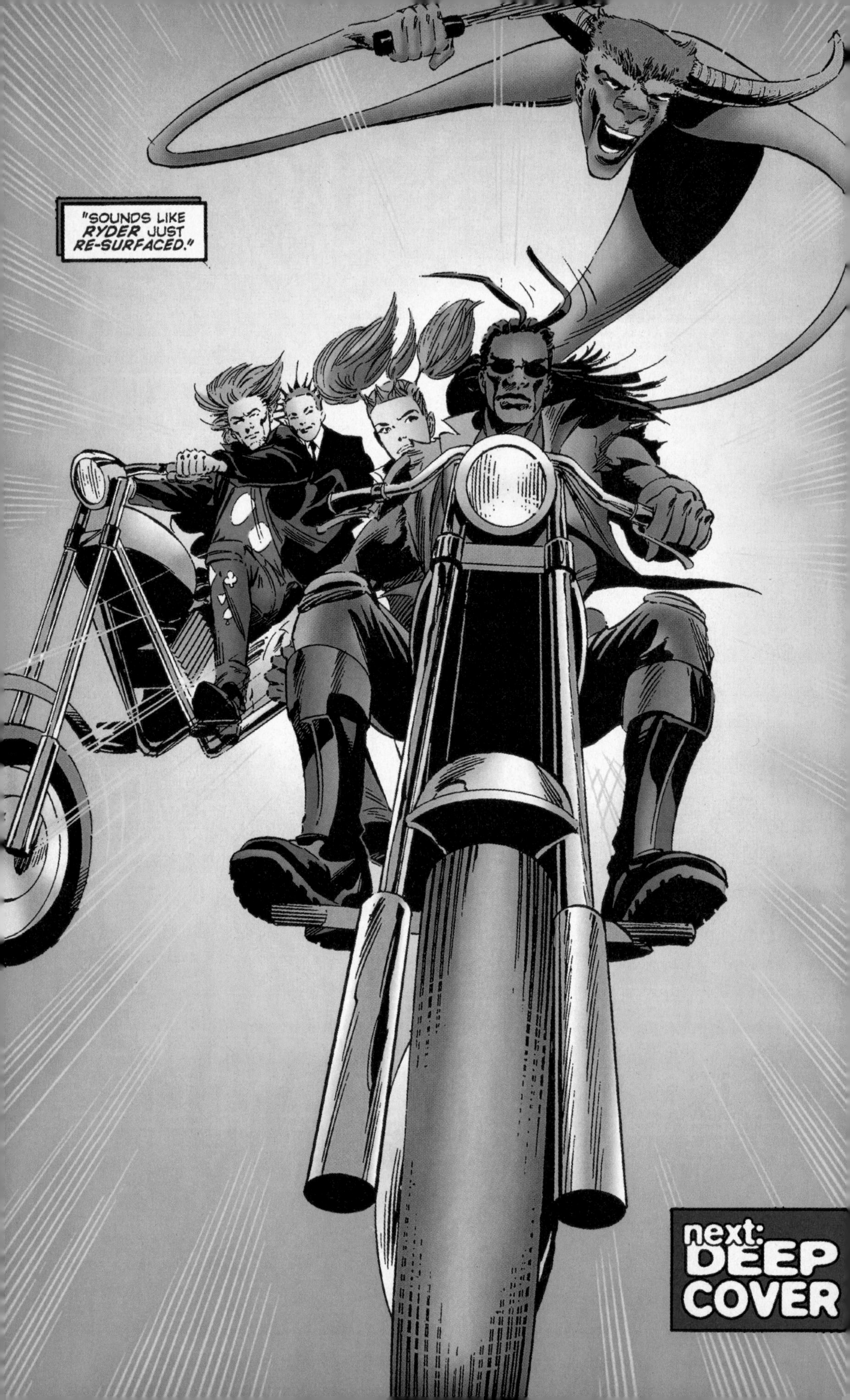
"SOUNDS LIKE RYDER JUST RE-SURFACED."
next: DEEP COVER

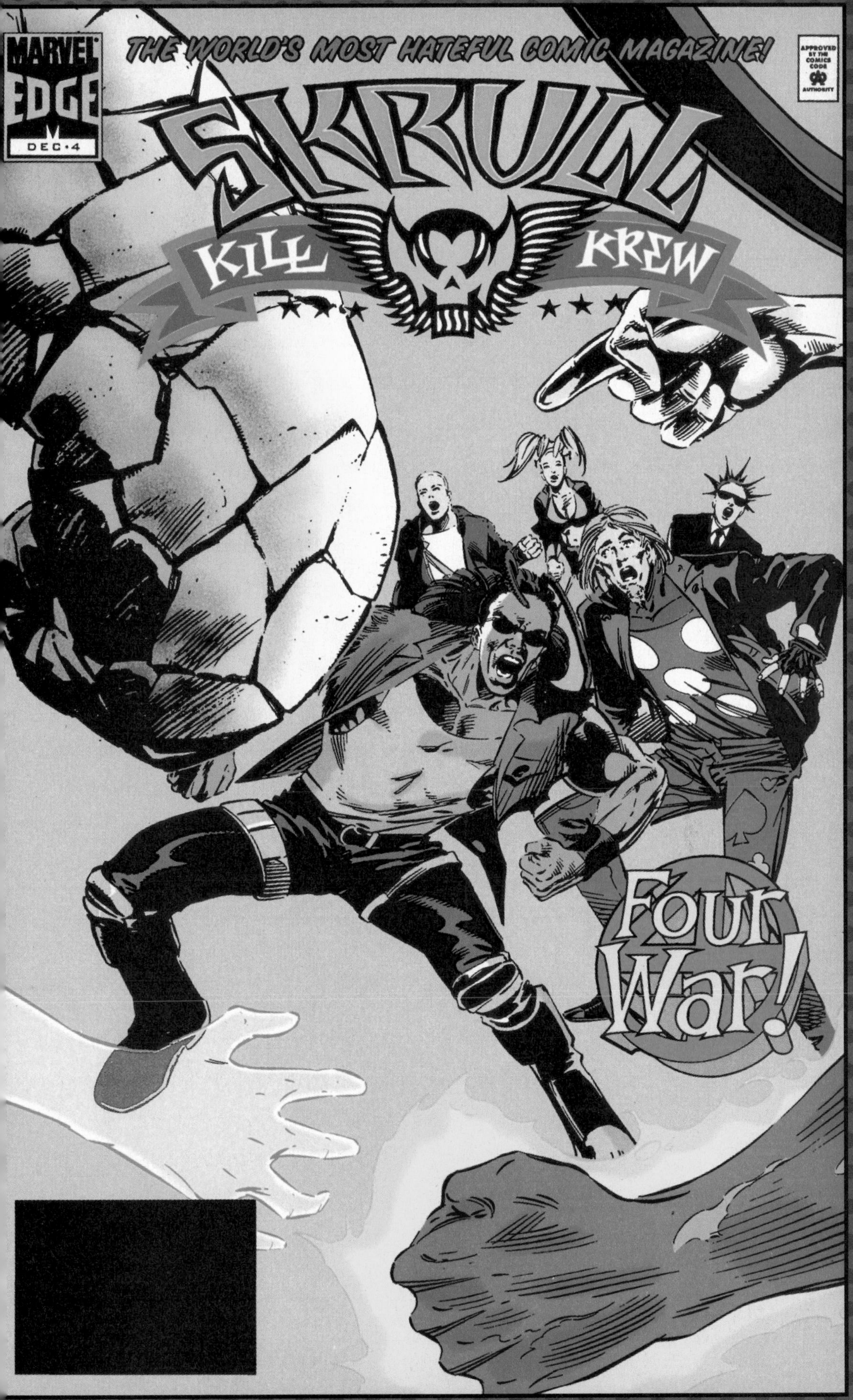
MARVEL EDGE
DEC•4
THE WORLD'S MOST HATEFUL COMIC MAGAZINE!
APPROVED BY THE COMICS CODE AUTHORITY
SKRULL
KILL KREW
Four War!

CONGRATULATIONS, MA'AM. AS OUR LUCKY *ONE HUNDREDTH* CUSTOMER, YOU'RE ENTITLED TO A *TWENTY-FIVE PERCENT* DISCOUNT ON ANY NUMBER OF *TOP QUALITY ITEMS* FROM OUR RANGE OF DOMESTIC *HYGIENE* PRODUCTS.

WOULD YOU LIKE ME TO COME INSIDE AND GIVE A FREE *DEMONSTRATION?*

AH, GOOD AFTERNOON, SIR. I SEE YOU'RE SOMETHING OF A GARDENER! WELL, AS THE GODFATHER SAYS, I'M ABOUT TO MAKE YOU AN OFFER YOU CAN'T TURN DOWN, RIGHT?

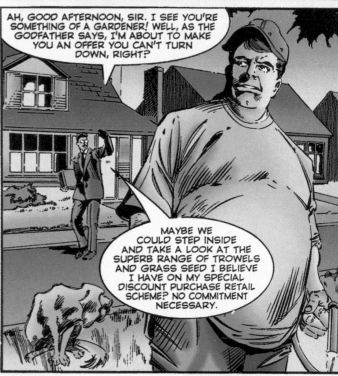

MAYBE WE COULD STEP INSIDE AND TAKE A LOOK AT THE SUPERB RANGE OF TROWELS AND GRASS SEED I BELIEVE I HAVE ON MY SPECIAL DISCOUNT PURCHASE RETAIL SCHEME? NO COMMITMENT NECESSARY.

WELL, THEN AGAIN, MAYBE NOT.

WHAT'S THE PROBLEM WITH THESE PEOPLE? I HAVEN'T BEEN ABLE TO SELL *SQUAT* SINCE I GOT HERE. NOBODY'S EVEN LETTING ME PAST THEIR FRONT DOOR!

JUST MAKES ME WONDER WHAT COMEDIAN DECIDED TO NAME THIS DUMP *"PLEASANT VALLEY."*

WUH!

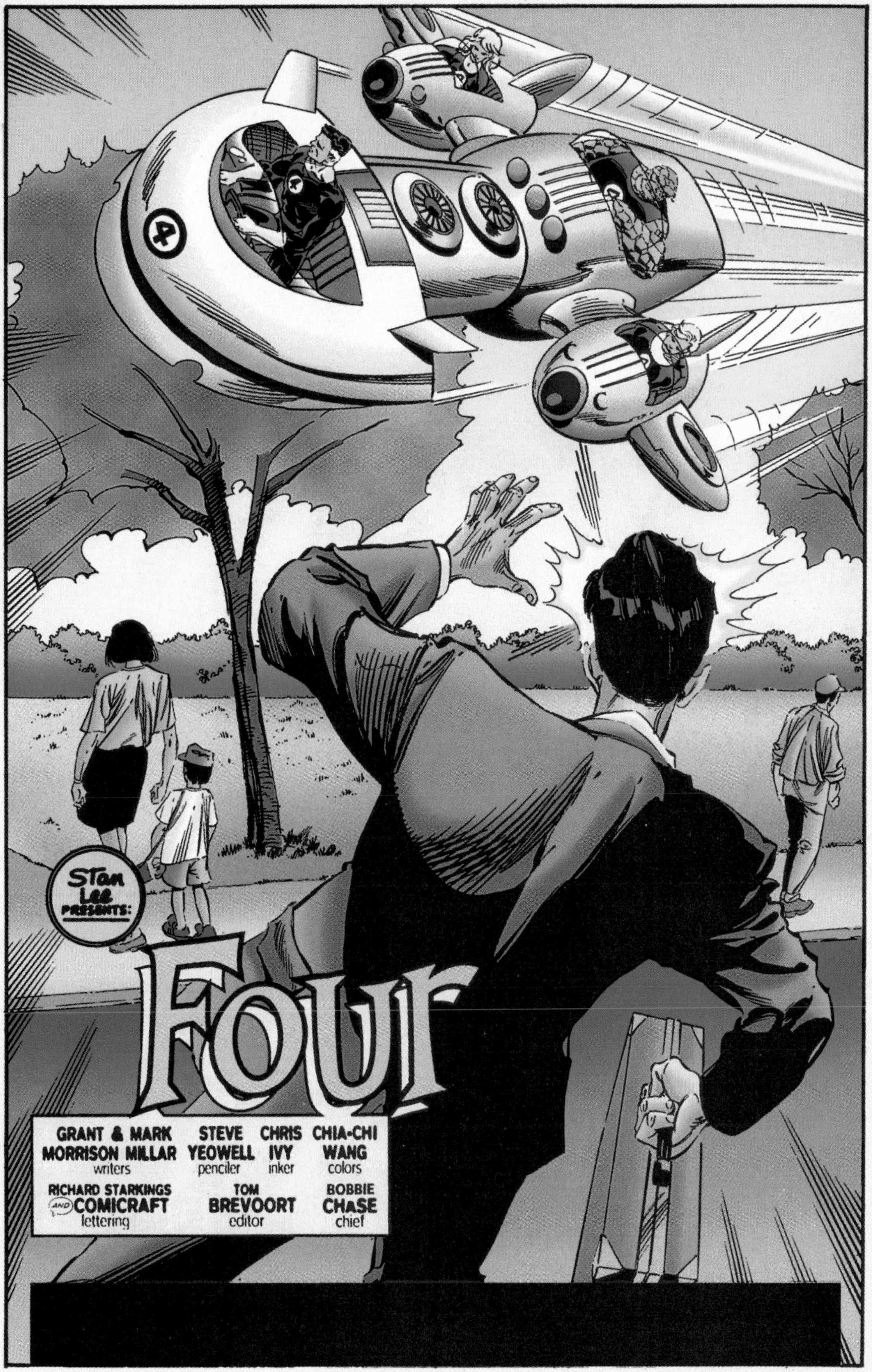

Stan Lee presents:
Four
GRANT & MARK MORRISON MILLAR writers
STEVE YEOWELL penciler
CHRIS IVY inker
CHIA-CHI WANG colors
RICHARD STARKINGS AND COMICRAFT lettering
TOM BREVOORT editor
BOBBIE CHASE chief

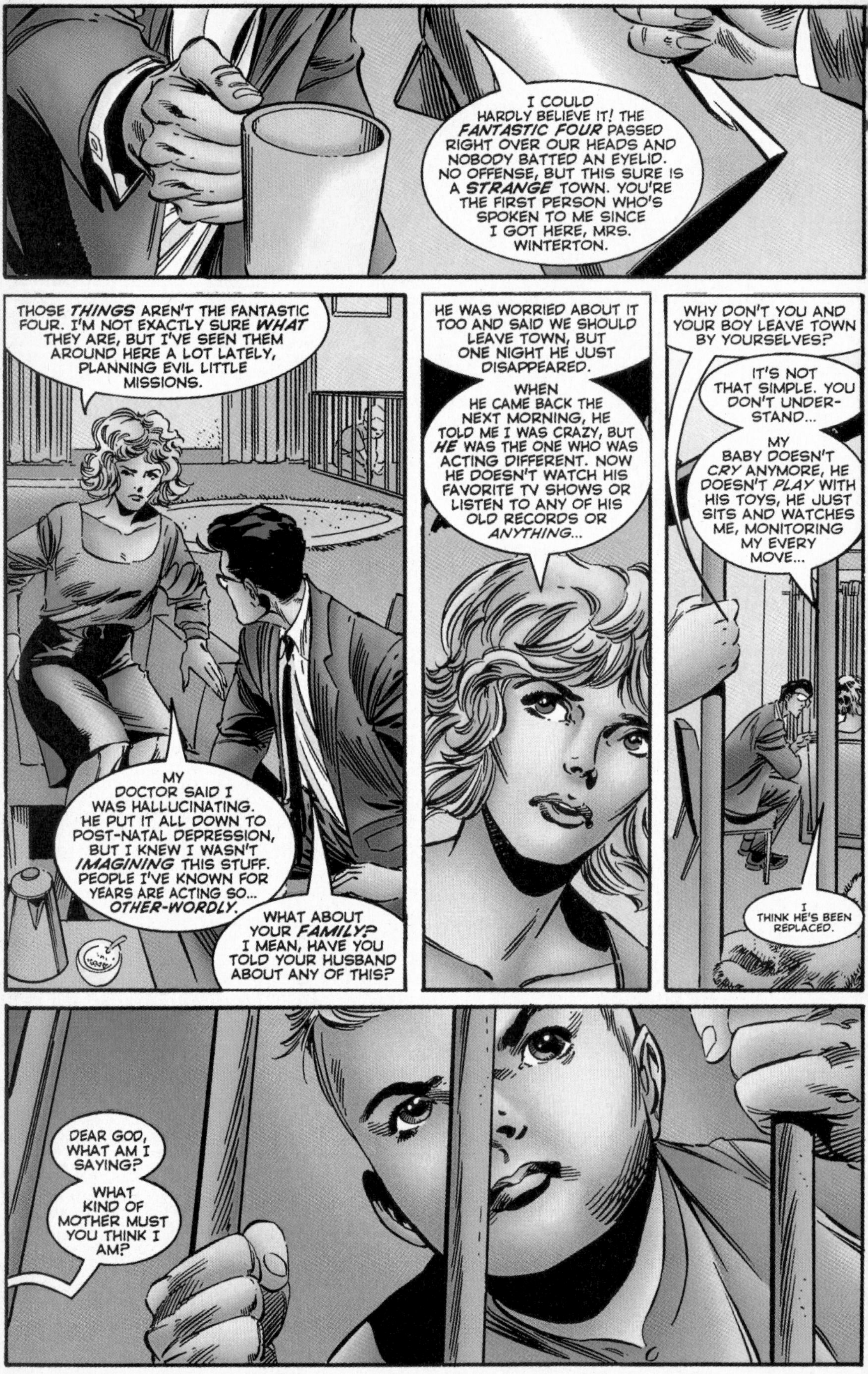
I COULD HARDLY BELIEVE IT! THE FANTASTIC FOUR PASSED RIGHT OVER OUR HEADS AND NOBODY BATTED AN EYELID. NO OFFENSE, BUT THIS SURE IS A STRANGE TOWN. YOU'RE THE FIRST PERSON WHO'S SPOKEN TO ME SINCE I GOT HERE, MRS. WINTERTON.
THOSE THINGS AREN'T THE FANTASTIC FOUR. I'M NOT EXACTLY SURE WHAT THEY ARE, BUT I'VE SEEN THEM AROUND HERE A LOT LATELY, PLANNING EVIL LITTLE MISSIONS.
MY DOCTOR SAID I WAS HALLUCINATING. HE PUT IT ALL DOWN TO POST-NATAL DEPRESSION, BUT I KNEW I WASN'T IMAGINING THIS STUFF. PEOPLE I'VE KNOWN FOR YEARS ARE ACTING SO... OTHER-WORDLY.
WHAT ABOUT YOUR FAMILY? I MEAN, HAVE YOU TOLD YOUR HUSBAND ABOUT ANY OF THIS?
HE WAS WORRIED ABOUT IT TOO AND SAID WE SHOULD LEAVE TOWN, BUT ONE NIGHT HE JUST DISAPPEARED.
WHEN HE CAME BACK THE NEXT MORNING, HE TOLD ME I WAS CRAZY, BUT HE WAS THE ONE WHO WAS ACTING DIFFERENT. NOW HE DOESN'T WATCH HIS FAVORITE TV SHOWS OR LISTEN TO ANY OF HIS OLD RECORDS OR ANYTHING...
WHY DON'T YOU AND YOUR BOY LEAVE TOWN BY YOURSELVES?
IT'S NOT THAT SIMPLE. YOU DON'T UNDER-STAND...
MY BABY DOESN'T CRY ANYMORE, HE DOESN'T PLAY WITH HIS TOYS, HE JUST SITS AND WATCHES ME, MONITORING MY EVERY MOVE...
I THINK HE'S BEEN REPLACED.
DEAR GOD, WHAT AM I SAYING?
WHAT KIND OF MOTHER MUST YOU THINK I AM?

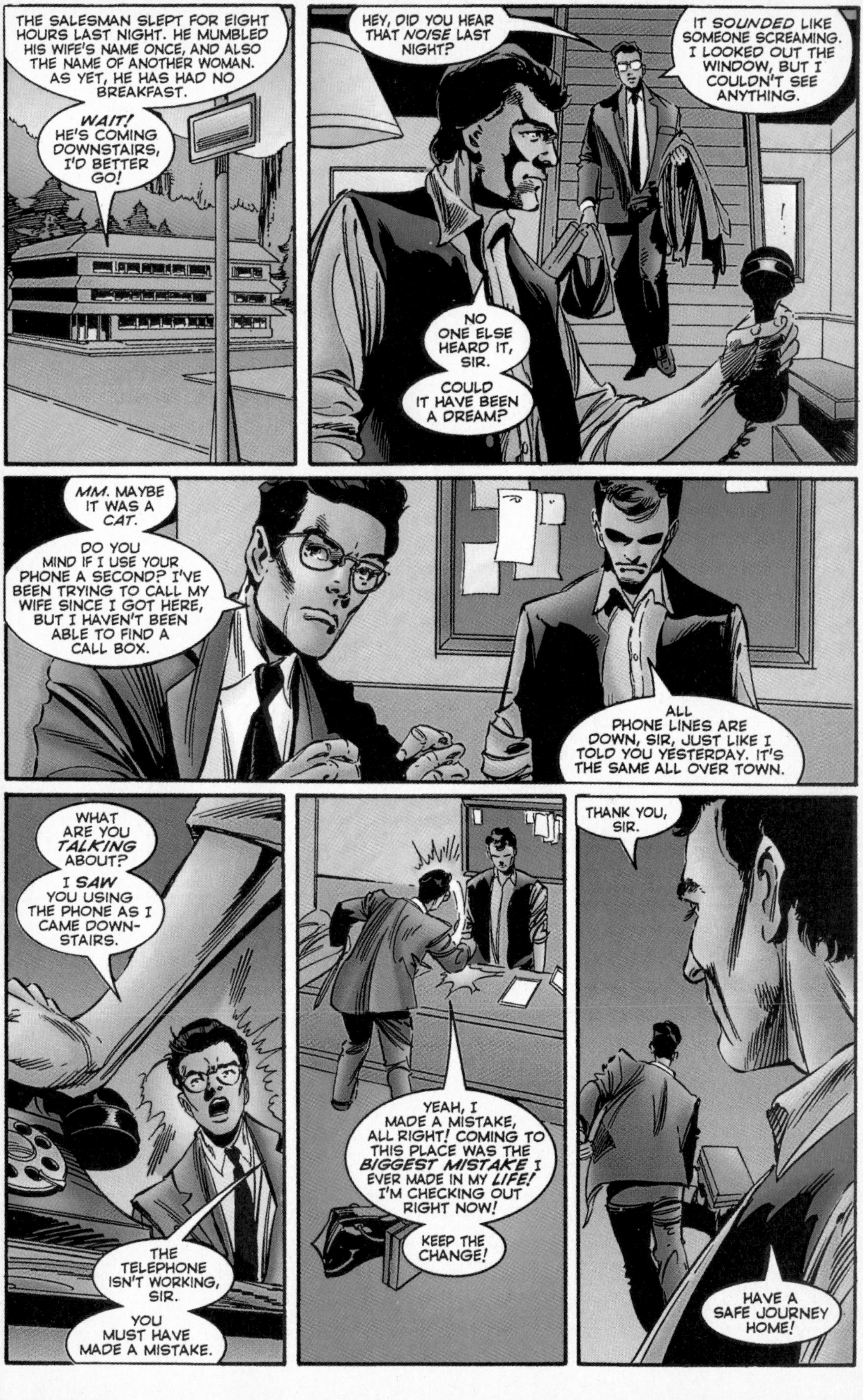
THE SALESMAN SLEPT FOR EIGHT HOURS LAST NIGHT. HE MUMBLED HIS WIFE'S NAME ONCE, AND ALSO THE NAME OF ANOTHER WOMAN. AS YET, HE HAS HAD NO BREAKFAST.
WAIT! HE'S COMING DOWNSTAIRS, I'D BETTER GO!
HEY, DID YOU HEAR THAT NOISE LAST NIGHT?
IT SOUNDED LIKE SOMEONE SCREAMING. I LOOKED OUT THE WINDOW, BUT I COULDN'T SEE ANYTHING.
NO ONE ELSE HEARD IT, SIR.
COULD IT HAVE BEEN A DREAM?
MM. MAYBE IT WAS A CAT.
DO YOU MIND IF I USE YOUR PHONE A SECOND? I'VE BEEN TRYING TO CALL MY WIFE SINCE I GOT HERE, BUT I HAVEN'T BEEN ABLE TO FIND A CALL BOX.
ALL PHONE LINES ARE DOWN, SIR, JUST LIKE I TOLD YOU YESTERDAY. IT'S THE SAME ALL OVER TOWN.
WHAT ARE YOU TALKING ABOUT?
I SAW YOU USING THE PHONE AS I CAME DOWN-STAIRS.
THE TELEPHONE ISN'T WORKING, SIR.
YOU MUST HAVE MADE A MISTAKE.
YEAH, I MADE A MISTAKE, ALL RIGHT! COMING TO THIS PLACE WAS THE BIGGEST MISTAKE I EVER MADE IN MY LIFE! I'M CHECKING OUT RIGHT NOW!
KEEP THE CHANGE!
THANK YOU, SIR.
HAVE A SAFE JOURNEY HOME!

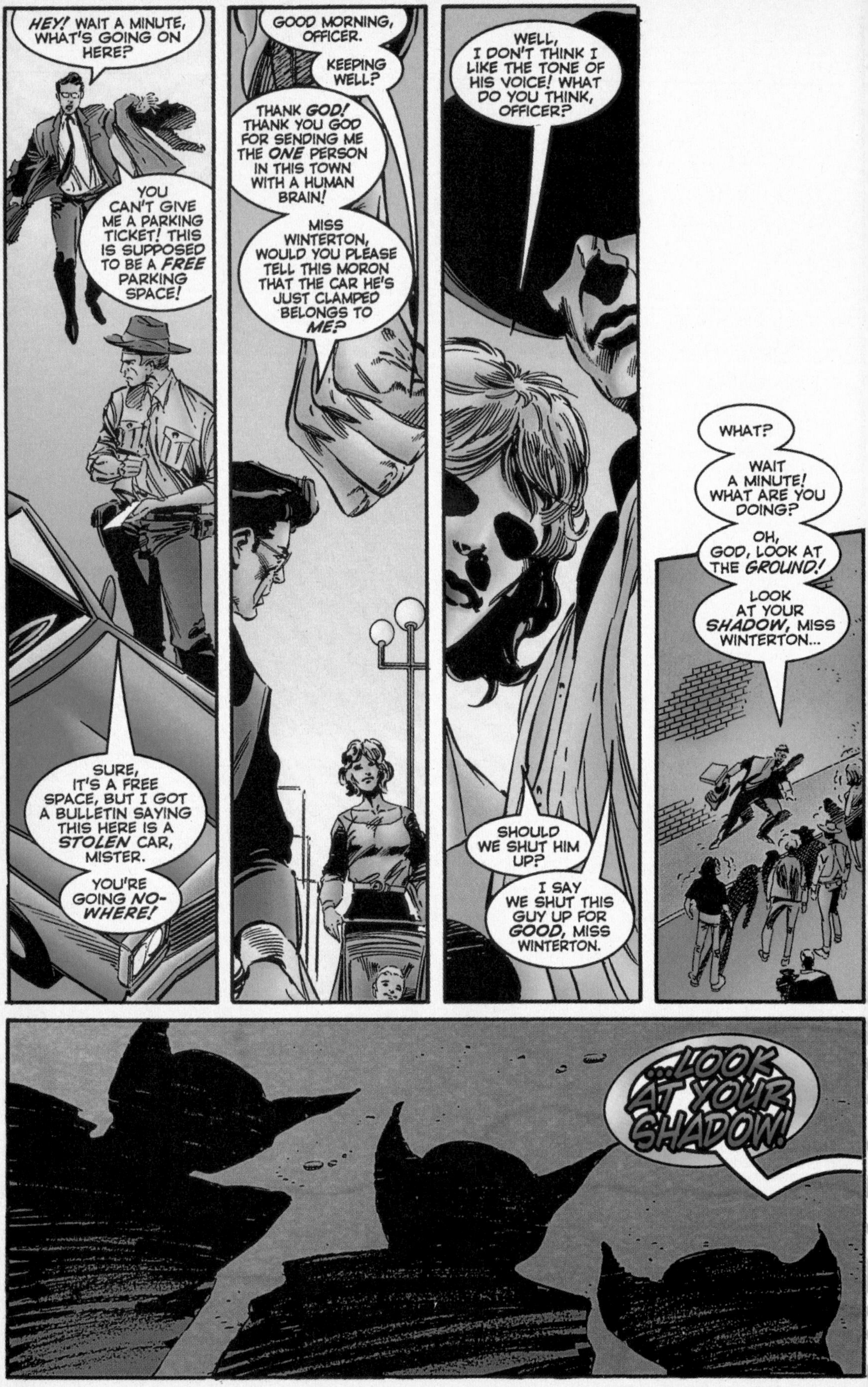
HEY! WAIT A MINUTE, WHAT'S GOING ON HERE?
YOU CAN'T GIVE ME A PARKING TICKET! THIS IS SUPPOSED TO BE A FREE PARKING SPACE!
SURE, IT'S A FREE SPACE, BUT I GOT A BULLETIN SAYING THIS HERE IS A STOLEN CAR, MISTER.
YOU'RE GOING NO-WHERE!
GOOD MORNING, OFFICER.
KEEPING WELL?
THANK GOD! THANK YOU GOD FOR SENDING ME THE ONE PERSON IN THIS TOWN WITH A HUMAN BRAIN!
MISS WINTERTON, WOULD YOU PLEASE TELL THIS MORON THAT THE CAR HE'S JUST CLAMPED BELONGS TO ME?
WELL, I DON'T THINK I LIKE THE TONE OF HIS VOICE! WHAT DO YOU THINK, OFFICER?
SHOULD WE SHUT HIM UP?
I SAY WE SHUT THIS GUY UP FOR GOOD, MISS WINTERTON.
WHAT?
WAIT A MINUTE! WHAT ARE YOU DOING?
OH, GOD, LOOK AT THE GROUND!
LOOK AT YOUR SHADOW, MISS WINTERTON...
...LOOK AT YOUR SHADOW!

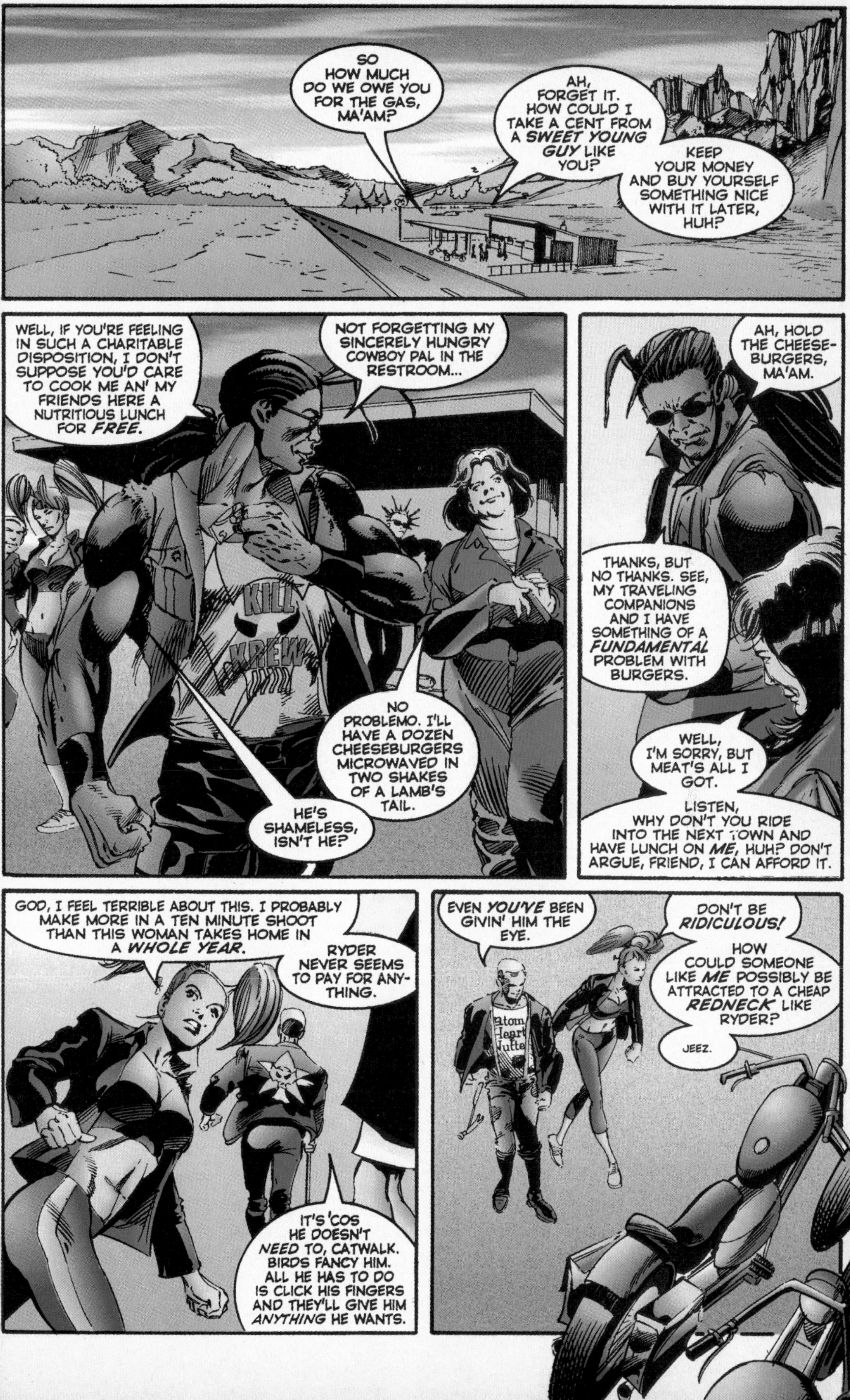
SO HOW MUCH DO WE OWE YOU FOR THE GAS, MA'AM?
AH, FORGET IT. HOW COULD I TAKE A CENT FROM A *SWEET YOUNG GUY* LIKE YOU?
KEEP YOUR MONEY AND BUY YOURSELF SOMETHING NICE WITH IT LATER, HUH?
WELL, IF YOU'RE FEELING IN SUCH A CHARITABLE DISPOSITION, I DON'T SUPPOSE YOU'D CARE TO COOK ME AN' MY FRIENDS HERE A NUTRITIOUS LUNCH FOR *FREE*.
NOT FORGETTING MY SINCERELY HUNGRY COWBOY PAL IN THE RESTROOM...
KILL KREW
NO PROBLEMO. I'LL HAVE A DOZEN CHEESEBURGERS MICROWAVED IN TWO SHAKES OF A LAMB'S TAIL.
HE'S SHAMELESS, ISN'T HE?
AH, HOLD THE CHEESE-BURGERS, MA'AM.
THANKS, BUT NO THANKS. SEE, MY TRAVELING COMPANIONS AND I HAVE SOMETHING OF A *FUNDAMENTAL* PROBLEM WITH BURGERS.
WELL, I'M SORRY, BUT MEAT'S ALL I GOT.
LISTEN, WHY DON'T YOU RIDE INTO THE NEXT TOWN AND HAVE LUNCH ON *ME*, HUH? DON'T ARGUE, FRIEND, I CAN AFFORD IT.
GOD, I FEEL TERRIBLE ABOUT THIS. I PROBABLY MAKE MORE IN A TEN MINUTE SHOOT THAN THIS WOMAN TAKES HOME IN A *WHOLE YEAR*.
RYDER NEVER SEEMS TO PAY FOR ANY-THING.
IT'S 'COS HE DOESN'T *NEED* TO, CATWALK. BIRDS FANCY HIM. ALL HE HAS TO DO IS CLICK HIS FINGERS AND THEY'LL GIVE HIM *ANYTHING* HE WANTS.
EVEN *YOU'VE* BEEN GIVIN' HIM THE EYE.
DON'T BE *RIDICULOUS!*
HOW COULD SOMEONE LIKE *ME* POSSIBLY BE ATTRACTED TO A CHEAP *REDNECK* LIKE RYDER?
JEEZ.

OH RYDER, I FANCY YOU SO MUCH! I'D DO ANYTHING TO GIVE YOU A KISS!

THAT'S YOU, THAT IS, CATWALK...

UUNGH!

MOONSTOMP!

HEY, NOW WHAT'S THE PROBLEM HERE?

IT'S MOON-STOMP! HE'S HAVING ANOTHER ATTACK! YOU'D BETTER DO SOMETHING, RYDER, HE'S IN AGONY!

I'M ALL RIGHT! IT WAS JUST A RELAPSE, RIGHT? IT WASN'T AS BAD AS IT LOOKED.

THOSE PATCHES ON HIS FACE... THEY'RE SPREADING.

THAT'S BECAUSE MY WHITE SUPREMACIST FRIEND HERE HAS A VIRUS WHICH IS FEEDING ON THE ANGER IN HIS BODY AND TURNING HIM INTO WHAT HE HATES MOST.

NAMELY NEGROES.

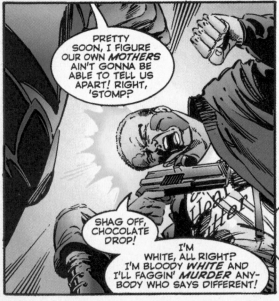

PRETTY SOON, I FIGURE OUR OWN MOTHERS AIN'T GONNA BE ABLE TO TELL US APART! RIGHT, 'STOMP?

SHAG OFF, CHOCOLATE DROP!

I'M WHITE, ALL RIGHT? I'M BLOODY WHITE AND I'LL FAGGIN' MURDER ANYBODY WHO SAYS DIFFERENT!

SURE YOU'RE WHITE, MOONSTOMP. WHITE LIKE SPIKE LEE AND BILL COSBY, RIGHT? WHITE LIKE MALCOLM X.

I WONDER IF THOSE GOOD OLE SKINHEAD BOYS YOU USED TO HANG OUT WITH IN BRIXTON ARE SIMILARLY COLOR-BLIND NOW TOO, HUH?

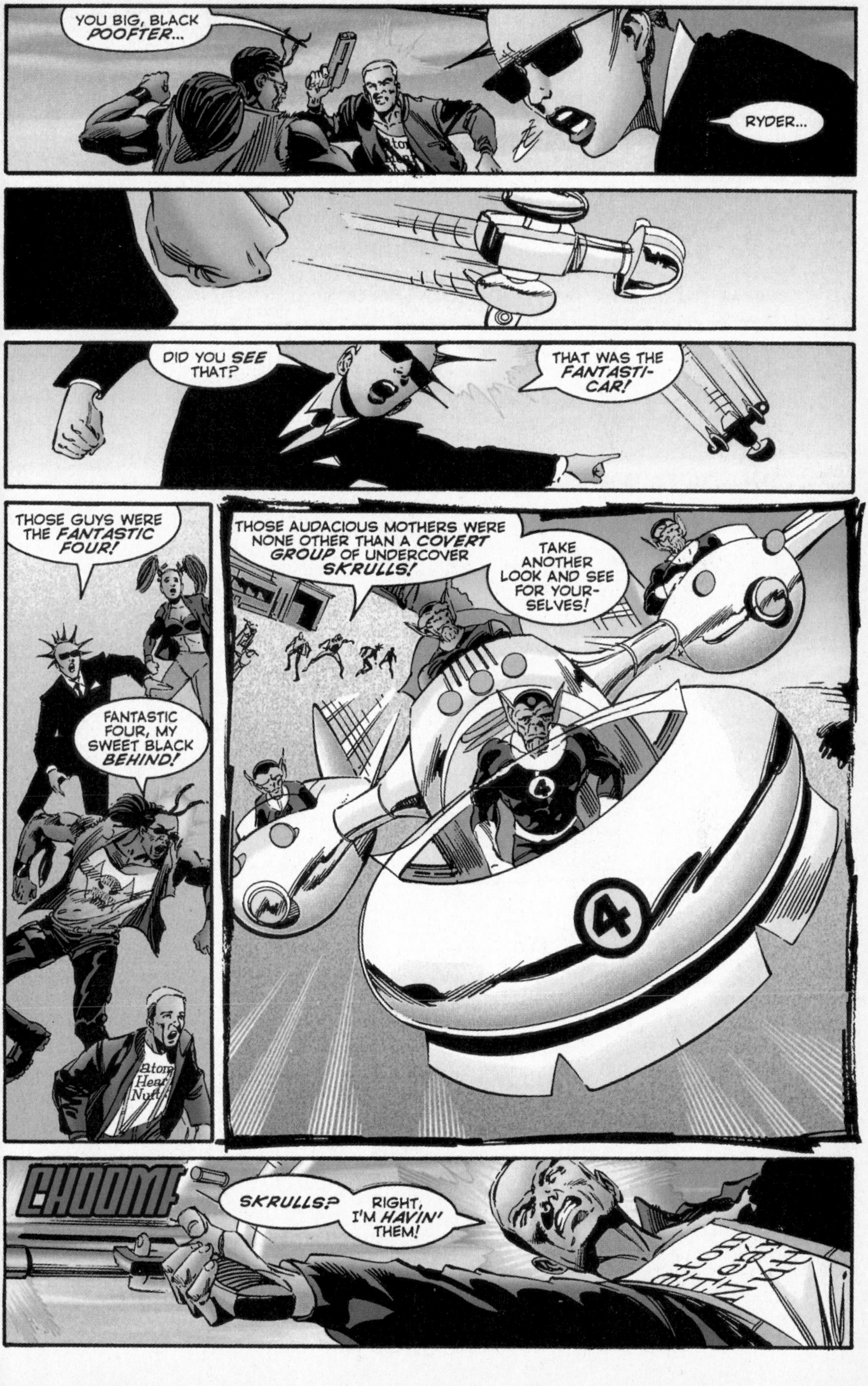
YOU BIG, BLACK POOFTER...
RYDER...
DID YOU SEE THAT?
THAT WAS THE FANTASTI-CAR!
THOSE GUYS WERE THE FANTASTIC FOUR!
FANTASTIC FOUR, MY SWEET BLACK BEHIND!
THOSE AUDACIOUS MOTHERS WERE NONE OTHER THAN A COVERT GROUP OF UNDERCOVER SKRULLS!
TAKE ANOTHER LOOK AND SEE FOR YOUR-SELVES!
CHOOMF
SKRULLS?
RIGHT, I'M HAVIN' THEM!

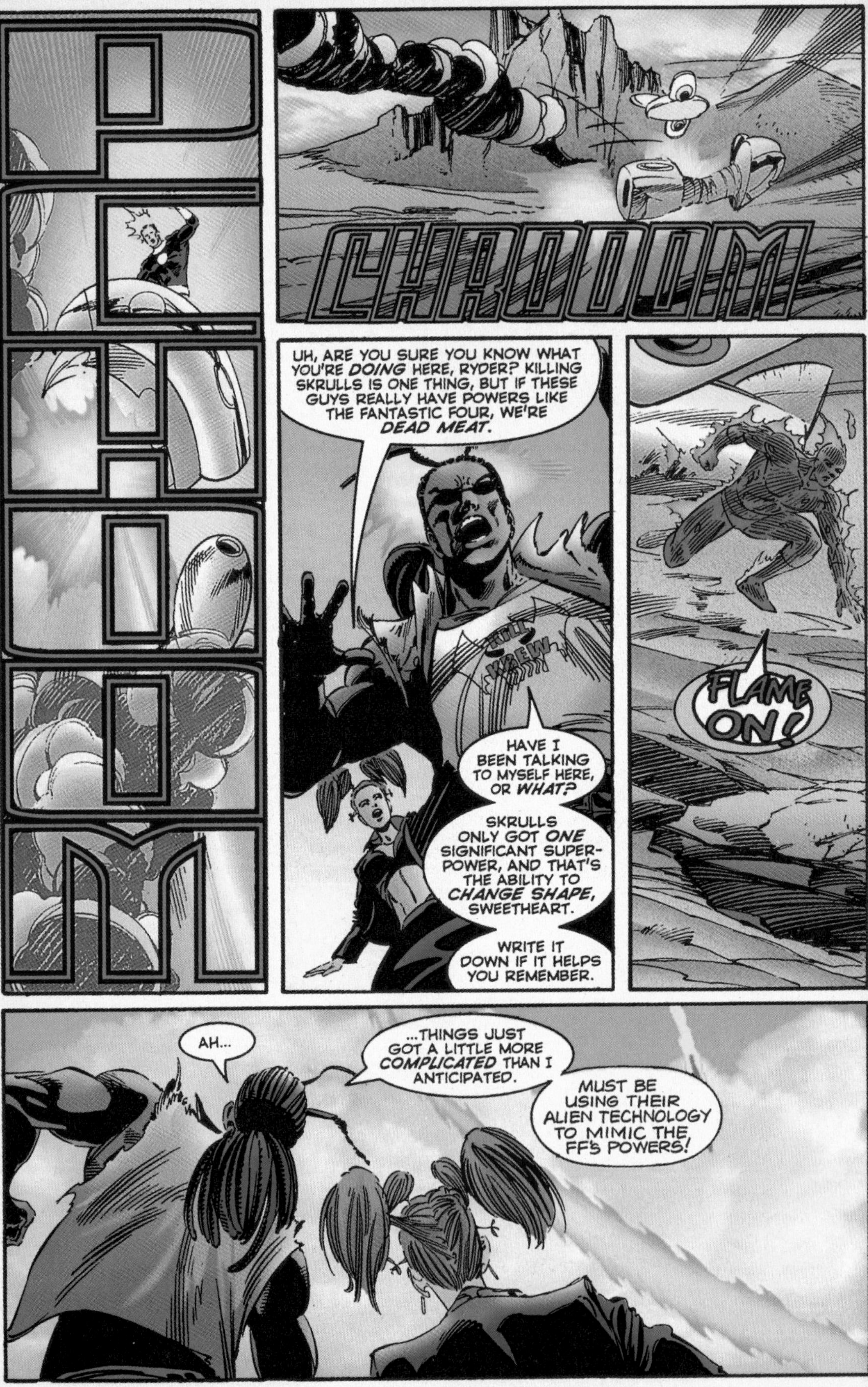
PHOOM
CHROOOM
UH, ARE YOU SURE YOU KNOW WHAT YOU'RE DOING HERE, RYDER? KILLING SKRULLS IS ONE THING, BUT IF THESE GUYS REALLY HAVE POWERS LIKE THE FANTASTIC FOUR, WE'RE DEAD MEAT.
HAVE I BEEN TALKING TO MYSELF HERE, OR WHAT?
SKRULLS ONLY GOT ONE SIGNIFICANT SUPER-POWER, AND THAT'S THE ABILITY TO CHANGE SHAPE, SWEETHEART.
WRITE IT DOWN IF IT HELPS YOU REMEMBER.
FLAME ON!
AH...
...THINGS JUST GOT A LITTLE MORE COMPLICATED THAN I ANTICIPATED.
MUST BE USING THEIR ALIEN TECHNOLOGY TO MIMIC THE FF'S POWERS!

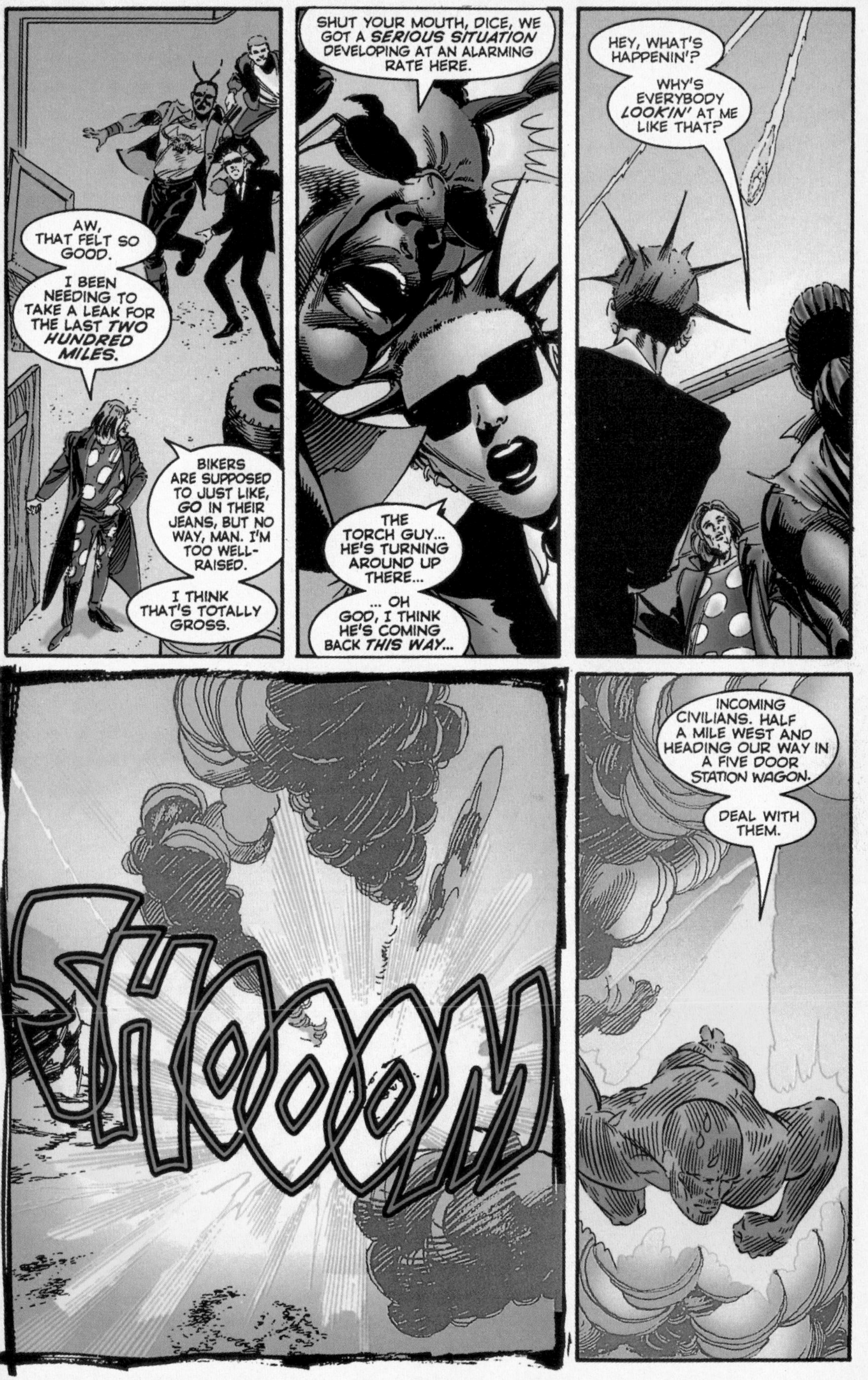

AW, THAT FELT SO GOOD.
I BEEN NEEDING TO TAKE A LEAK FOR THE LAST *TWO HUNDRED MILES*.
BIKERS ARE SUPPOSED TO JUST LIKE, *GO* IN THEIR JEANS, BUT NO WAY, MAN. I'M TOO WELL-RAISED.
I THINK THAT'S TOTALLY GROSS.
SHUT YOUR MOUTH, DICE, WE GOT A *SERIOUS SITUATION* DEVELOPING AT AN ALARMING RATE HERE.
THE TORCH GUY... HE'S TURNING AROUND UP THERE...
... OH GOD, I THINK HE'S COMING BACK *THIS WAY*...
HEY, WHAT'S HAPPENIN'?
WHY'S EVERYBODY *LOOKIN'* AT ME LIKE THAT?
SHOOOOM
INCOMING CIVILIANS. HALF A MILE WEST AND HEADING OUR WAY IN A FIVE DOOR STATION WAGON.
DEAL WITH THEM.

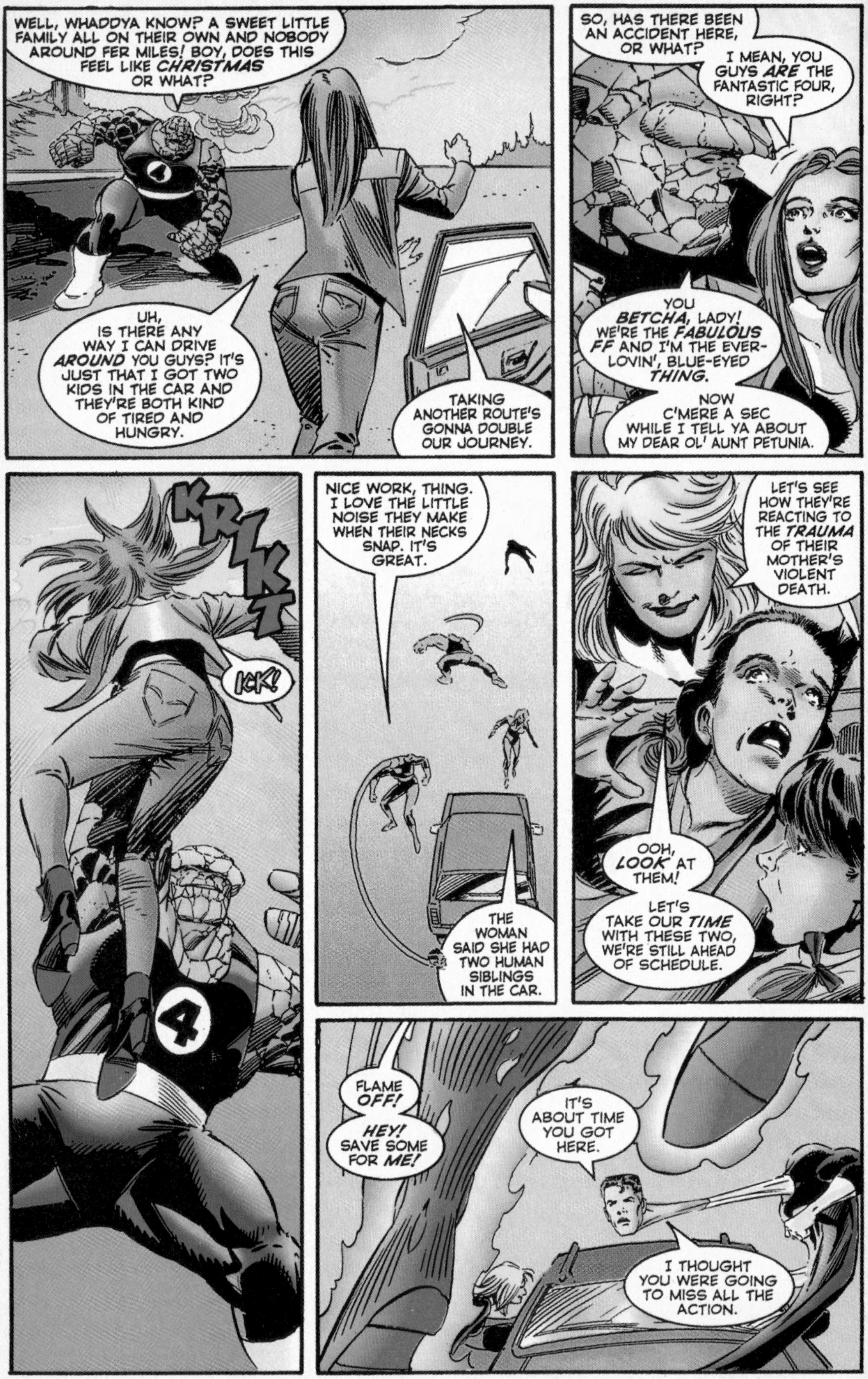

WELL, WHADDYA KNOW? A SWEET LITTLE FAMILY ALL ON THEIR OWN AND NOBODY AROUND FER MILES! BOY, DOES THIS FEEL LIKE CHRISTMAS OR WHAT?
UH, IS THERE ANY WAY I CAN DRIVE AROUND YOU GUYS? IT'S JUST THAT I GOT TWO KIDS IN THE CAR AND THEY'RE BOTH KIND OF TIRED AND HUNGRY.
TAKING ANOTHER ROUTE'S GONNA DOUBLE OUR JOURNEY.
SO, HAS THERE BEEN AN ACCIDENT HERE, OR WHAT?
I MEAN, YOU GUYS ARE THE FANTASTIC FOUR, RIGHT?
YOU BETCHA, LADY! WE'RE THE FABULOUS FF AND I'M THE EVER-LOVIN', BLUE-EYED THING.
NOW C'MERE A SEC WHILE I TELL YA ABOUT MY DEAR OL' AUNT PETUNIA.
KRIKT
ICK!
NICE WORK, THING. I LOVE THE LITTLE NOISE THEY MAKE WHEN THEIR NECKS SNAP. IT'S GREAT.
THE WOMAN SAID SHE HAD TWO HUMAN SIBLINGS IN THE CAR.
LET'S SEE HOW THEY'RE REACTING TO THE TRAUMA OF THEIR MOTHER'S VIOLENT DEATH.
OOH, LOOK AT THEM!
LET'S TAKE OUR TIME WITH THESE TWO, WE'RE STILL AHEAD OF SCHEDULE.
FLAME OFF!
HEY! SAVE SOME FOR ME!
IT'S ABOUT TIME YOU GOT HERE.
I THOUGHT YOU WERE GOING TO MISS ALL THE ACTION.

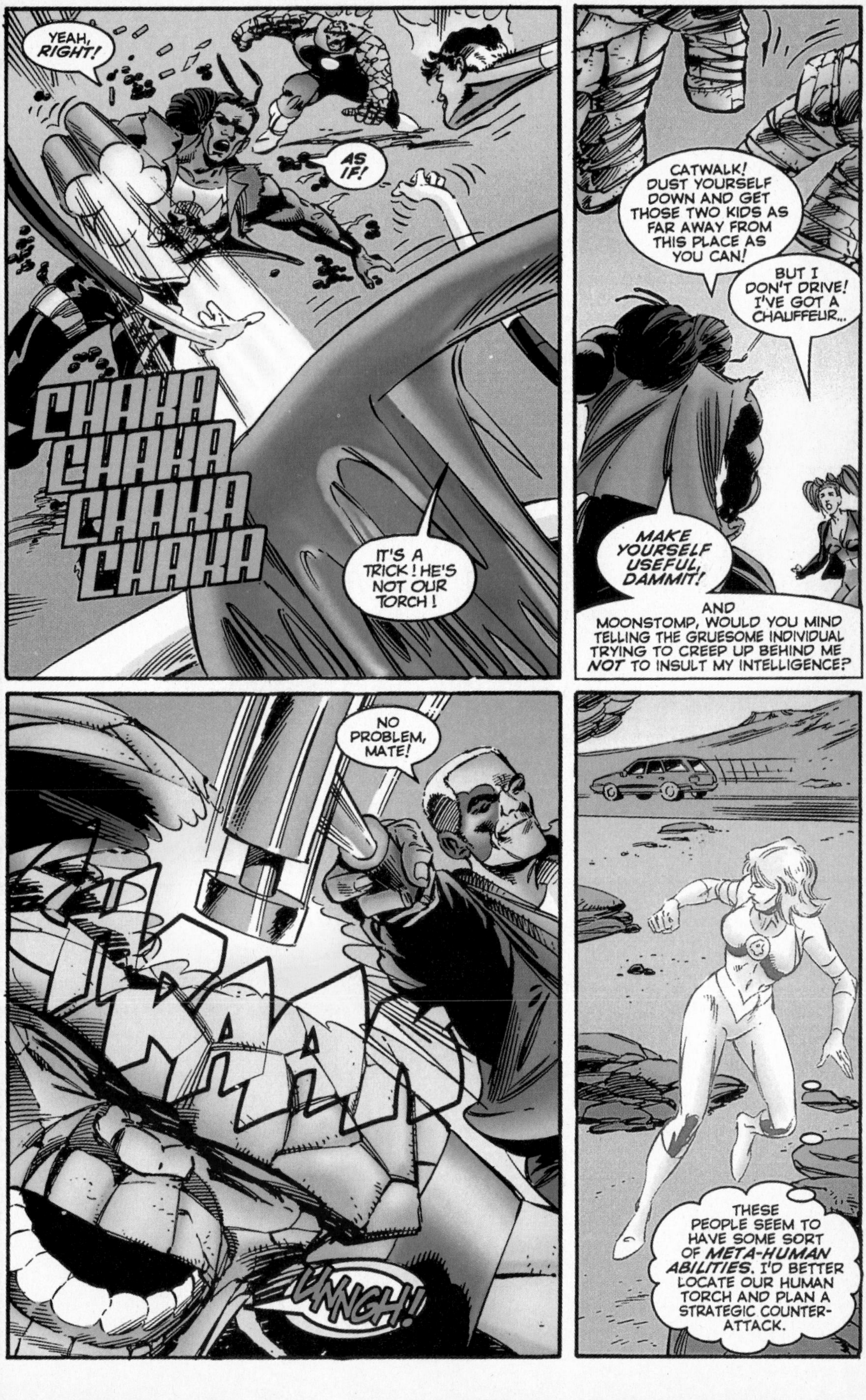
YEAH, RIGHT!
AS IF!
CHAKA CHAKA CHAKA CHAKA
IT'S A TRICK! HE'S NOT OUR TORCH!
CATWALK! DUST YOURSELF DOWN AND GET THOSE TWO KIDS AS FAR AWAY FROM THIS PLACE AS YOU CAN!
BUT I DON'T DRIVE! I'VE GOT A CHAUFFEUR...
MAKE YOURSELF USEFUL, DAMMIT!
AND MOONSTOMP, WOULD YOU MIND TELLING THE GRUESOME INDIVIDUAL TRYING TO CREEP UP BEHIND ME NOT TO INSULT MY INTELLIGENCE?
NO PROBLEM, MATE!
UNNGH!
THESE PEOPLE SEEM TO HAVE SOME SORT OF META-HUMAN ABILITIES. I'D BETTER LOCATE OUR HUMAN TORCH AND PLAN A STRATEGIC COUNTER-ATTACK.

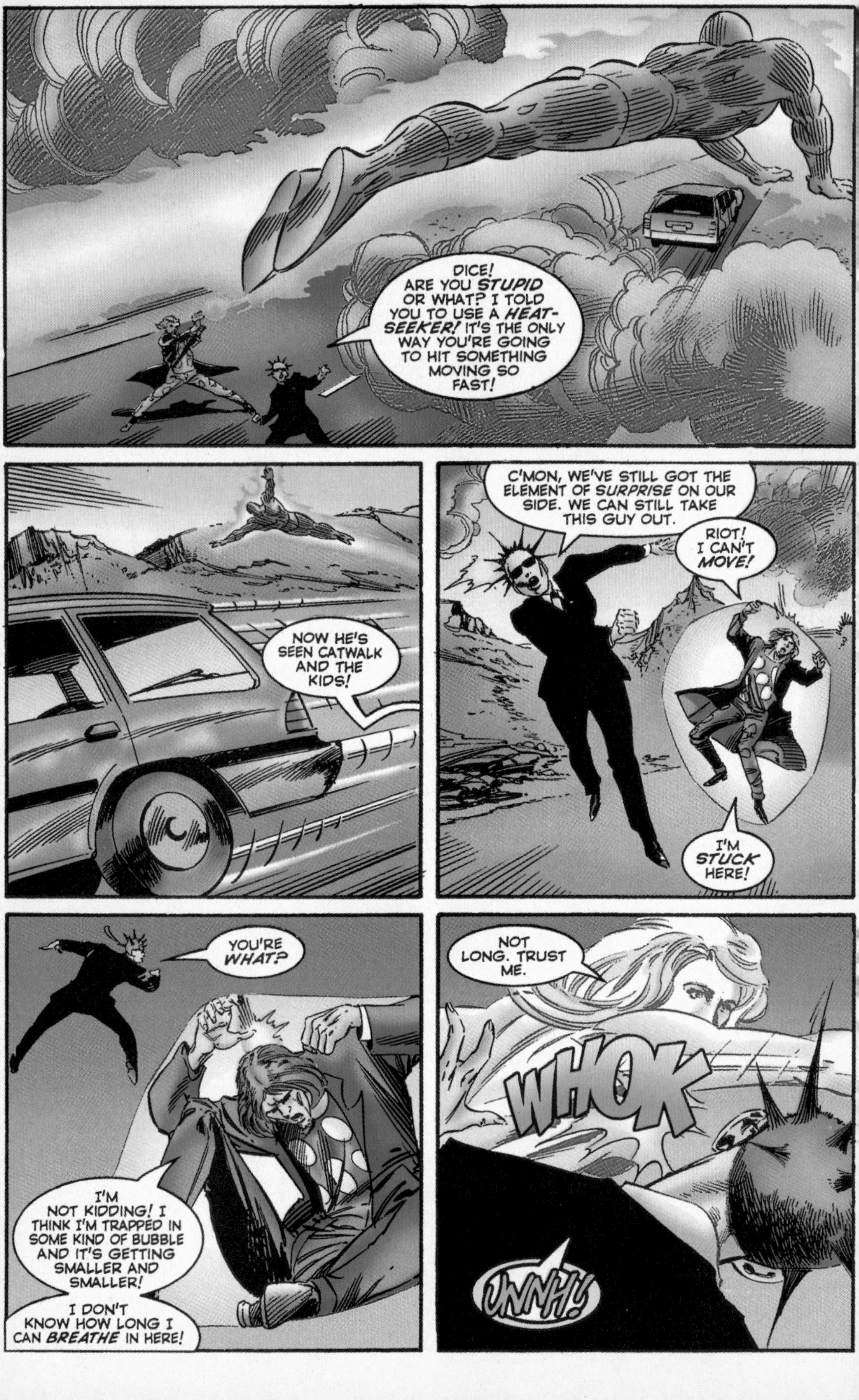
DICE! ARE YOU STUPID OR WHAT? I TOLD YOU TO USE A HEAT-SEEKER! IT'S THE ONLY WAY YOU'RE GOING TO HIT SOMETHING MOVING SO FAST!
NOW HE'S SEEN CATWALK AND THE KIDS!
C'MON, WE'VE STILL GOT THE ELEMENT OF SURPRISE ON OUR SIDE. WE CAN STILL TAKE THIS GUY OUT.
RIOT! I CAN'T MOVE!
I'M STUCK HERE!
YOU'RE WHAT?
I'M NOT KIDDING! I THINK I'M TRAPPED IN SOME KIND OF BUBBLE AND IT'S GETTING SMALLER AND SMALLER!
I DON'T KNOW HOW LONG I CAN BREATHE IN HERE!
NOT LONG. TRUST ME.
WHOK
UNNH!

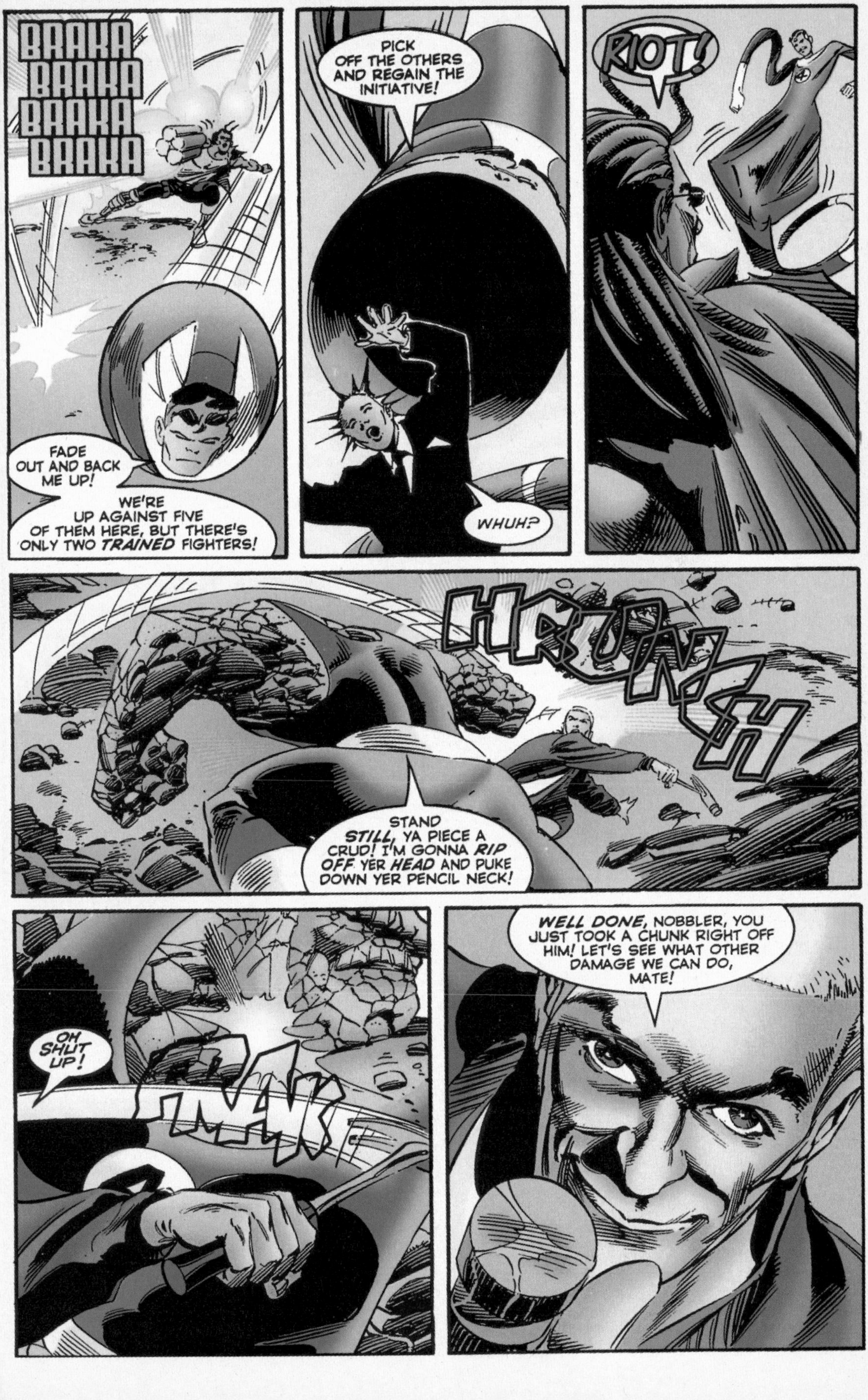
BRAKA BRAKA BRAKA BRAKA
FADE OUT AND BACK ME UP!
WE'RE UP AGAINST FIVE OF THEM HERE, BUT THERE'S ONLY TWO *TRAINED* FIGHTERS!
PICK OFF THE OTHERS AND REGAIN THE INITIATIVE!
WHUH?
RIOT!
STAND *STILL*, YA PIECE A CRUD! I'M GONNA *RIP OFF* YER *HEAD* AND PUKE DOWN YER PENCIL NECK!
OH SHUT UP!
*WELL DONE*, NOBBLER, YOU JUST TOOK A CHUNK RIGHT OFF HIM! LET'S SEE WHAT OTHER DAMAGE WE CAN DO, MATE!

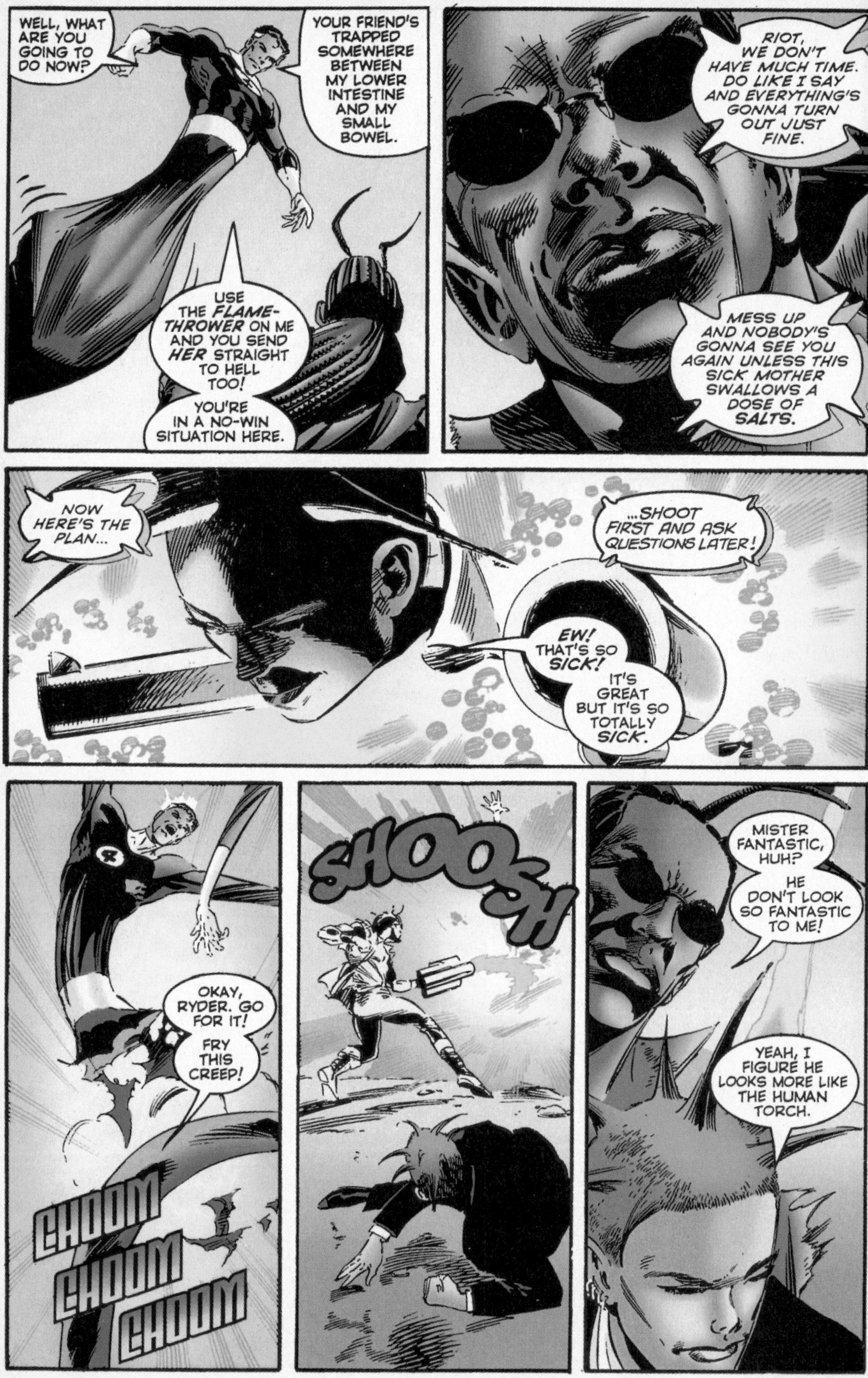
WELL, WHAT ARE YOU GOING TO DO NOW?
YOUR FRIEND'S TRAPPED SOMEWHERE BETWEEN MY LOWER INTESTINE AND MY SMALL BOWEL.
USE THE FLAME-THROWER ON ME AND YOU SEND HER STRAIGHT TO HELL TOO!
YOU'RE IN A NO-WIN SITUATION HERE.
RIOT, WE DON'T HAVE MUCH TIME. DO LIKE I SAY AND EVERYTHING'S GONNA TURN OUT JUST FINE.
MESS UP AND NOBODY'S GONNA SEE YOU AGAIN UNLESS THIS SICK MOTHER SWALLOWS A DOSE OF SALTS.
NOW HERE'S THE PLAN...
...SHOOT FIRST AND ASK QUESTIONS LATER!
EW! THAT'S SO SICK!
IT'S GREAT BUT IT'S SO TOTALLY SICK.
OKAY, RYDER. GO FOR IT!
FRY THIS CREEP!
CHOOM
CHOOM
CHOOM
SHOOSH
MISTER FANTASTIC, HUH?
HE DON'T LOOK SO FANTASTIC TO ME!
YEAH, I FIGURE HE LOOKS MORE LIKE THE HUMAN TORCH.

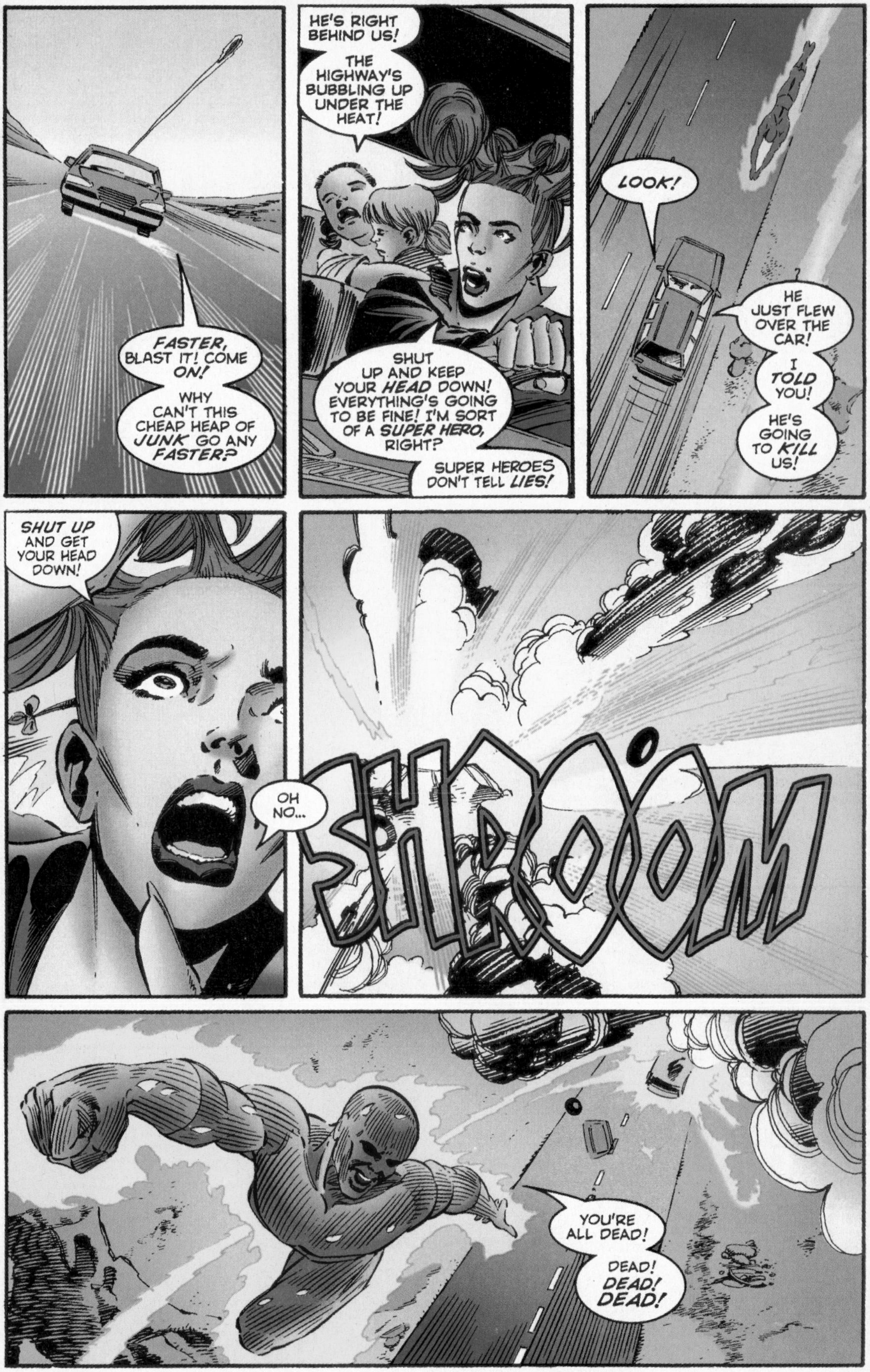
FASTER, BLAST IT! COME ON!
WHY CAN'T THIS CHEAP HEAP OF JUNK GO ANY FASTER?
HE'S RIGHT BEHIND US!
THE HIGHWAY'S BUBBLING UP UNDER THE HEAT!
SHUT UP AND KEEP YOUR HEAD DOWN! EVERYTHING'S GOING TO BE FINE! I'M SORT OF A SUPER HERO, RIGHT?
SUPER HEROES DON'T TELL LIES!
LOOK!
HE JUST FLEW OVER THE CAR!
I TOLD YOU!
HE'S GOING TO KILL US!
SHUT UP AND GET YOUR HEAD DOWN!
OH NO...
SHROOOM
YOU'RE ALL DEAD!
DEAD! DEAD! DEAD!

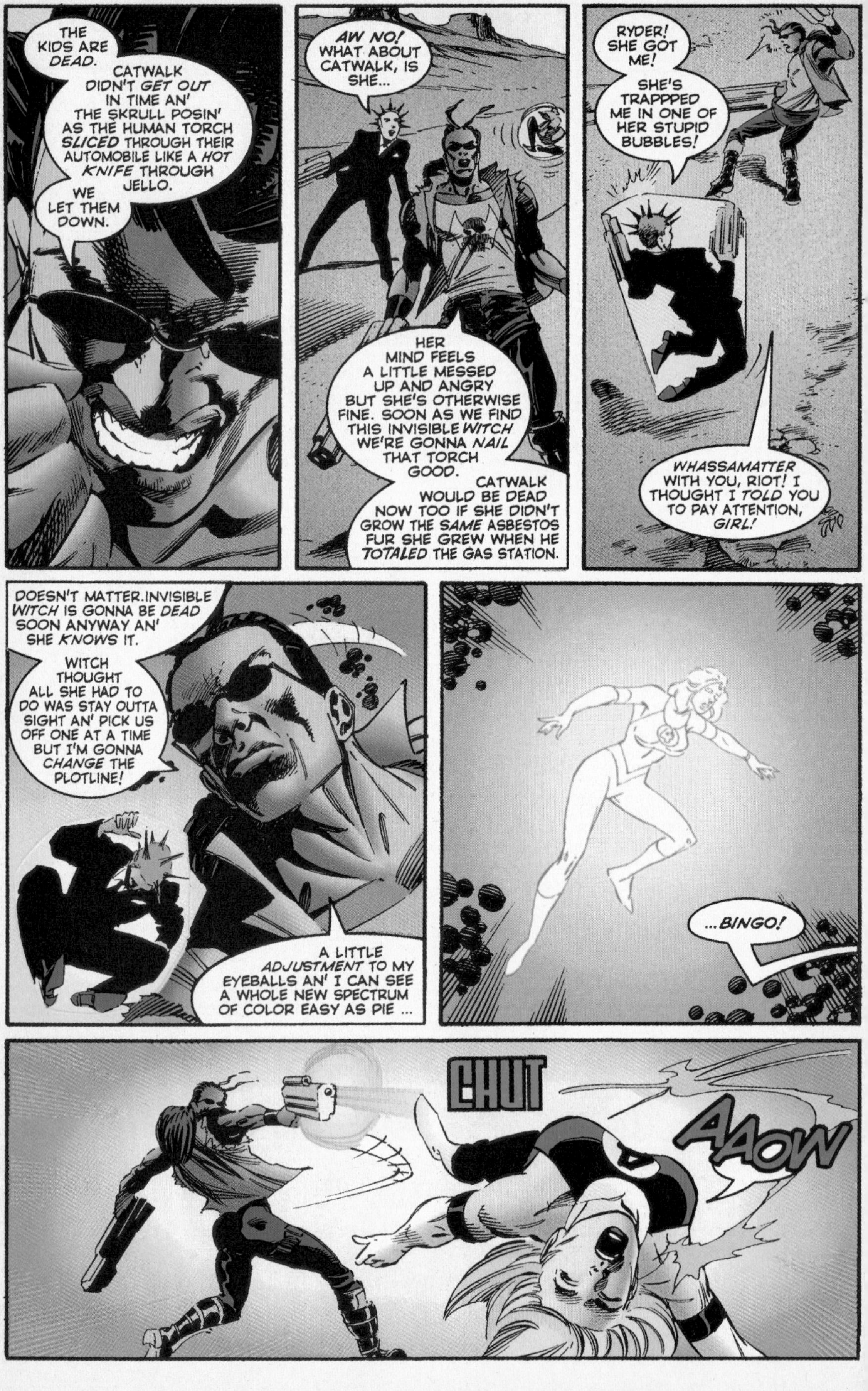
THE KIDS ARE DEAD.
CATWALK DIDN'T GET OUT IN TIME AN' THE SKRULL POSIN' AS THE HUMAN TORCH SLICED THROUGH THEIR AUTOMOBILE LIKE A HOT KNIFE THROUGH JELLO.
WE LET THEM DOWN.
AW NO! WHAT ABOUT CATWALK, IS SHE...
HER MIND FEELS A LITTLE MESSED UP AND ANGRY BUT SHE'S OTHERWISE FINE. SOON AS WE FIND THIS INVISIBLE WITCH WE'RE GONNA NAIL THAT TORCH GOOD.
CATWALK WOULD BE DEAD NOW TOO IF SHE DIDN'T GROW THE SAME ASBESTOS FUR SHE GREW WHEN HE TOTALED THE GAS STATION.
RYDER! SHE GOT ME!
SHE'S TRAPPPED ME IN ONE OF HER STUPID BUBBLES!
WHASSAMATTER WITH YOU, RIOT! I THOUGHT I TOLD YOU TO PAY ATTENTION, GIRL!
DOESN'T MATTER.INVISIBLE WITCH IS GONNA BE DEAD SOON ANYWAY AN' SHE KNOWS IT.
WITCH THOUGHT ALL SHE HAD TO DO WAS STAY OUTTA SIGHT AN' PICK US OFF ONE AT A TIME BUT I'M GONNA CHANGE THE PLOTLINE!
A LITTLE ADJUSTMENT TO MY EYEBALLS AN' I CAN SEE A WHOLE NEW SPECTRUM OF COLOR EASY AS PIE ...
...BINGO!
CHUT
AAOW

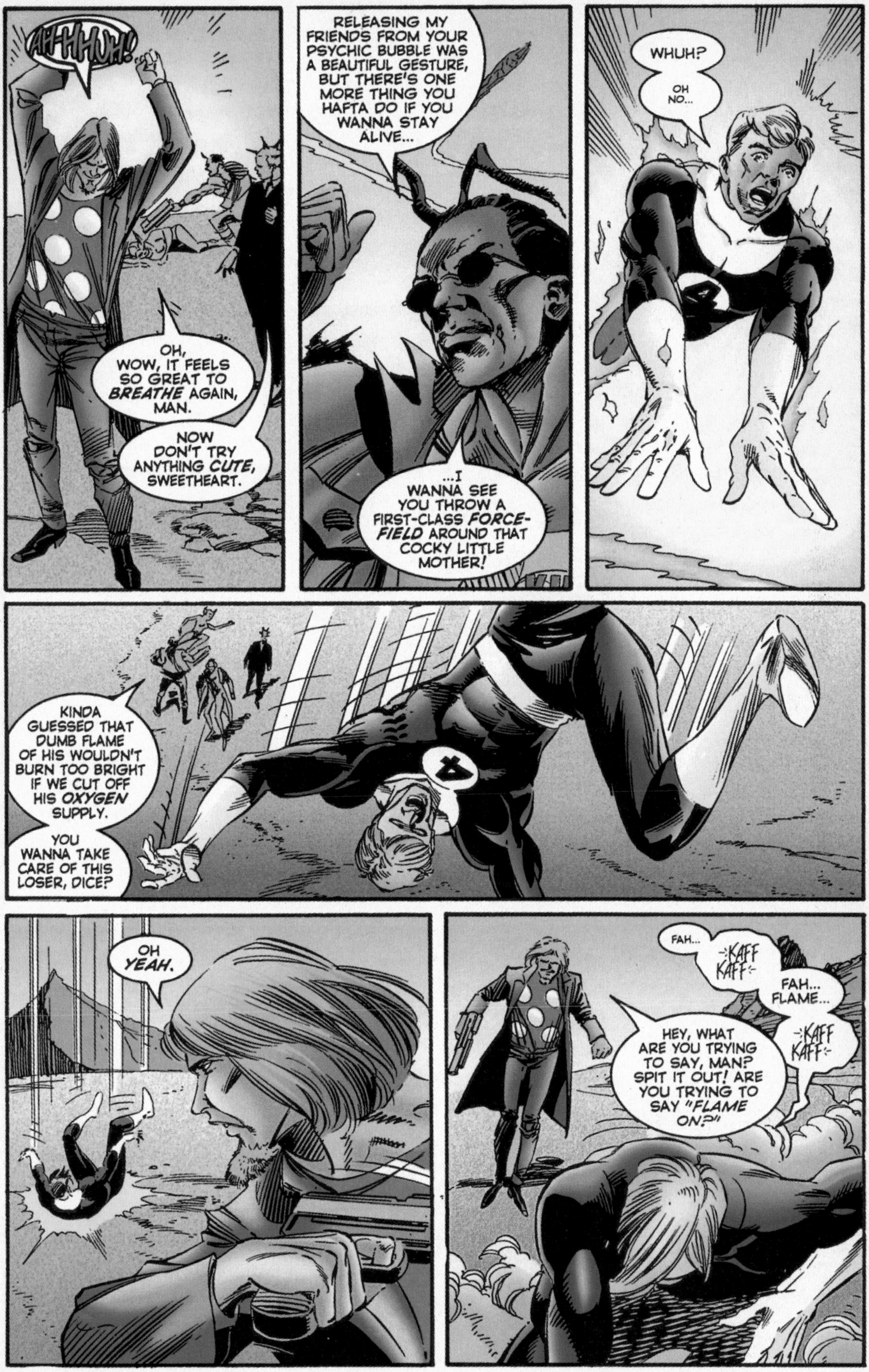
AH-HHUH!
OH, WOW, IT FEELS SO GREAT TO BREATHE AGAIN, MAN.
NOW DON'T TRY ANYTHING CUTE, SWEETHEART.
RELEASING MY FRIENDS FROM YOUR PSYCHIC BUBBLE WAS A BEAUTIFUL GESTURE, BUT THERE'S ONE MORE THING YOU HAFTA DO IF YOU WANNA STAY ALIVE...
...I WANNA SEE YOU THROW A FIRST-CLASS FORCE-FIELD AROUND THAT COCKY LITTLE MOTHER!
WHUH?
OH NO...
KINDA GUESSED THAT DUMB FLAME OF HIS WOULDN'T BURN TOO BRIGHT IF WE CUT OFF HIS OXYGEN SUPPLY.
YOU WANNA TAKE CARE OF THIS LOSER, DICE?
OH YEAH.
FAH...
KAFF KAFF
FAH... FLAME...
KAFF KAFF
HEY, WHAT ARE YOU TRYING TO SAY, MAN? SPIT IT OUT! ARE YOU TRYING TO SAY "FLAME ON?"

WELL, *NO DICE!*

*CATWALK!* OH WOW, ARE YOU OKAY?

HE DESERVED THAT SO MUCH! I JUST WISH *I* WAS THE ONE WHO PULLED THE TRIGGER!

H-HEY, WHAT'S THAT *RUMBLING* SOUND?

*MOONSTOMP!* HURRY UP AND FINISH THE FIGHT, HUH? WE GOT NO TIME TO FOOL AROUND.

YOU THINK I'M *STUPID* OR SOMETHIN'?

I KNOW WHAT *TIME* IT IS, NIG-NOG...

--IT'S *CLOBBERIN' TIME!*

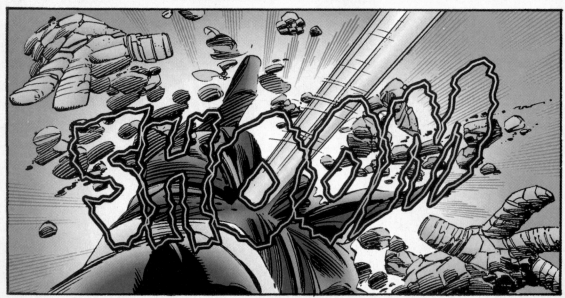

SHOOOM

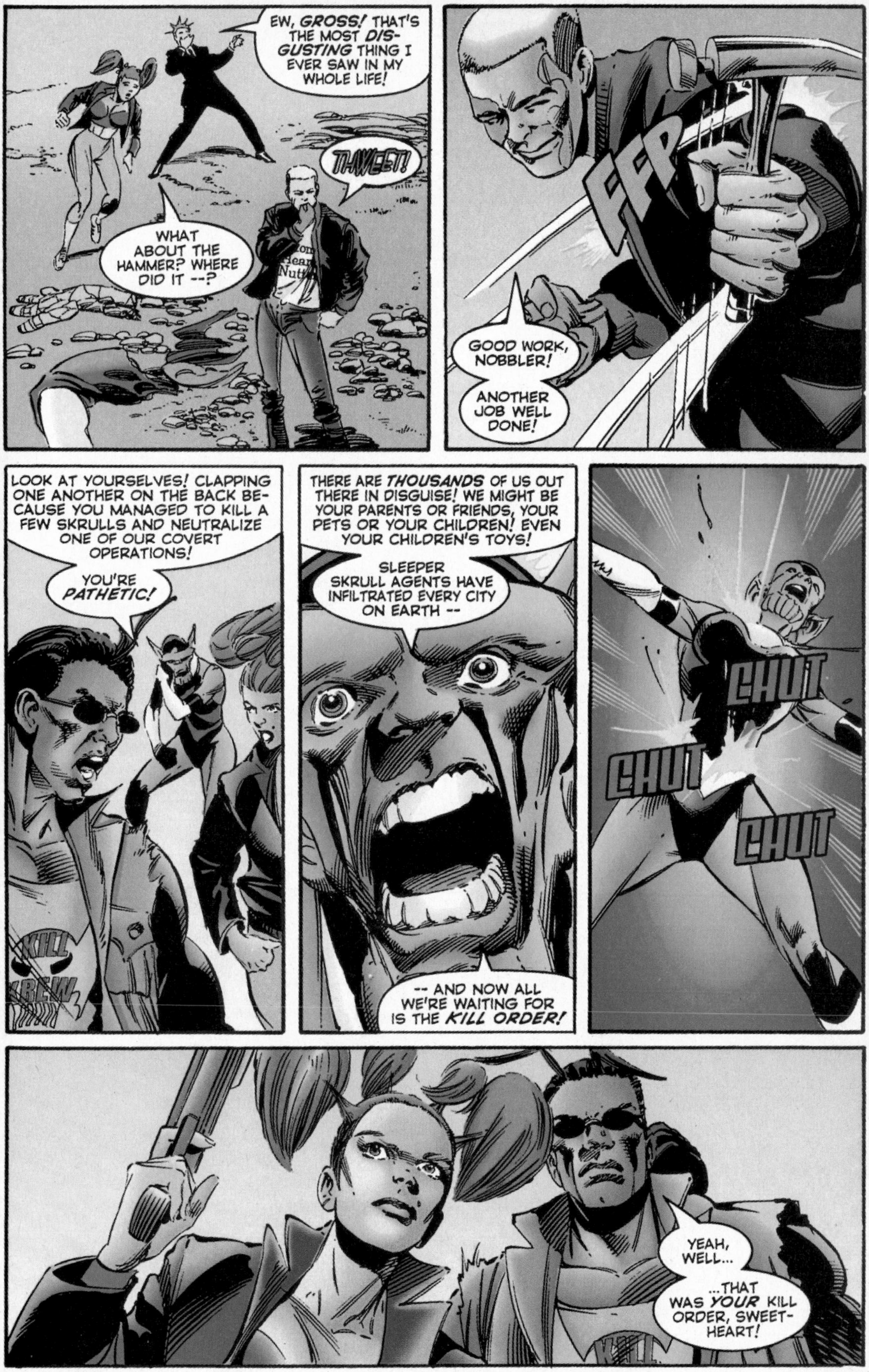
EW, *GROSS!* THAT'S THE MOST *DIS-GUSTING* THING I EVER SAW IN MY WHOLE LIFE!
THWEET!
WHAT ABOUT THE HAMMER? WHERE DID IT --?
FFP
GOOD WORK, NOBBLER!
ANOTHER JOB WELL DONE!
LOOK AT YOURSELVES! CLAPPING ONE ANOTHER ON THE BACK BE-CAUSE YOU MANAGED TO KILL A FEW SKRULLS AND NEUTRALIZE ONE OF OUR COVERT OPERATIONS!
YOU'RE *PATHETIC!*
THERE ARE *THOUSANDS* OF US OUT THERE IN DISGUISE! WE MIGHT BE YOUR PARENTS OR FRIENDS, YOUR PETS OR YOUR CHILDREN! EVEN YOUR CHILDREN'S TOYS!
SLEEPER SKRULL AGENTS HAVE INFILTRATED EVERY CITY ON EARTH --
-- AND NOW ALL WE'RE WAITING FOR IS THE *KILL ORDER!*
CHUT
CHUT
CHUT
YEAH, WELL...
...THAT WAS *YOUR* KILL ORDER, SWEET-HEART!

YOU REALLY *HATE* SKRULLS, DON'T YOU, RYDER?

I MEAN, REALLY, *REALLY HATE* THEM, RIGHT?

YOU *SAID* IT, COWBOY. SKRULLS ARE *SCUM.*

IN FACT, THERE'S NOTHING RAISES MY SPIRITS FASTER THAN WATCHING ONE OF THOSE GREEN MOTHERS PERSPIRE THROUGH THE SIGHT OF A HIGH-VELOCITY *RIFLE.*

YOU SEE, SKRULLS ONLY GOT TWO BASIC FUNCTIONS IN LIFE: THEY LIKE GETTIN' IT TOGETHER AND MAKIN' UGLY BABY SKRULLS AND THEY LIKE HURTING ORDINARY, DECENT EARTH PEOPLE WHO CAN'T FIGHT BACK.

IT'S UP TO US TO EVEN THE SCORE.

THAT WAS BRILLIANT, WASN'T IT? THAT WAS TOTALLY FAGGIN' *AMAZING!* I BET I COULD TAKE THE REAL *THING* NO PROBLEM! WHY DON'T WE DO IT, RYDER? LET'S GIVE THE *REAL* FANTASTIC FOUR A GOOD HIDING, EH?

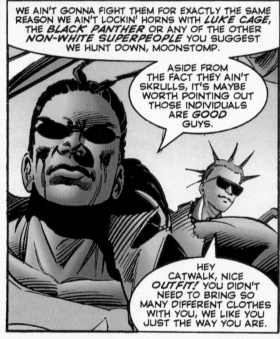

WE AIN'T GONNA FIGHT THEM FOR EXACTLY THE SAME REASON WE AIN'T LOCKIN' HORNS WITH *LUKE CAGE,* THE *BLACK PANTHER* OR ANY OF THE OTHER *NON-WHITE SUPERPEOPLE* YOU SUGGEST WE HUNT DOWN, MOONSTOMP.

ASIDE FROM THE FACT THEY AIN'T SKRULLS, IT'S MAYBE WORTH POINTING OUT THOSE INDIVIDUALS ARE *GOOD* GUYS.

HEY CATWALK, NICE *OUTFIT!* YOU DIDN'T NEED TO BRING SO MANY DIFFERENT CLOTHES WITH YOU, WE LIKE YOU JUST THE WAY YOU ARE.

I DIDN'T SPEND A FORTUNE ON DESIGNER LABELS JUST TO KEEP THEM LOCKED UP IN MY APARTMENT, RIOT!

YEAH, WELL, IF YOU HAVE TO GET CHANGED EVERY FIVE MINUTES, TRY NOT TO DO IT IN FRONT OF RYDER NEXT TIME, HUH?

OH, SHUT UP, YOU WEIRD LITTLE WITCH! I THOUGHT WE WERE SUPPOSED TO BE LOOKING AROUND FOR SOMEPLACE NICE TO EAT!

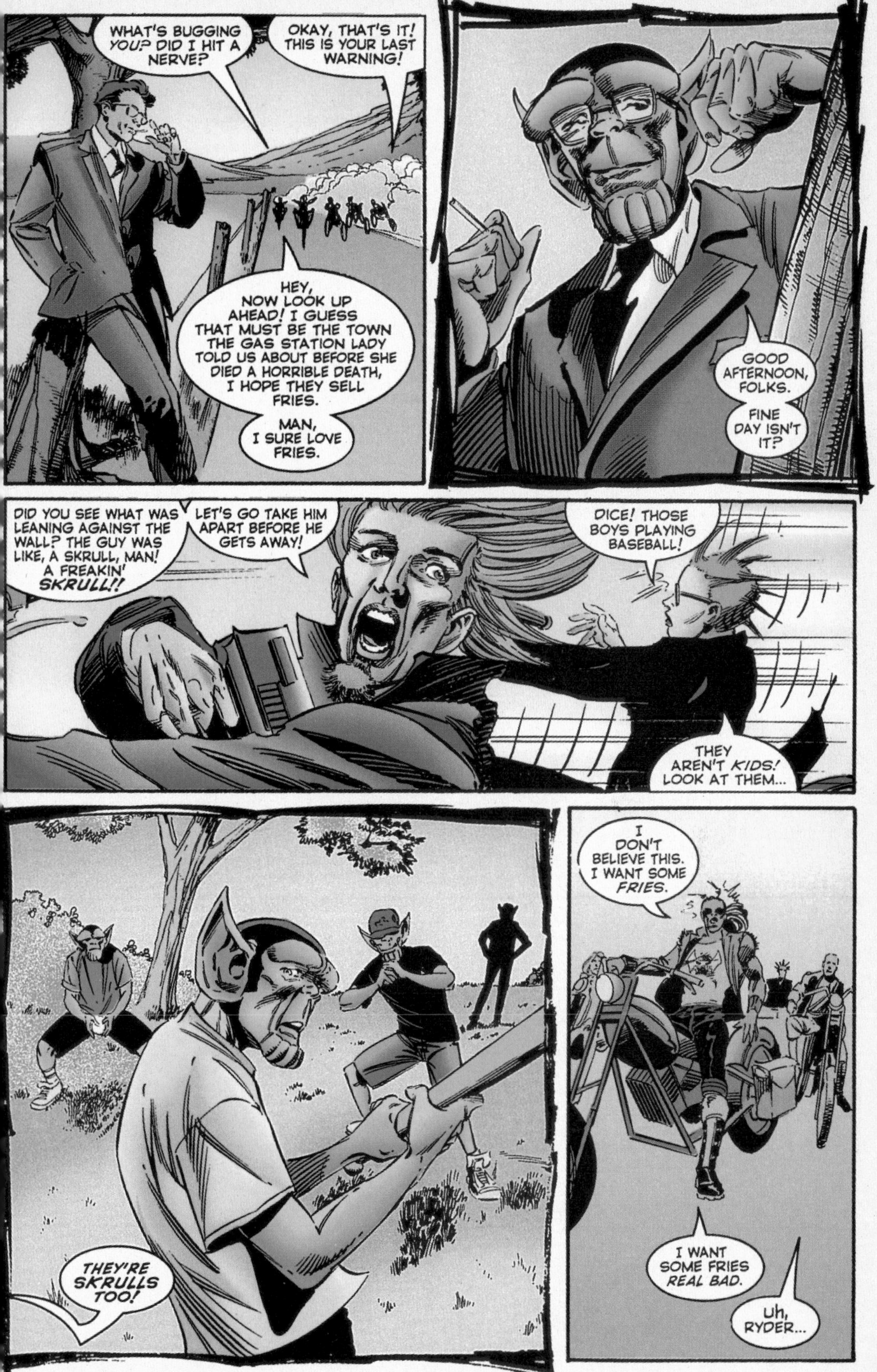
WHAT'S BUGGING YOU? DID I HIT A NERVE?
OKAY, THAT'S IT! THIS IS YOUR LAST WARNING!
HEY, NOW LOOK UP AHEAD! I GUESS THAT MUST BE THE TOWN THE GAS STATION LADY TOLD US ABOUT BEFORE SHE DIED A HORRIBLE DEATH, I HOPE THEY SELL FRIES.
MAN, I SURE LOVE FRIES.
GOOD AFTERNOON, FOLKS.
FINE DAY ISN'T IT?
DID YOU SEE WHAT WAS LEANING AGAINST THE WALL? THE GUY WAS LIKE, A SKRULL, MAN! A FREAKIN' SKRULL!!
LET'S GO TAKE HIM APART BEFORE HE GETS AWAY!
DICE! THOSE BOYS PLAYING BASEBALL!
THEY AREN'T KIDS! LOOK AT THEM...
THEY'RE SKRULLS TOO!
I DON'T BELIEVE THIS. I WANT SOME FRIES.
I WANT SOME FRIES REAL BAD.
UH, RYDER...

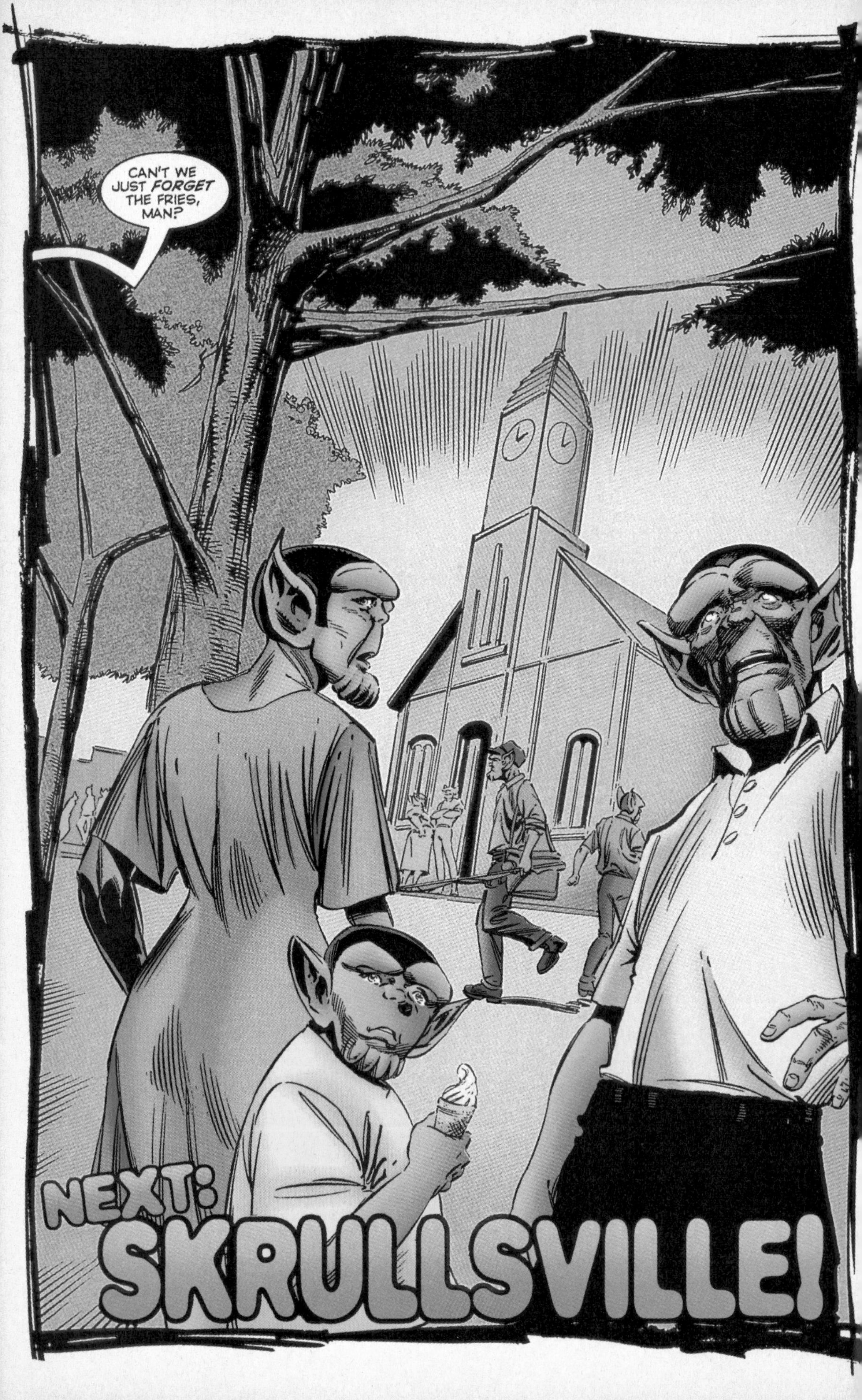
CAN'T WE JUST FORGET THE FRIES, MAN?
NEXT: SKRULLSVILLE!

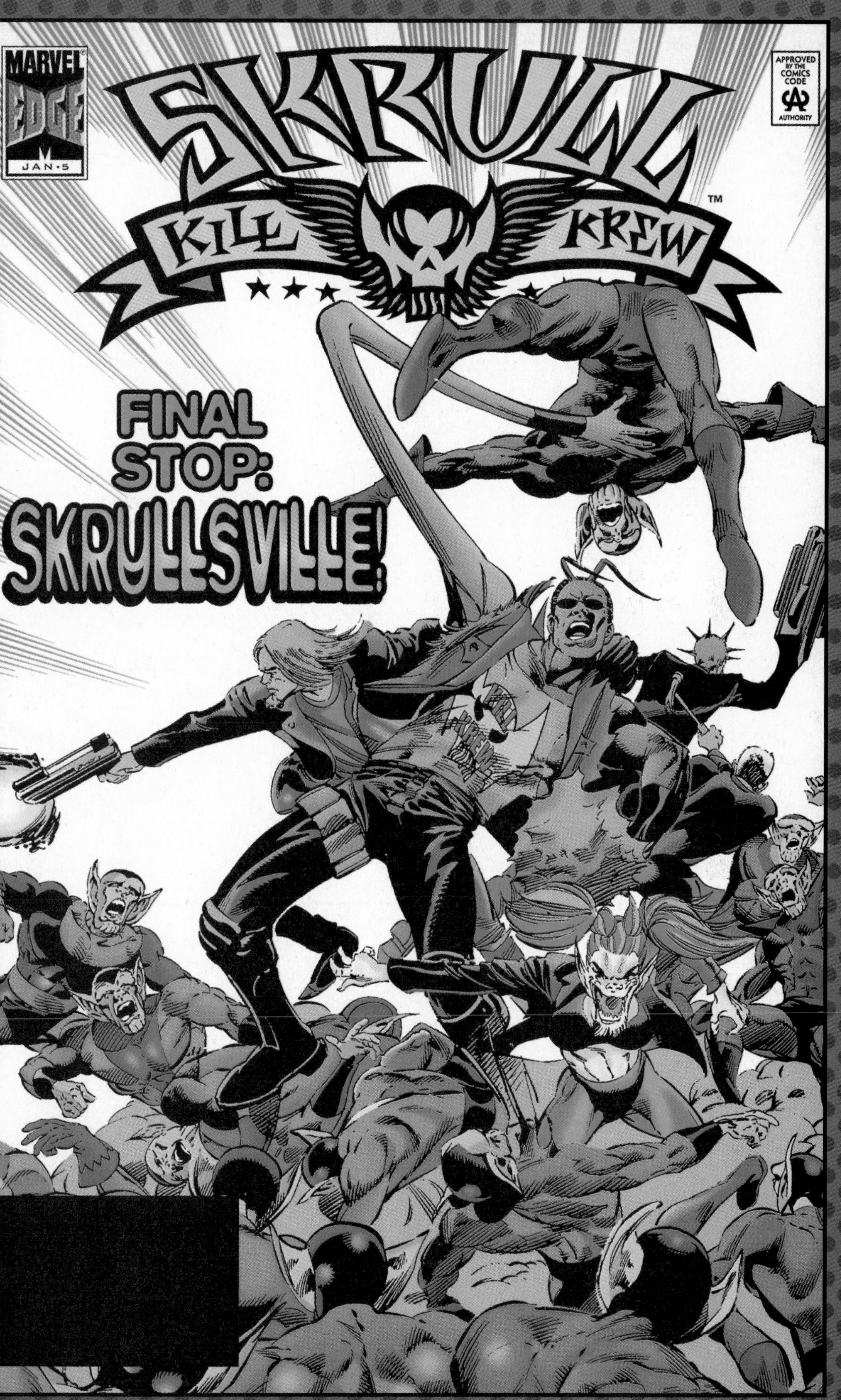
MARVEL EDGE
JAN • 5
APPROVED BY THE COMICS CODE AUTHORITY
SKRULL KILL KREW™
FINAL STOP: SKRULLSVILLE!

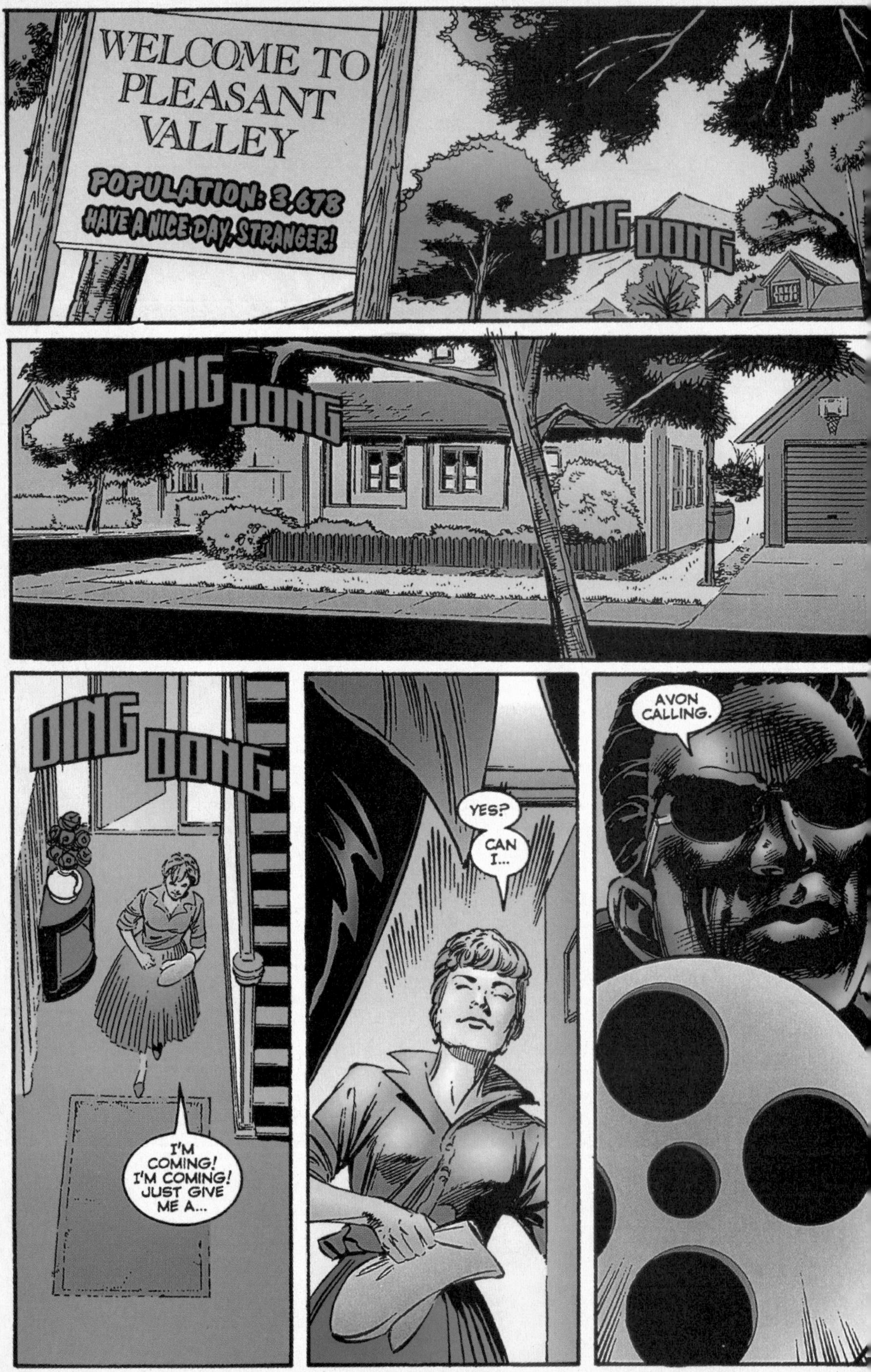
WELCOME TO
PLEASANT
VALLEY
POPULATION: 3,678
HAVE A NICE DAY, STRANGER!
DING DONG
DING DONG
DING DONG.
I'M COMING! I'M COMING! JUST GIVE ME A...
YES?
CAN I...
AVON CALLING.

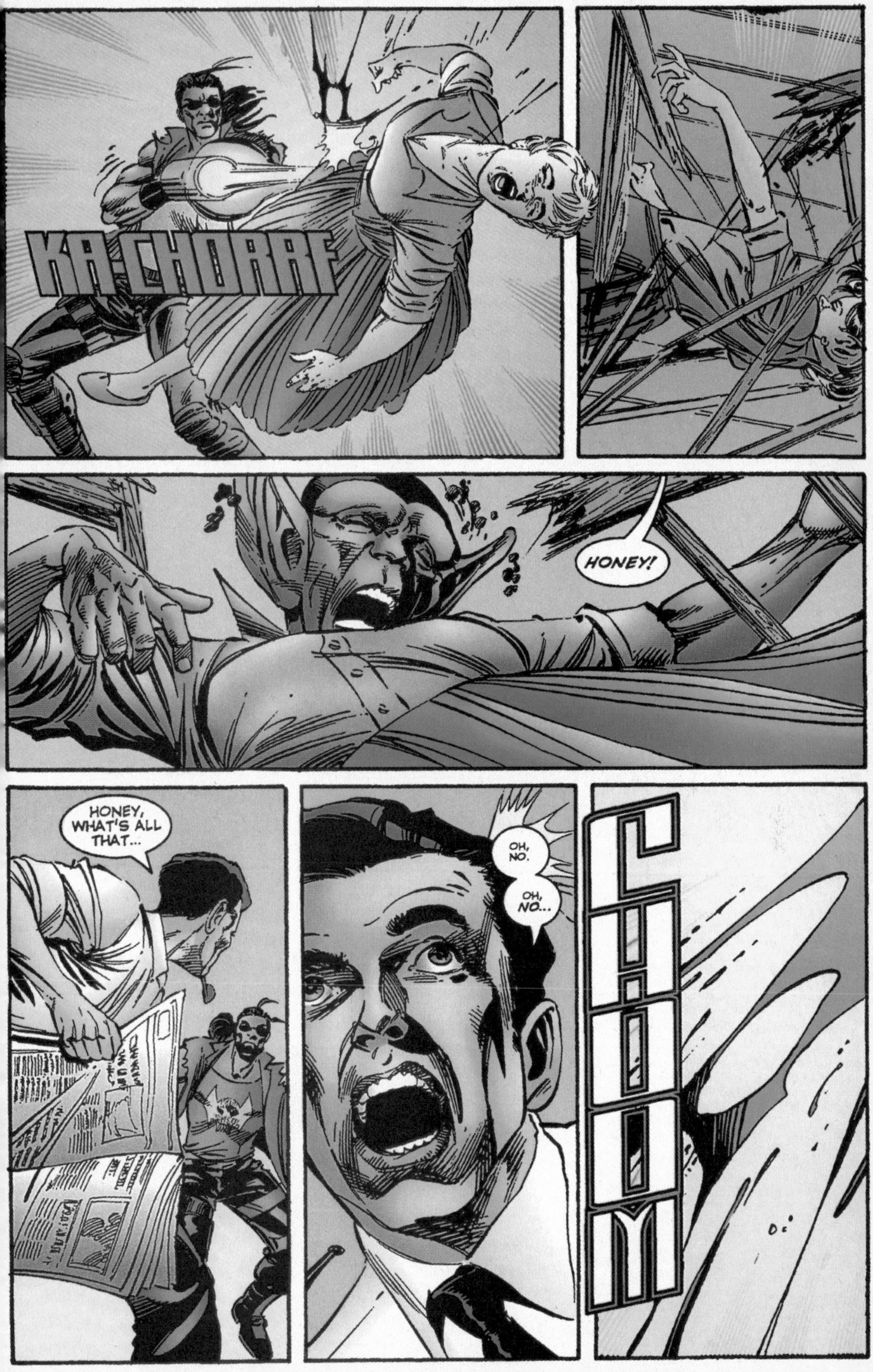
KA-CHORRF
HONEY!
HONEY, WHAT'S ALL THAT...
OH, NO.
OH, NO...

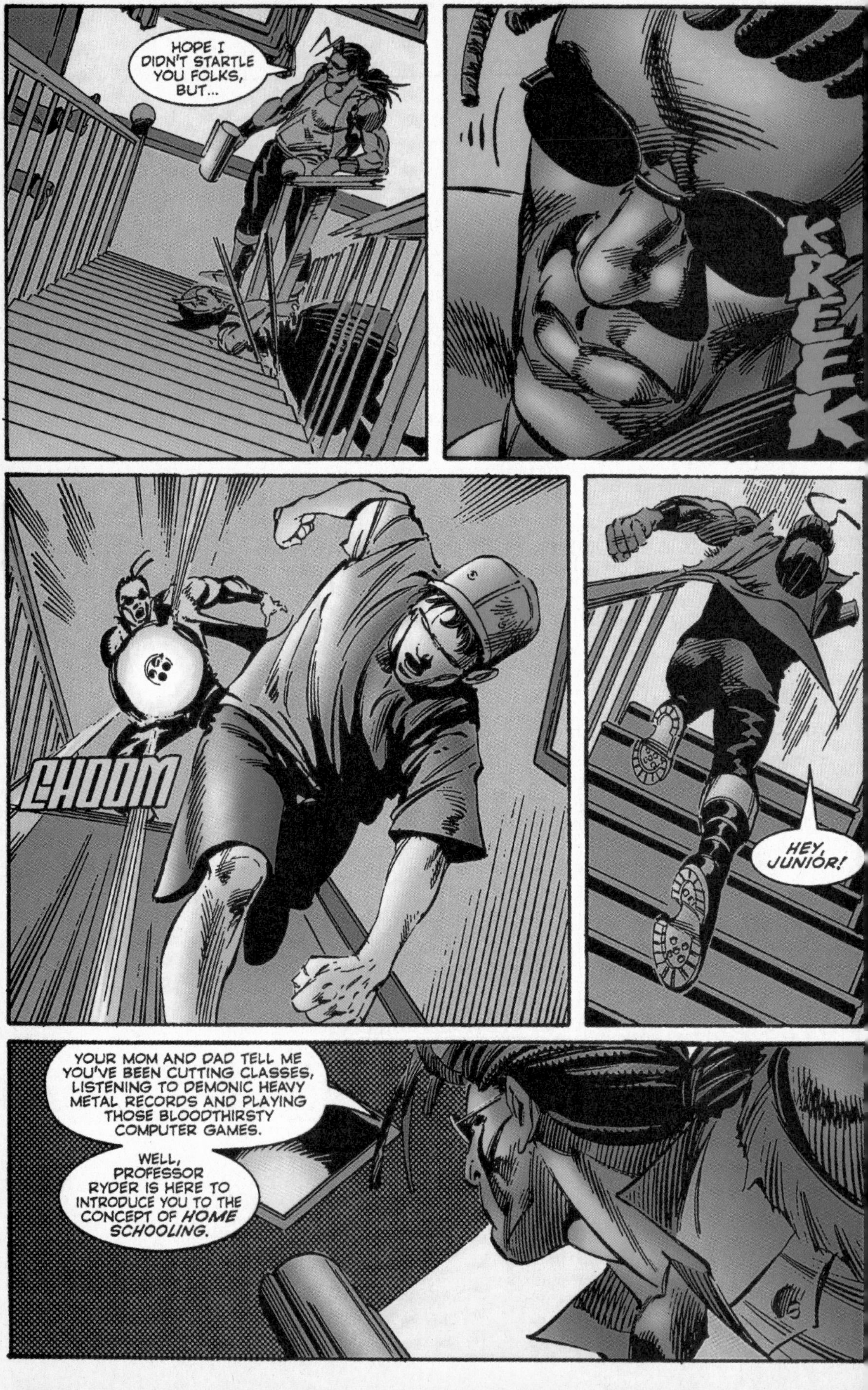
HOPE I DIDN'T STARTLE YOU FOLKS, BUT...
KREEK
CHOOM
HEY, JUNIOR!
YOUR MOM AND DAD TELL ME YOU'VE BEEN CUTTING CLASSES, LISTENING TO DEMONIC HEAVY METAL RECORDS AND PLAYING THOSE BLOODTHIRSTY COMPUTER GAMES.
WELL, PROFESSOR RYDER IS HERE TO INTRODUCE YOU TO THE CONCEPT OF HOME SCHOOLING.

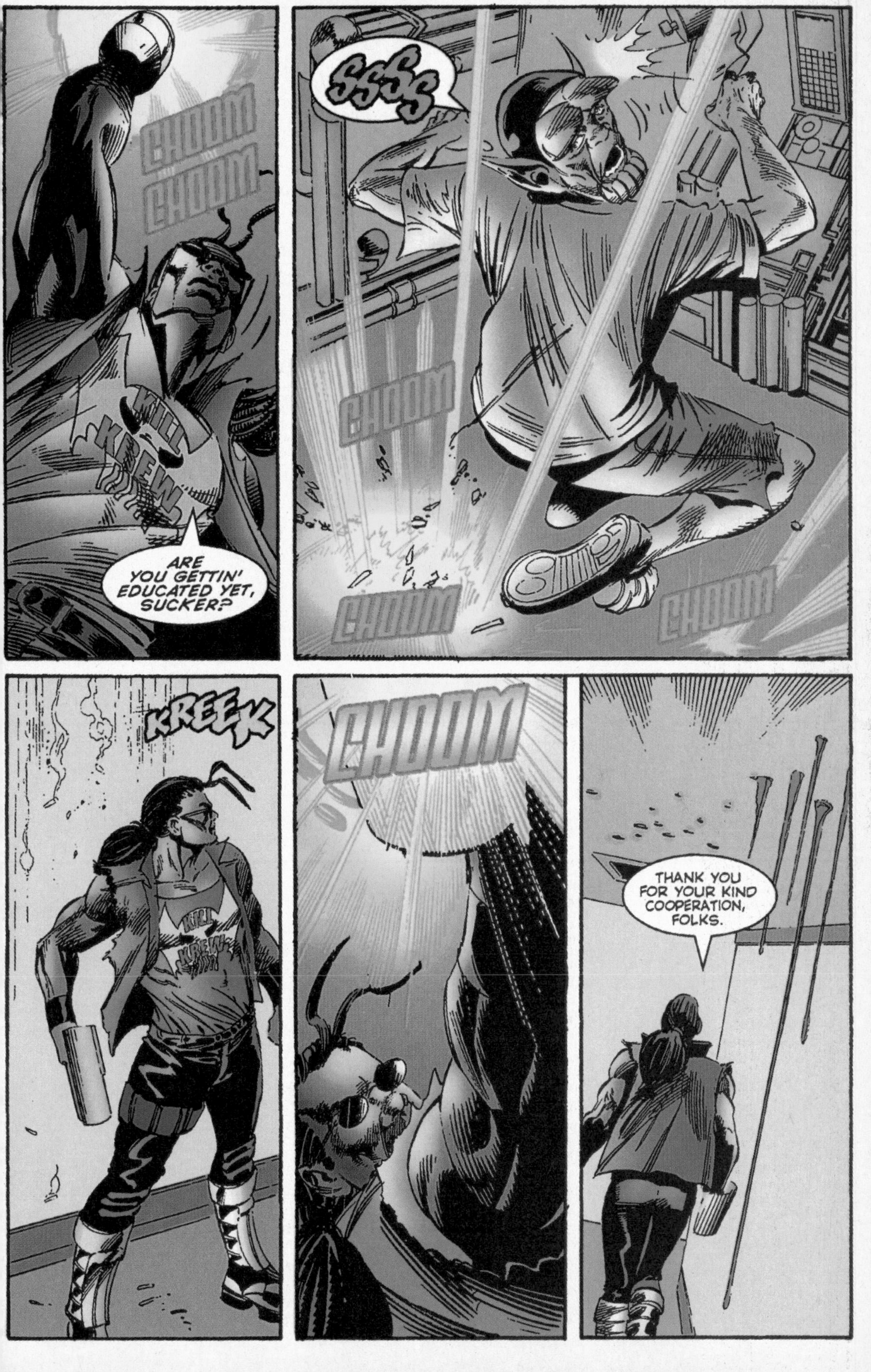
CHOOM
CHOOM
KILL KREW
ARE YOU GETTIN' EDUCATED YET, SUCKER?
SSSS
CHOOM
CHOOM
CHOOM
KREEK
KILL KREW
CHOOM
THANK YOU FOR YOUR KIND COOPERATION, FOLKS.

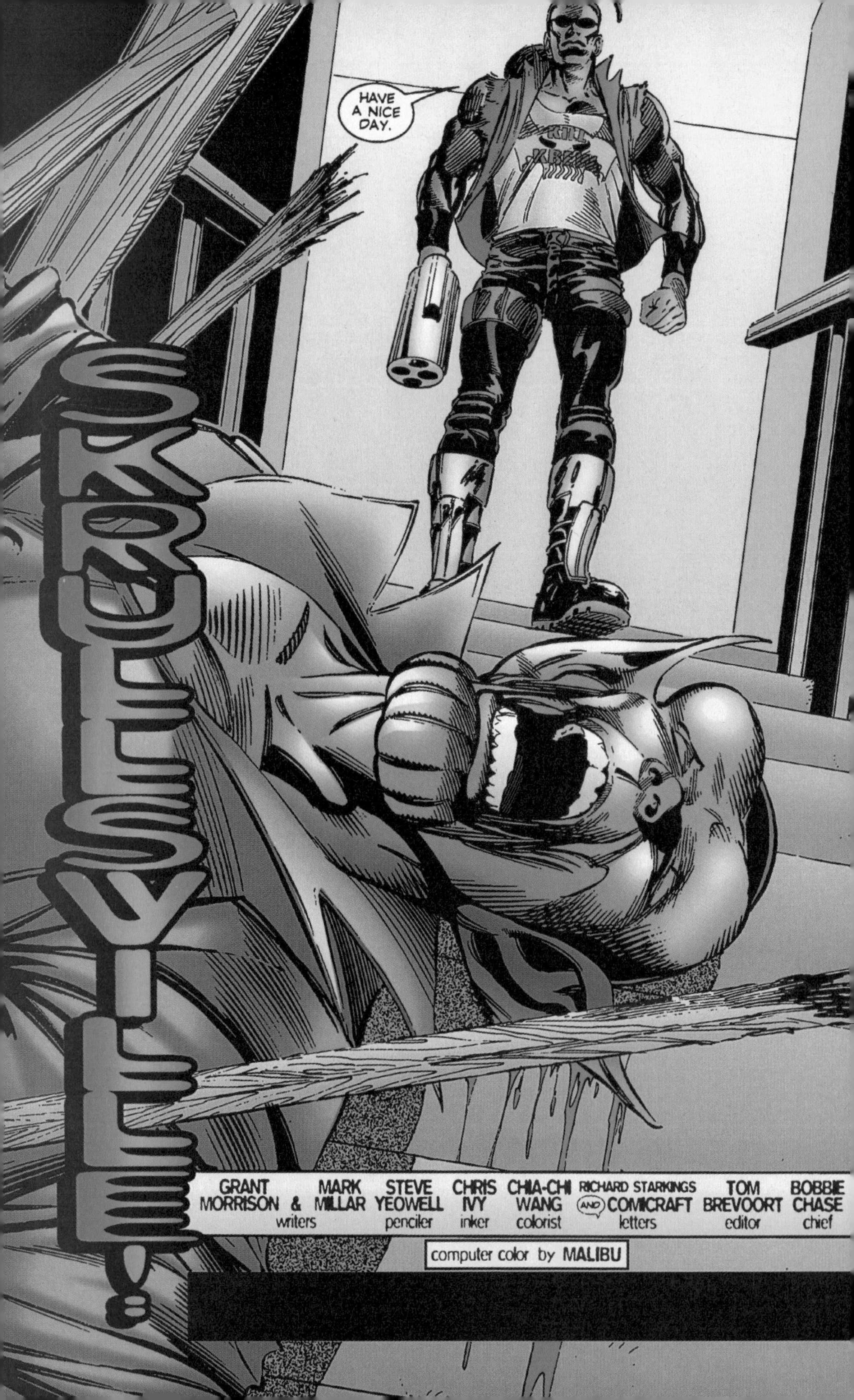
HAVE A NICE DAY.
SKRULLSVILLE!
GRANT MORRISON & MARK MILLAR writers
STEVE YEOWELL penciler
CHRIS IVY inker
CHIA-CHI WANG colorist
RICHARD STARKINGS AND COMICRAFT letters
TOM BREVOORT editor
BOBBIE CHASE chief
computer color by MALIBU

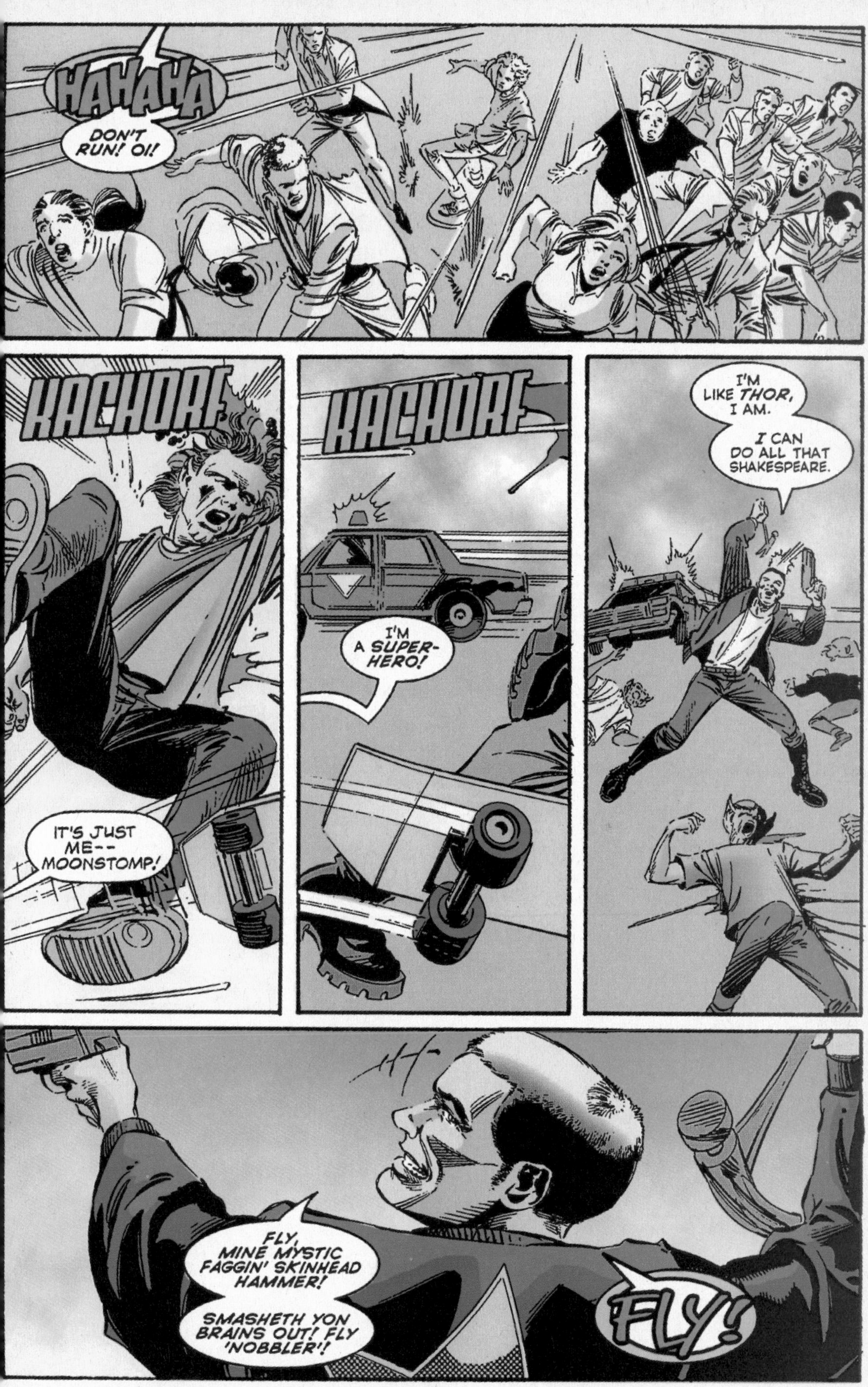
HAHAHA
DON'T RUN! OI!
KACHORF
IT'S JUST ME-- MOONSTOMP!
KACHORF
I'M A SUPER-HERO!
I'M LIKE THOR, I AM.
I CAN DO ALL THAT SHAKESPEARE.
FLY, MINE MYSTIC FAGGIN' SKINHEAD HAMMER!
SMASHETH YON BRAINS OUT! FLY 'NOBBLER'!
FLY!

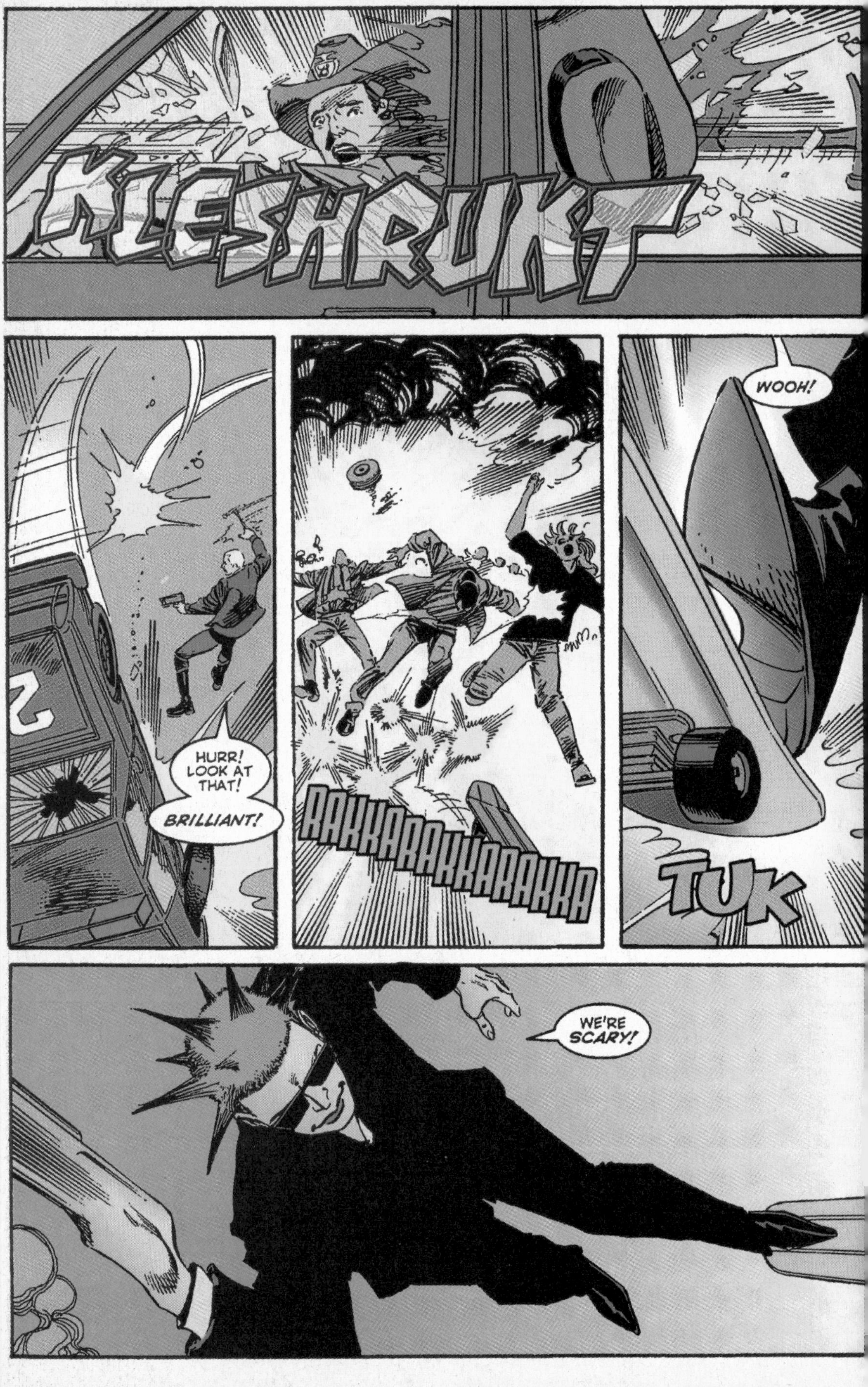
KLESHRUKT
HURR! LOOK AT THAT!
BRILLIANT!
RAKKARAKKARAKKA
WOOH!
TUK
WE'RE SCARY!

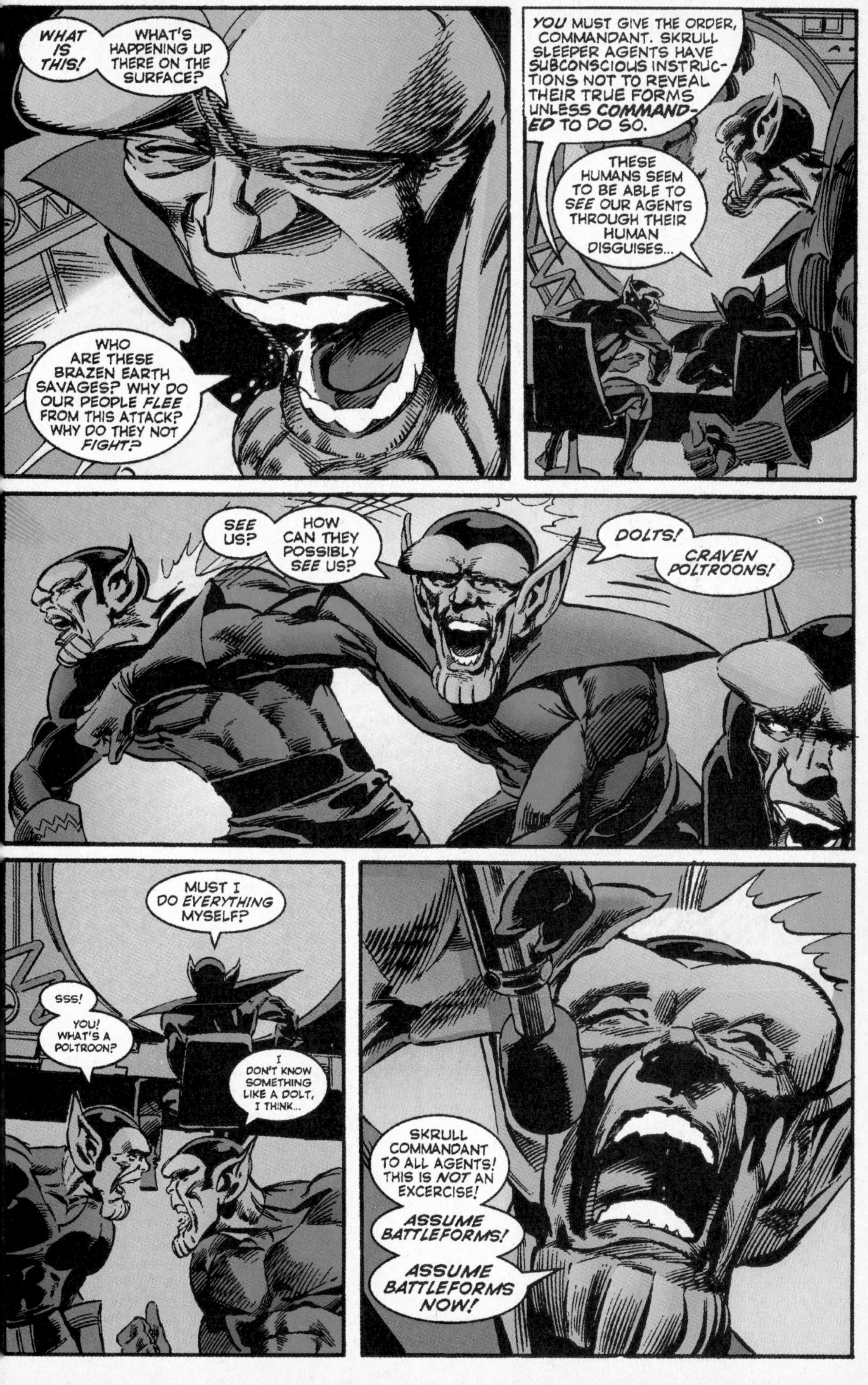
WHAT IS THIS!
WHAT'S HAPPENING UP THERE ON THE SURFACE?
WHO ARE THESE BRAZEN EARTH SAVAGES? WHY DO OUR PEOPLE FLEE FROM THIS ATTACK? WHY DO THEY NOT FIGHT?
YOU MUST GIVE THE ORDER, COMMANDANT. SKRULL SLEEPER AGENTS HAVE SUBCONSCIOUS INSTRUCTIONS NOT TO REVEAL THEIR TRUE FORMS UNLESS COMMANDED TO DO SO.
THESE HUMANS SEEM TO BE ABLE TO SEE OUR AGENTS THROUGH THEIR HUMAN DISGUISES...
SEE US?
HOW CAN THEY POSSIBLY SEE US?
DOLTS!
CRAVEN POLTROONS!
MUST I DO EVERYTHING MYSELF?
SSS!
YOU! WHAT'S A POLTROON?
I DON'T KNOW SOMETHING LIKE A DOLT, I THINK...
SKRULL COMMANDANT TO ALL AGENTS! THIS IS NOT AN EXCERCISE!
ASSUME BATTLEFORMS!
ASSUME BATTLEFORMS NOW!

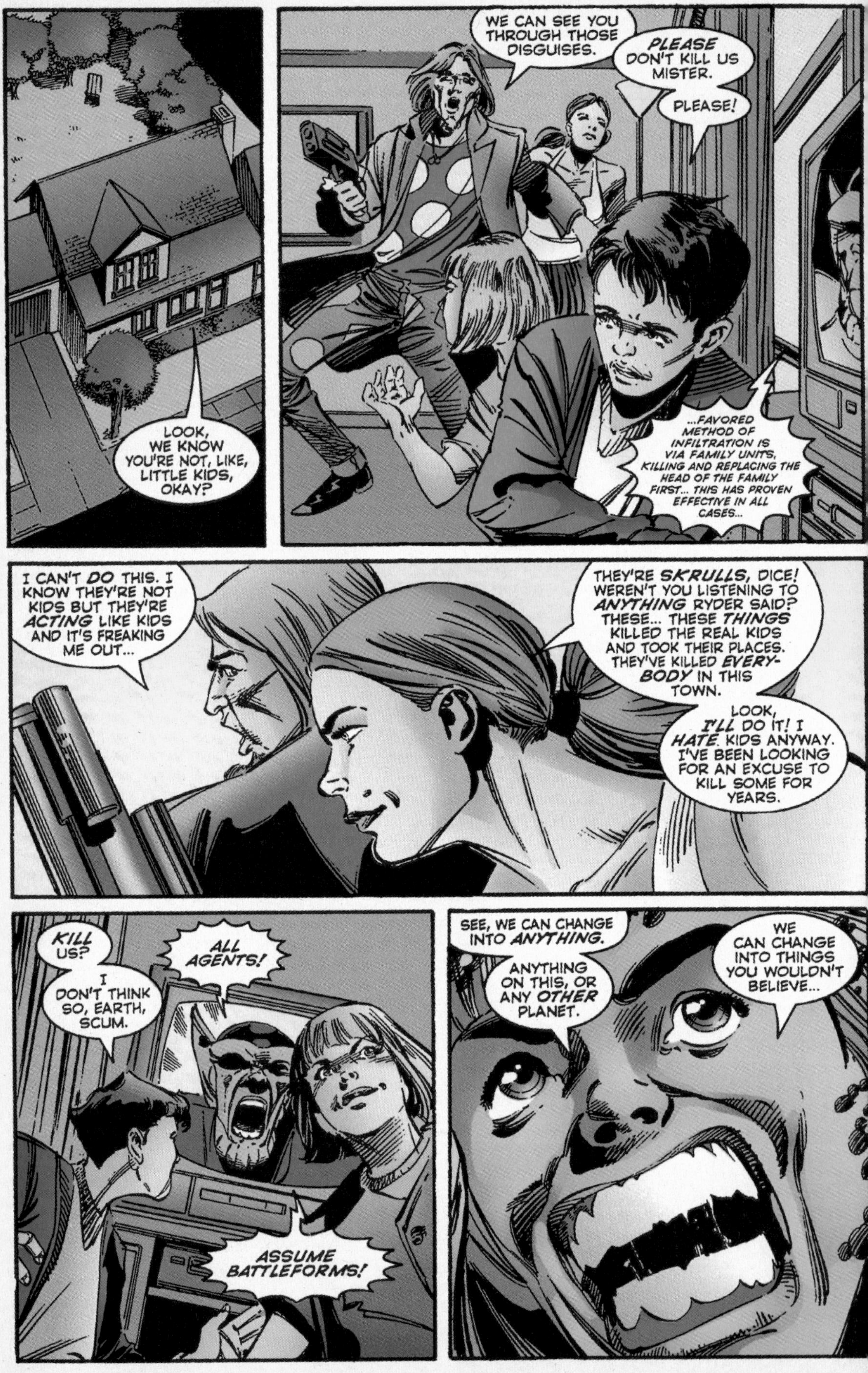

LOOK, WE KNOW YOU'RE NOT, LIKE, LITTLE KIDS, OKAY?
WE CAN SEE YOU THROUGH THOSE DISGUISES.
PLEASE DON'T KILL US MISTER.
PLEASE!
...FAVORED METHOD OF INFILTRATION IS VIA FAMILY UNITS, KILLING AND REPLACING THE HEAD OF THE FAMILY FIRST... THIS HAS PROVEN EFFECTIVE IN ALL CASES...
I CAN'T DO THIS. I KNOW THEY'RE NOT KIDS BUT THEY'RE ACTING LIKE KIDS AND IT'S FREAKING ME OUT...
THEY'RE SKRULLS, DICE! WEREN'T YOU LISTENING TO ANYTHING RYDER SAID? THESE... THESE THINGS KILLED THE REAL KIDS AND TOOK THEIR PLACES. THEY'VE KILLED EVERY-BODY IN THIS TOWN.
LOOK, I'LL DO IT! I HATE. KIDS ANYWAY. I'VE BEEN LOOKING FOR AN EXCUSE TO KILL SOME FOR YEARS.
KILL US?
I DON'T THINK SO, EARTH, SCUM.
ALL AGENTS!
ASSUME BATTLEFORMS!
SEE, WE CAN CHANGE INTO ANYTHING.
ANYTHING ON THIS, OR ANY OTHER PLANET.
WE CAN CHANGE INTO THINGS YOU WOULDN'T BELIEVE...

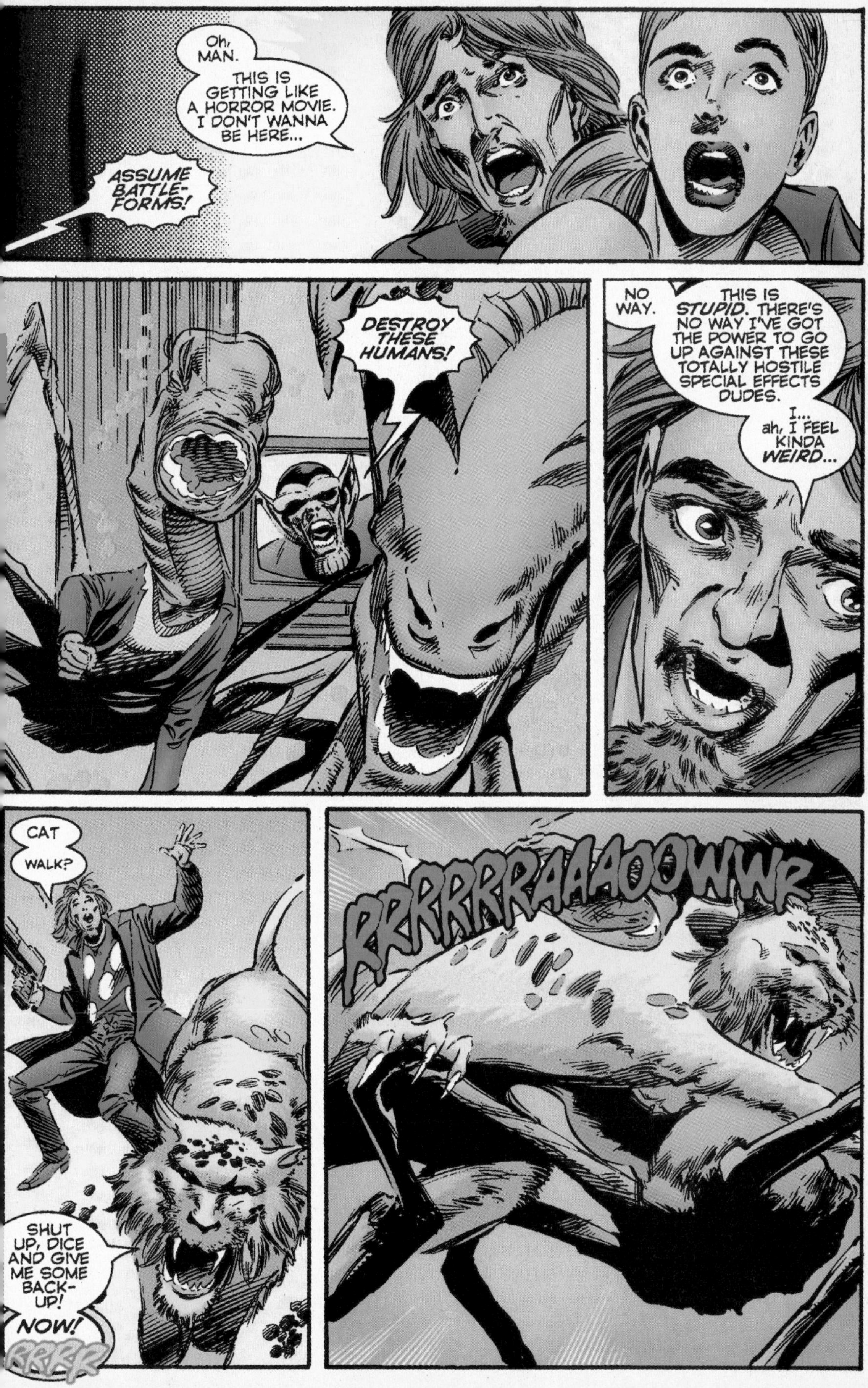

Oh, MAN.
THIS IS GETTING LIKE A HORROR MOVIE. I DON'T WANNA BE HERE...
ASSUME BATTLE-FORMS!
DESTROY THESE HUMANS!
NO WAY.
THIS IS STUPID. THERE'S NO WAY I'VE GOT THE POWER TO GO UP AGAINST THESE TOTALLY HOSTILE SPECIAL EFFECTS DUDES.
I... ah, I FEEL KINDA WEIRD...
CAT
WALK?
SHUT UP, DICE AND GIVE ME SOME BACK-UP!
NOW!
RRRR
RRRRRRAAAOOWWR

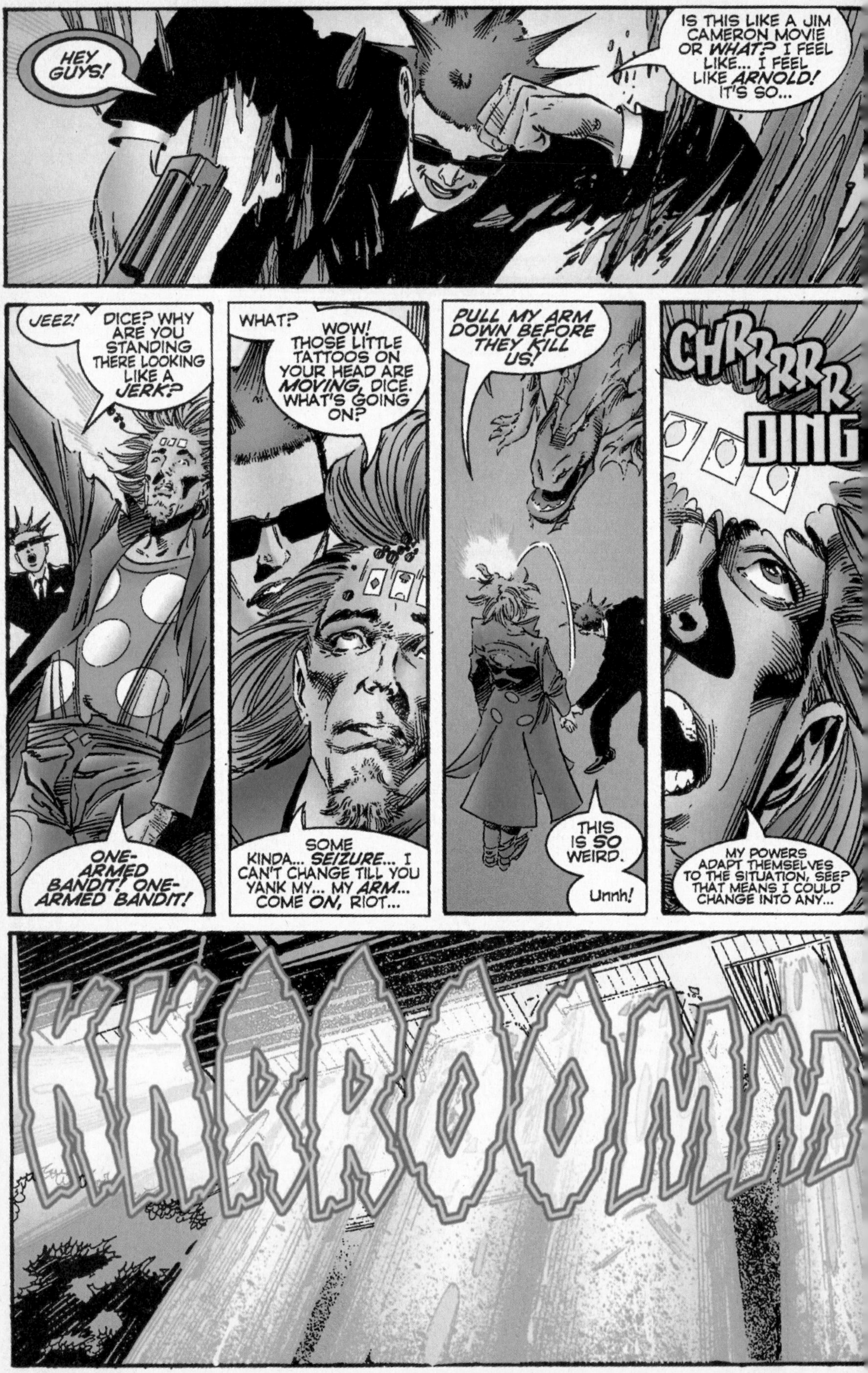

HEY GUYS!
IS THIS LIKE A JIM CAMERON MOVIE OR WHAT? I FEEL LIKE... I FEEL LIKE ARNOLD! IT'S SO...
JEEZ!
DICE? WHY ARE YOU STANDING THERE LOOKING LIKE A JERK?
ONE-ARMED BANDIT! ONE-ARMED BANDIT!
WHAT?
WOW! THOSE LITTLE TATTOOS ON YOUR HEAD ARE MOVING, DICE. WHAT'S GOING ON?
SOME KINDA... SEIZURE... I CAN'T CHANGE TILL YOU YANK MY... MY ARM... COME ON, RIOT...
PULL MY ARM DOWN BEFORE THEY KILL US!
THIS IS SO WEIRD.
Unnh!
CHRRRRR
DING
MY POWERS ADAPT THEMSELVES TO THE SITUATION, SEE? THAT MEANS I COULD CHANGE INTO ANY...
KKRROOMM

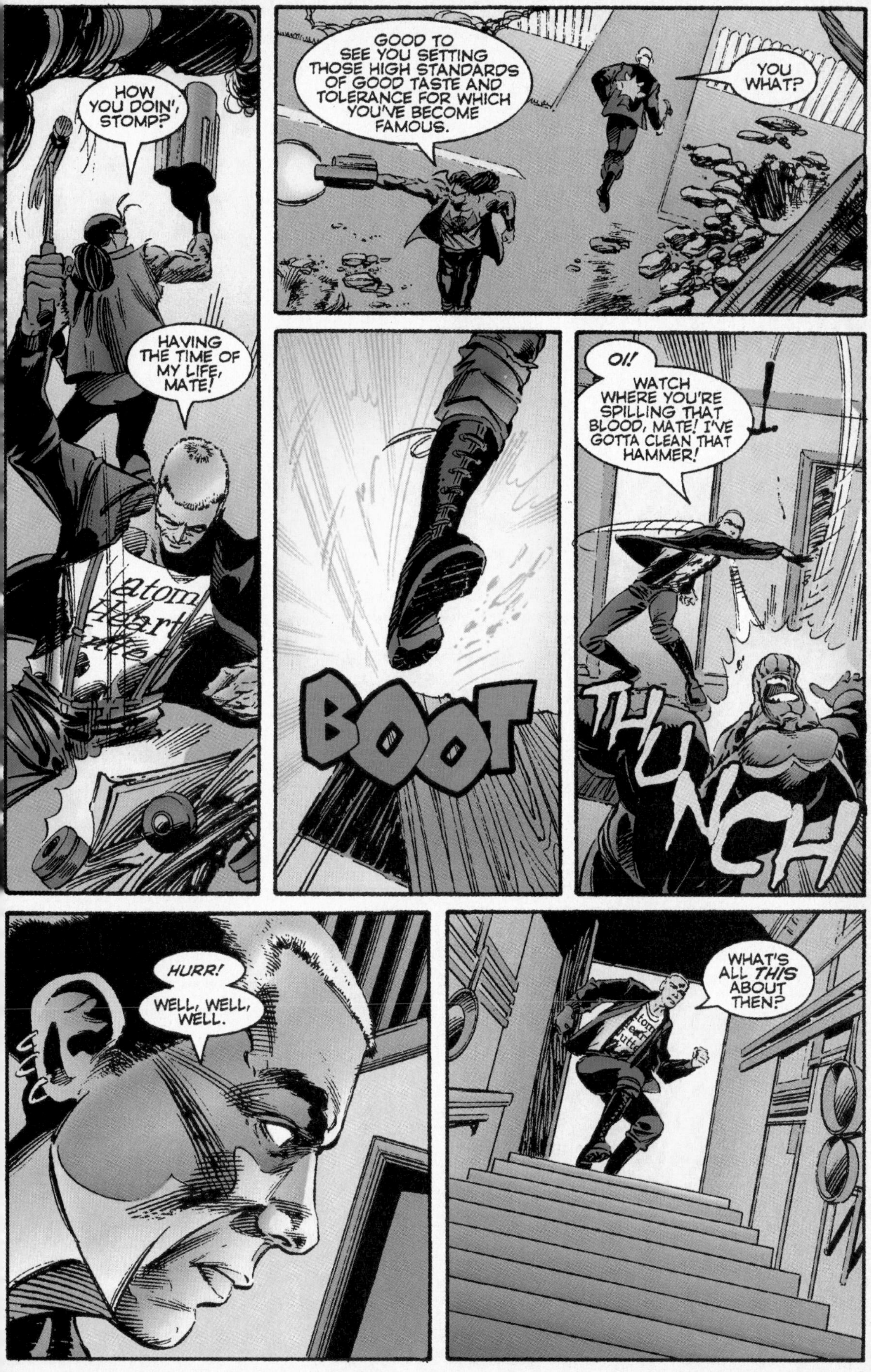
HOW YOU DOIN', STOMP?
HAVING THE TIME OF MY LIFE, MATE!
GOOD TO SEE YOU SETTING THOSE HIGH STANDARDS OF GOOD TASTE AND TOLERANCE FOR WHICH YOU'VE BECOME FAMOUS.
YOU WHAT?
BOOT
OI!
WATCH WHERE YOU'RE SPILLING THAT BLOOD, MATE! I'VE GOTTA CLEAN THAT HAMMER!
THUNCH
HURR!
WELL, WELL, WELL.
WHAT'S ALL *THIS* ABOUT THEN?

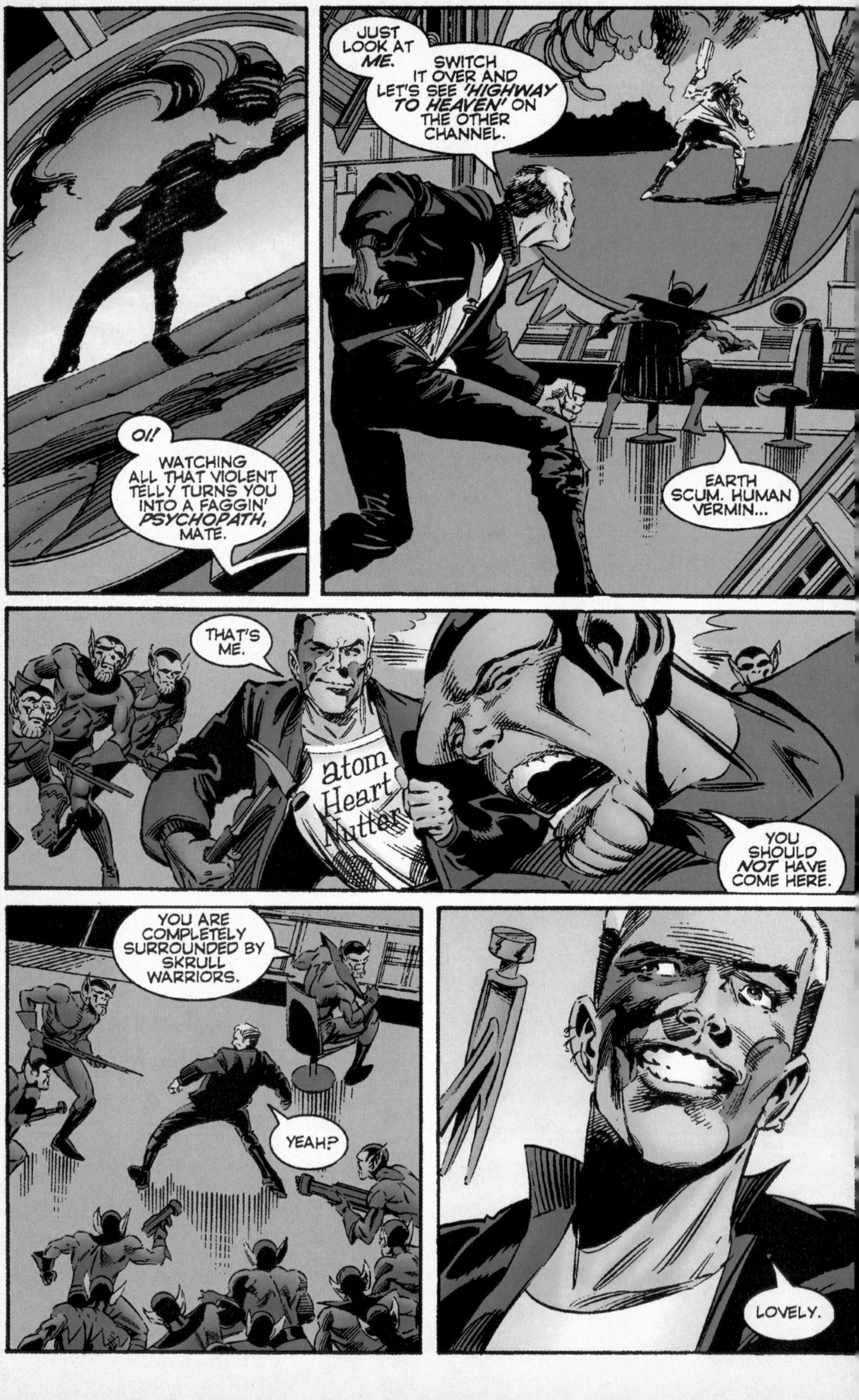
OI!
WATCHING ALL THAT VIOLENT TELLY TURNS YOU INTO A FAGGIN' PSYCHOPATH, MATE.
JUST LOOK AT ME. SWITCH IT OVER AND LET'S SEE 'HIGHWAY TO HEAVEN' ON THE OTHER CHANNEL.
EARTH SCUM. HUMAN VERMIN...
THAT'S ME.
atom Heart Nutter
YOU SHOULD NOT HAVE COME HERE.
YOU ARE COMPLETELY SURROUNDED BY SKRULL WARRIORS.
YEAH?
LOVELY.

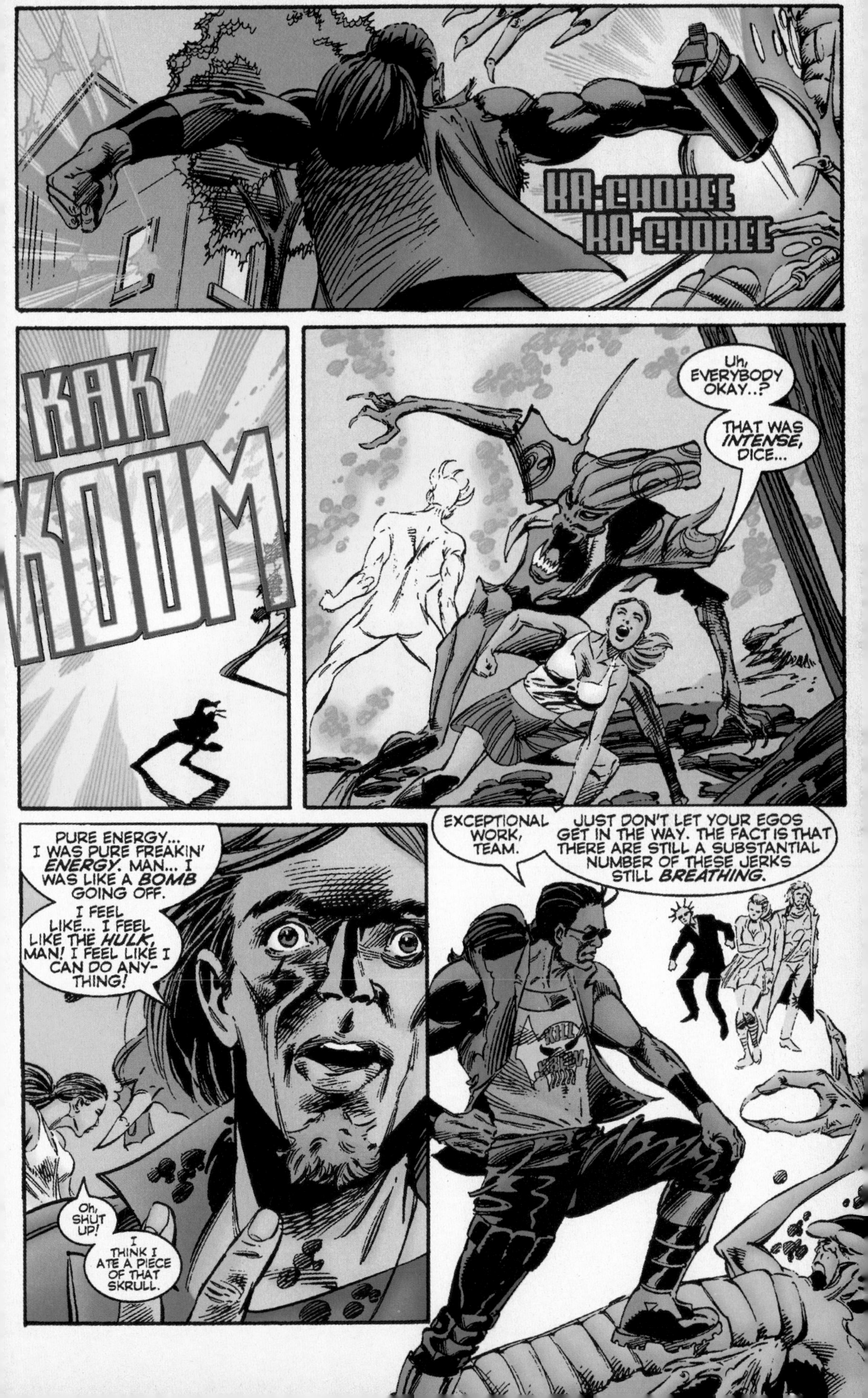

KA-CHOREE KA-CHOREE
KAK KOOM
Uh, EVERYBODY OKAY..?
THAT WAS *INTENSE,* DICE...
PURE ENERGY... I WAS PURE FREAKIN' *ENERGY*. MAN... I WAS LIKE A *BOMB* GOING OFF.
I FEEL LIKE... I FEEL LIKE THE *HULK,* MAN! I FEEL LIKE I CAN DO ANYTHING!
Oh, SHUT UP!
I THINK I ATE A PIECE OF THAT SKRULL.
EXCEPTIONAL WORK, TEAM.
JUST DON'T LET YOUR EGOS GET IN THE WAY. THE FACT IS THAT THERE ARE STILL A SUBSTANTIAL NUMBER OF THESE JERKS STILL *BREATHING*.

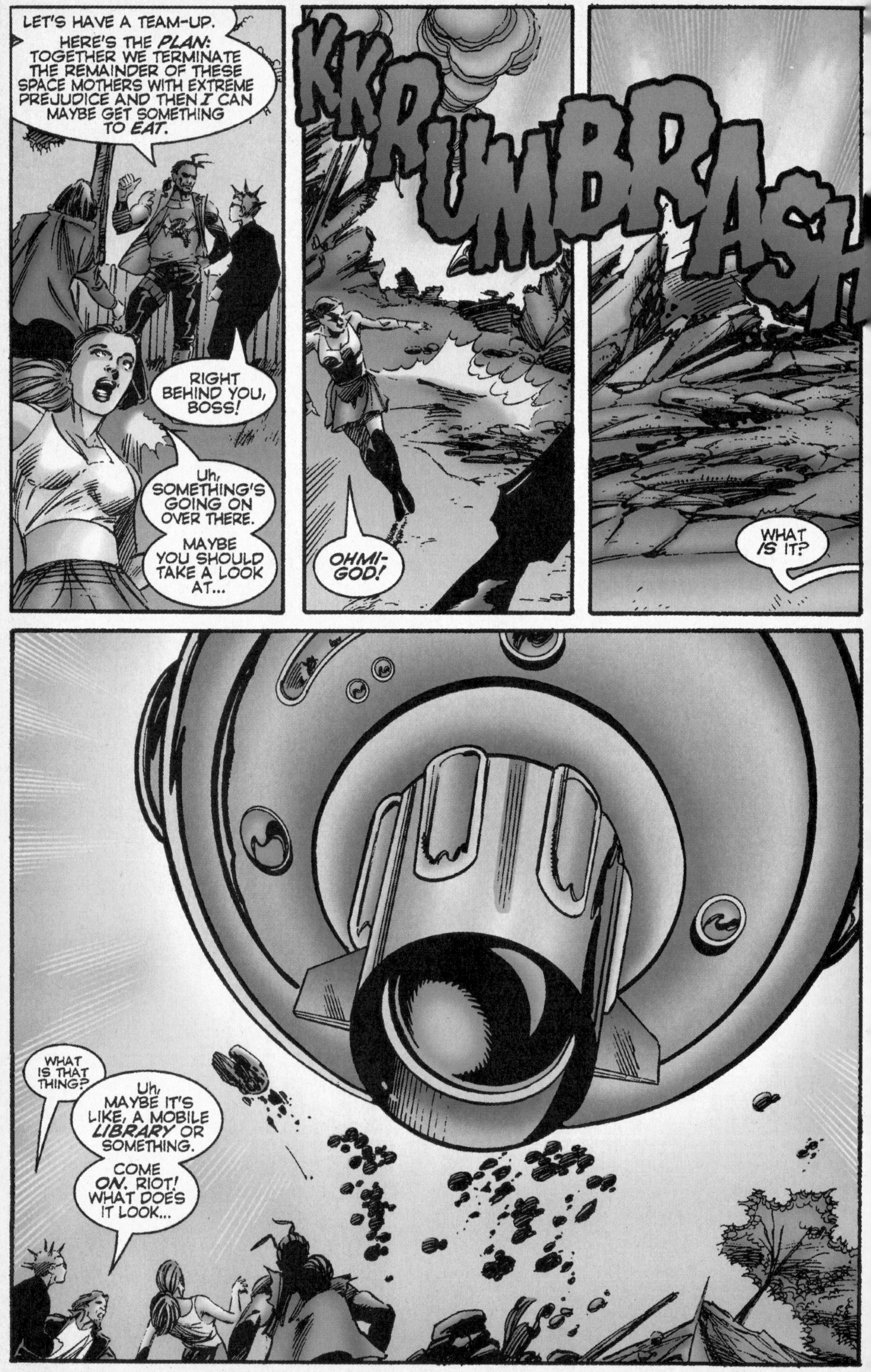

LET'S HAVE A TEAM-UP. HERE'S THE PLAN: TOGETHER WE TERMINATE THE REMAINDER OF THESE SPACE MOTHERS WITH EXTREME PREJUDICE AND THEN I CAN MAYBE GET SOMETHING TO EAT.
RIGHT BEHIND YOU, BOSS!
Uh, SOMETHING'S GOING ON OVER THERE.
MAYBE YOU SHOULD TAKE A LOOK AT...
KKRUMBRASH
OHMI-GOD!
WHAT IS IT?
WHAT IS THAT THING?
Uh, MAYBE IT'S LIKE, A MOBILE LIBRARY OR SOMETHING.
COME ON. RIOT! WHAT DOES IT LOOK...

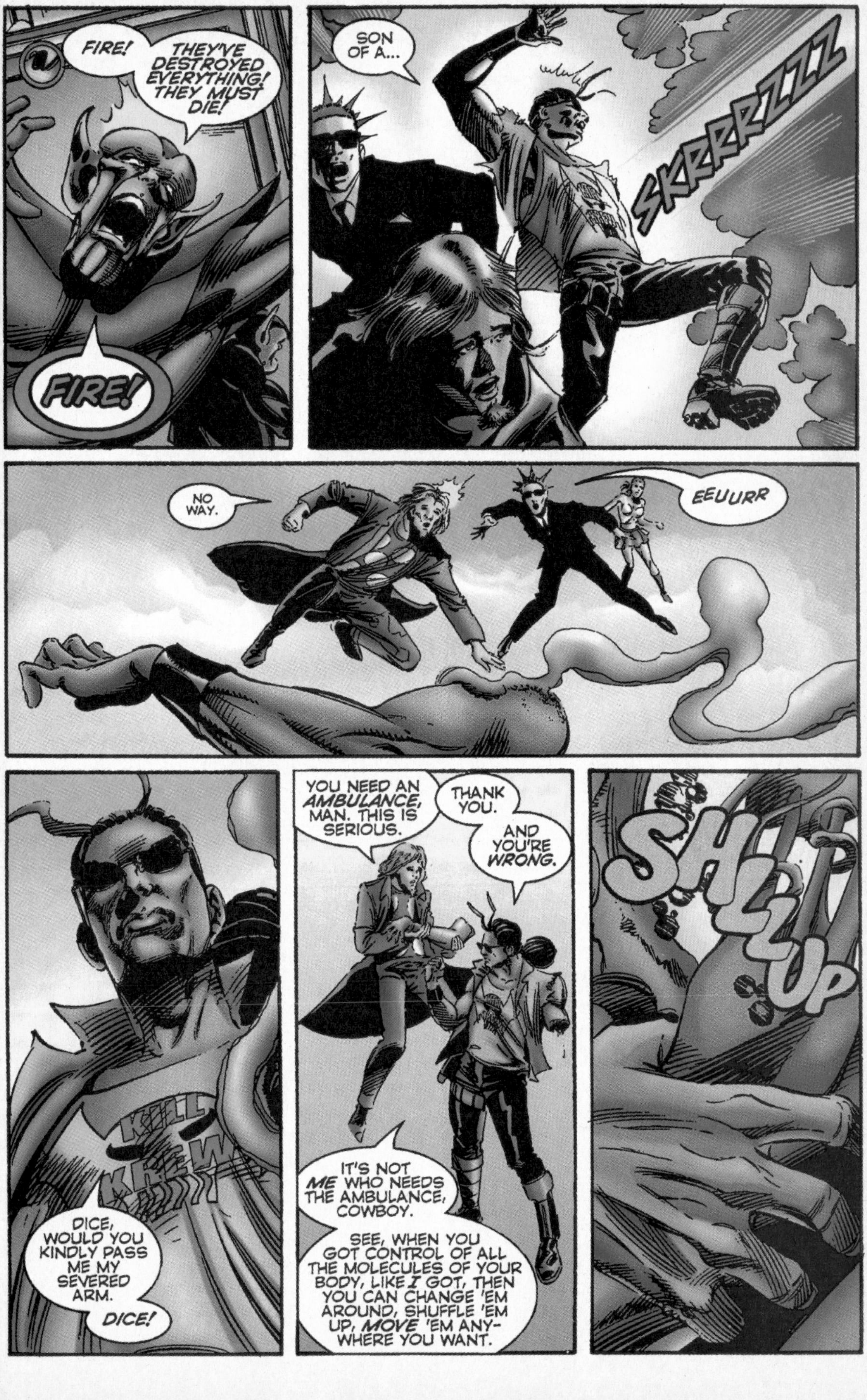
FIRE!
THEY'VE DESTROYED EVERYTHING! THEY MUST DIE!
FIRE!
SON OF A...
SKRRRZZZZ
NO WAY.
EEUURR
YOU NEED AN AMBULANCE, MAN. THIS IS SERIOUS.
THANK YOU.
AND YOU'RE WRONG.
IT'S NOT ME WHO NEEDS THE AMBULANCE, COWBOY.
SEE, WHEN YOU GOT CONTROL OF ALL THE MOLECULES OF YOUR BODY, LIKE I GOT, THEN YOU CAN CHANGE 'EM AROUND, SHUFFLE 'EM UP, MOVE 'EM ANYWHERE YOU WANT.
KILL KREW
DICE, WOULD YOU KINDLY PASS ME MY SEVERED ARM.
DICE!
SHLLUP

THEY'RE COMING BACK!

IN FACT, NOW THAT I THINK ABOUT IT, FORGET THE AMBULANCE. MAKE THAT A HEARSE.

WE'VE LOST ONE OF THEM, COMMANDANT! HE JUST VANISHED...

THEN DESTROY THE OTHERS, OAF.

AND OPEN A CHANNEL TO THE HOMEWORLD! TELL THEM WE MUST...

"PHONE-HOME", HUH?

HERE ARE THE NEWS HEAD-LINES, SUCKERS.

YOUR CALL HAS BEEN DIS-CONNECTED.

RYDER REALLY, REALLY HATES SKRULLS DOESN'T HE.

THROOM

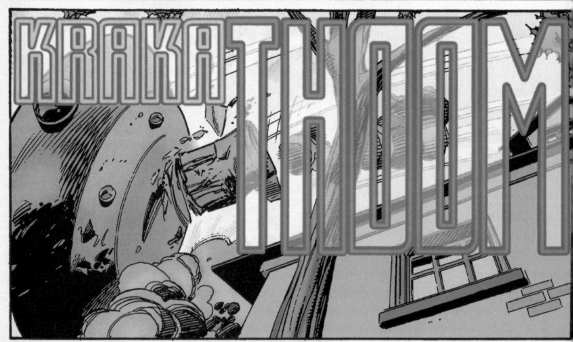

KRAKATHOOM

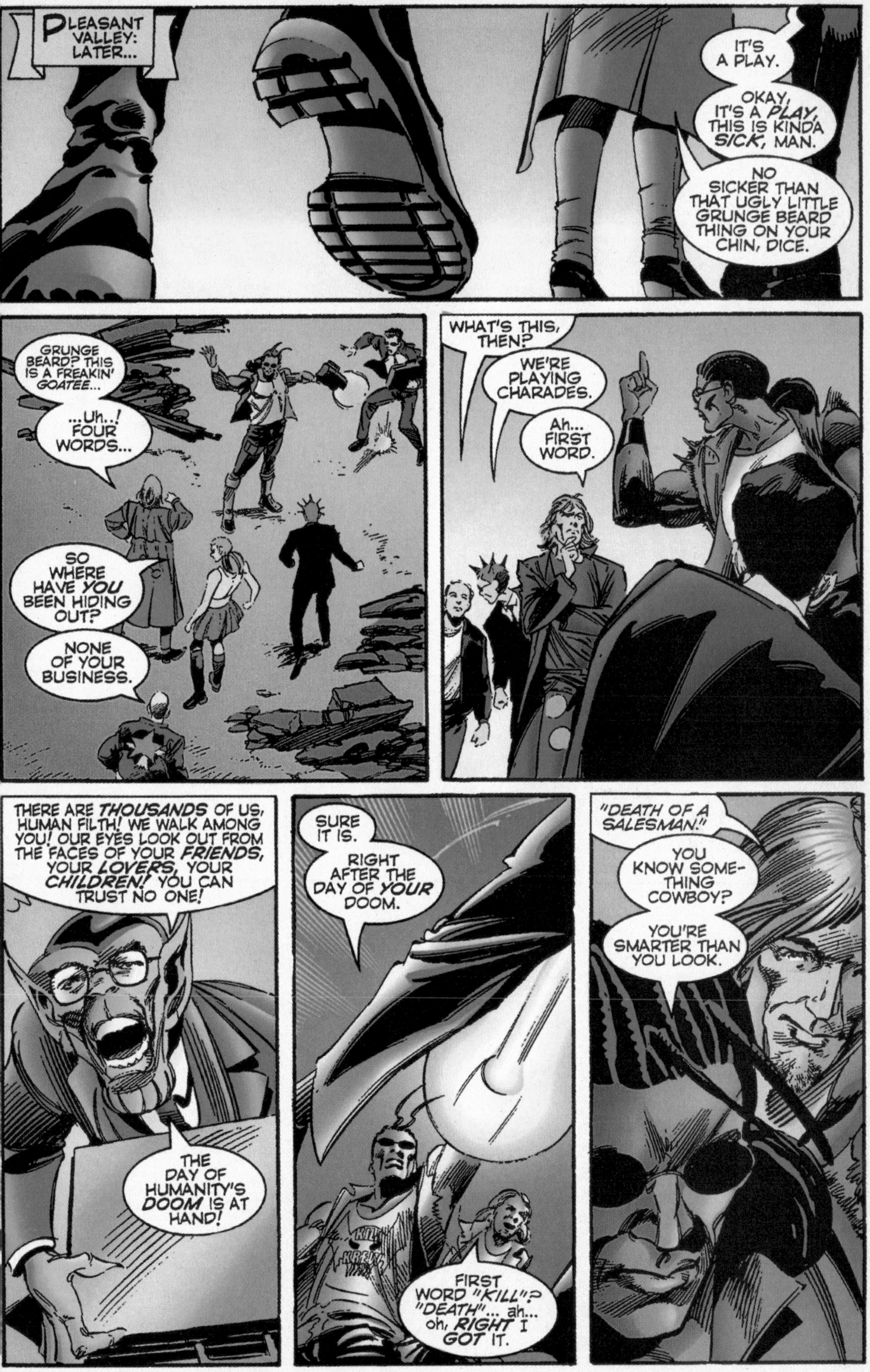
PLEASANT VALLEY: LATER...
IT'S A PLAY.
OKAY, IT'S A PLAY, THIS IS KINDA SICK, MAN.
NO SICKER THAN THAT UGLY LITTLE GRUNGE BEARD THING ON YOUR CHIN, DICE.
GRUNGE BEARD? THIS IS A FREAKIN' GOATEE...
...Uh..! FOUR WORDS...
SO WHERE HAVE YOU BEEN HIDING OUT?
NONE OF YOUR BUSINESS.
WHAT'S THIS, THEN?
WE'RE PLAYING CHARADES.
Ah... FIRST WORD.
THERE ARE THOUSANDS OF US, HUMAN FILTH! WE WALK AMONG YOU! OUR EYES LOOK OUT FROM THE FACES OF YOUR FRIENDS, YOUR LOVERS, YOUR CHILDREN! YOU CAN TRUST NO ONE!
THE DAY OF HUMANITY'S DOOM IS AT HAND!
SURE IT IS.
RIGHT AFTER THE DAY OF YOUR DOOM.
FIRST WORD "KILL"? "DEATH"... ah... oh, RIGHT I GOT IT.
"DEATH OF A SALESMAN."
YOU KNOW SOME-THING COWBOY?
YOU'RE SMARTER THAN YOU LOOK.

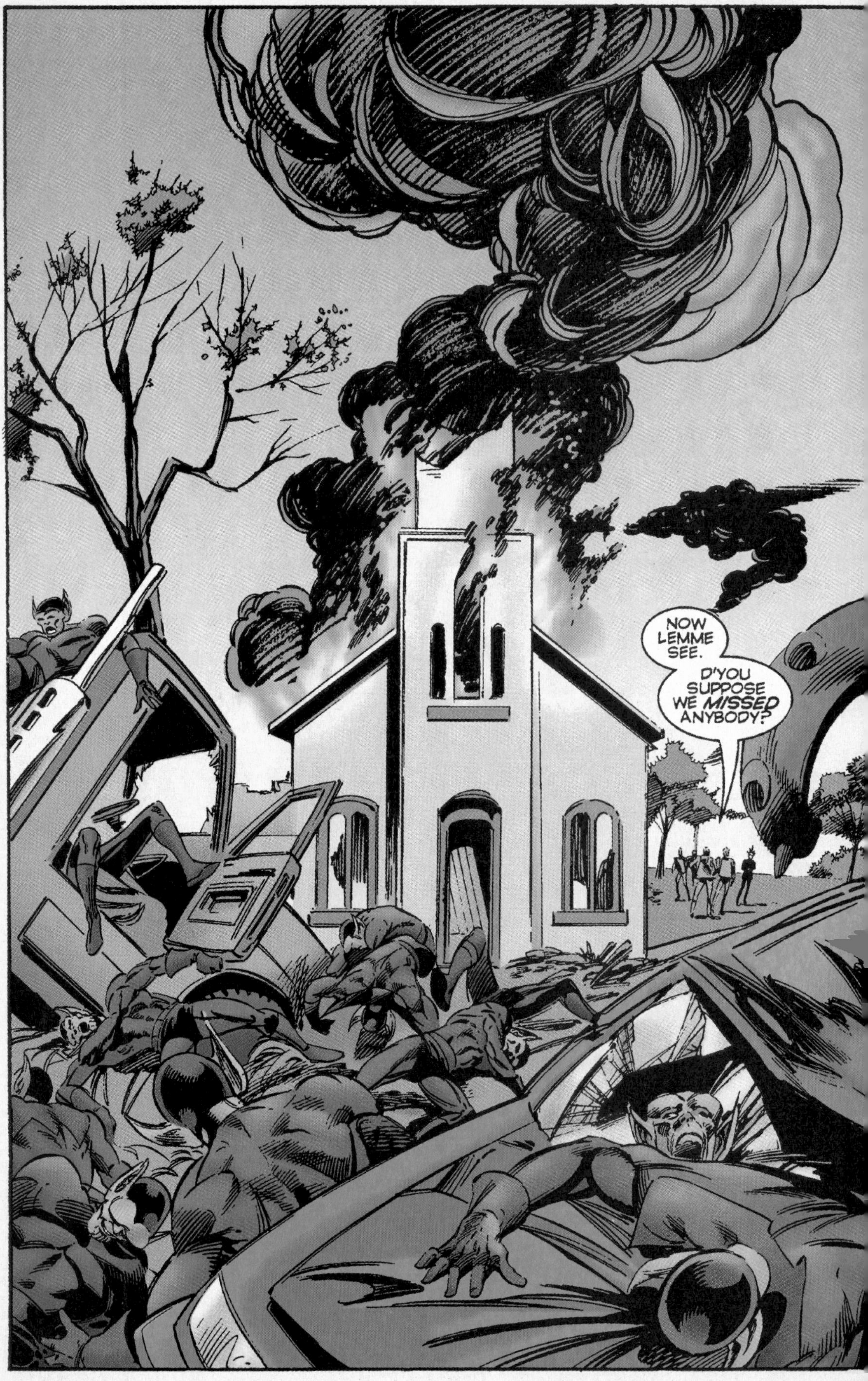
NOW LEMME SEE.
D'YOU SUPPOSE WE *MISSED* ANYBODY?

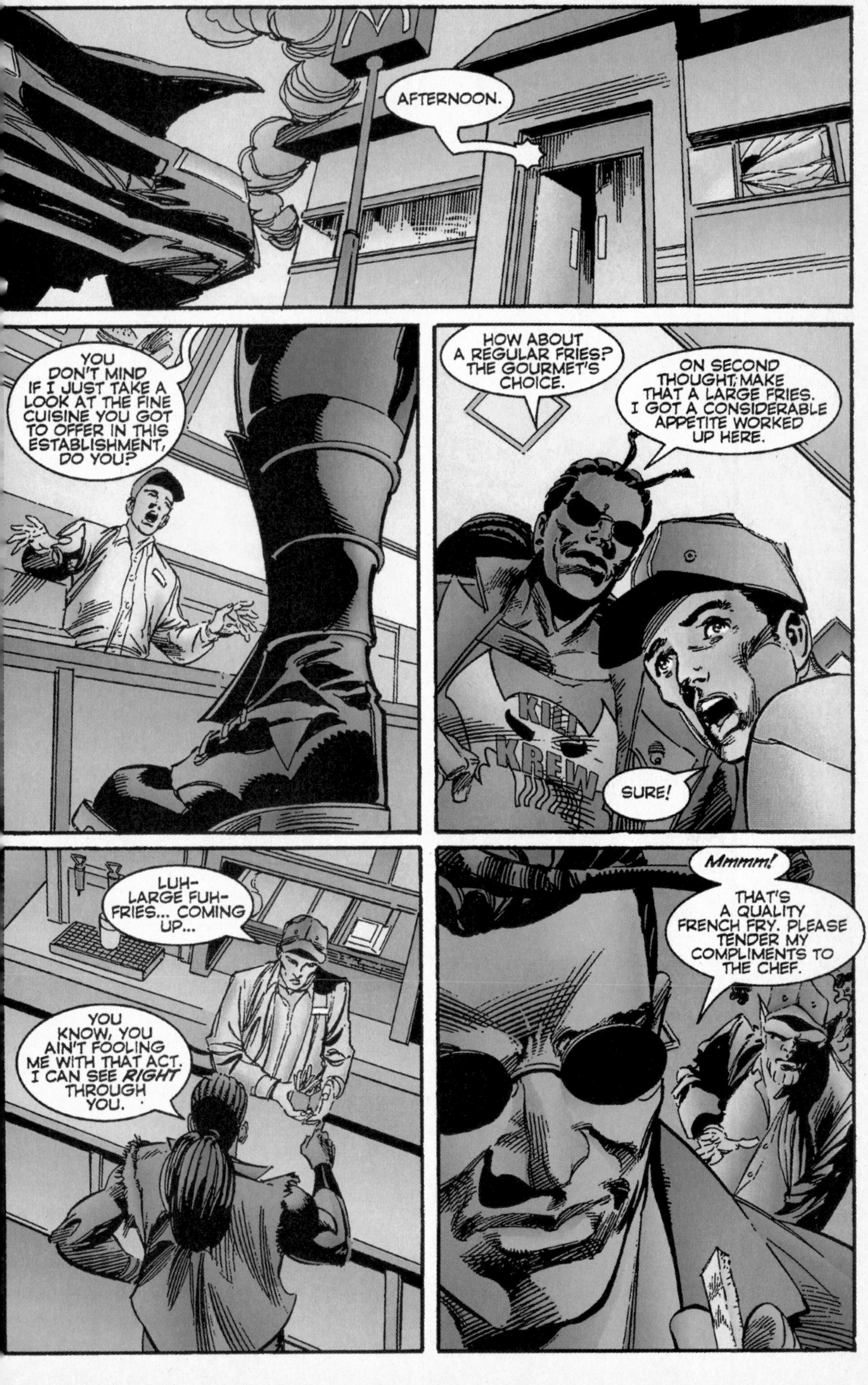
AFTERNOON.
YOU DON'T MIND IF I JUST TAKE A LOOK AT THE FINE CUISINE YOU GOT TO OFFER IN THIS ESTABLISHMENT, DO YOU?
HOW ABOUT A REGULAR FRIES? THE GOURMET'S CHOICE.
ON SECOND THOUGHT, MAKE THAT A LARGE FRIES. I GOT A CONSIDERABLE APPETITE WORKED UP HERE.
KILL KREW
SURE!
LUH-LARGE FUH-FRIES... COMING UP...
YOU KNOW, YOU AIN'T FOOLING ME WITH THAT ACT. I CAN SEE *RIGHT* THROUGH YOU.
*Mmmm!*
THAT'S A QUALITY FRENCH FRY. PLEASE TENDER MY COMPLIMENTS TO THE CHEF.

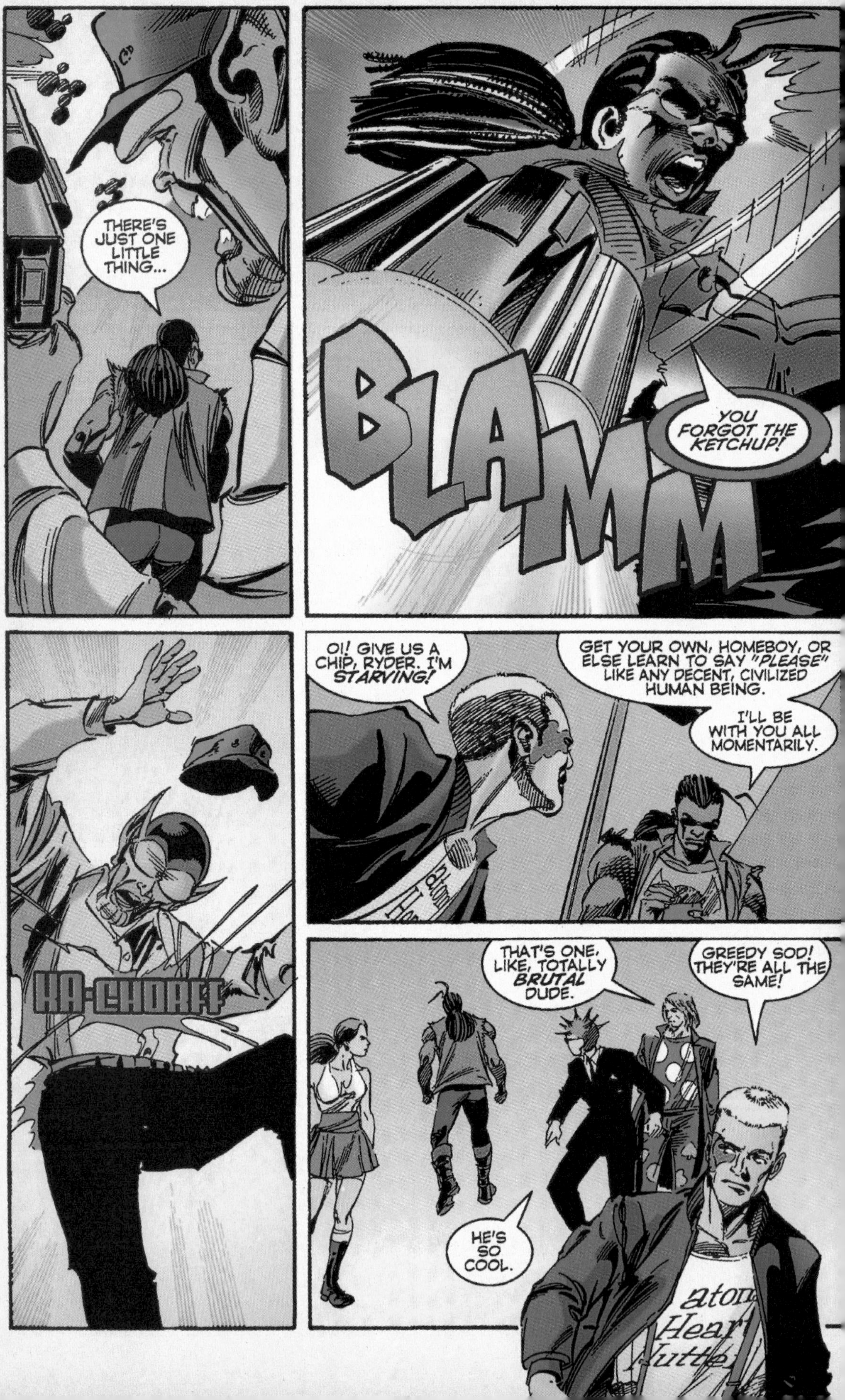
THERE'S JUST ONE LITTLE THING...
BLAMM
YOU FORGOT THE KETCHUP!
KA-CHOFF
OI! GIVE US A CHIP, RYDER. I'M *STARVING!*
GET YOUR OWN, HOMEBOY, OR ELSE LEARN TO SAY *"PLEASE"* LIKE ANY DECENT, CIVILIZED HUMAN BEING.
I'LL BE WITH YOU ALL MOMENTARILY.
THAT'S ONE, LIKE, TOTALLY *BRUTAL* DUDE.
GREEDY SOD! THEY'RE ALL THE SAME!
HE'S SO COOL.

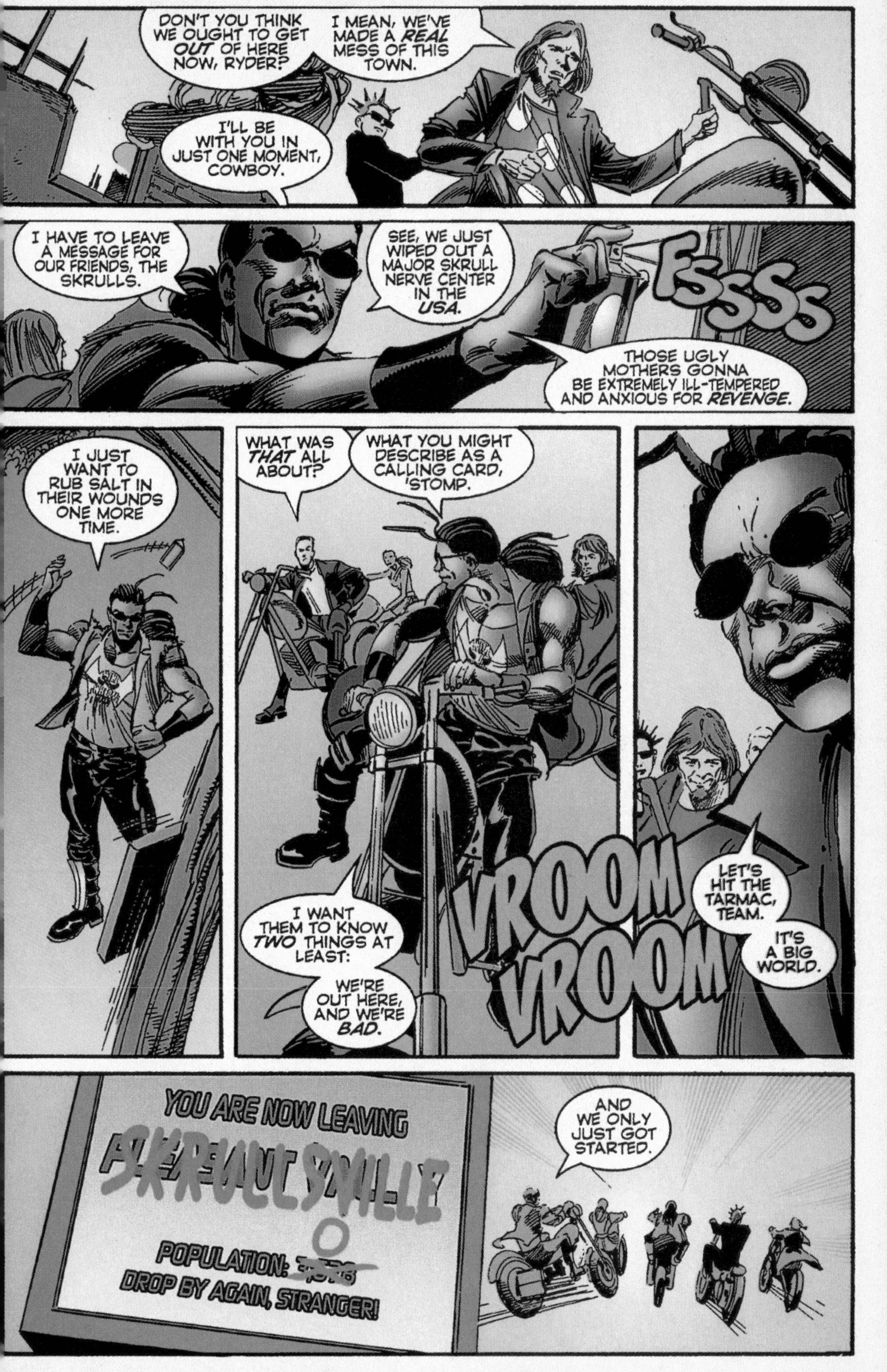
DON'T YOU THINK WE OUGHT TO GET *OUT* OF HERE NOW, RYDER?
I MEAN, WE'VE MADE A *REAL* MESS OF THIS TOWN.
I'LL BE WITH YOU IN JUST ONE MOMENT, COWBOY.
I HAVE TO LEAVE A MESSAGE FOR OUR FRIENDS, THE SKRULLS.
SEE, WE JUST WIPED OUT A MAJOR SKRULL NERVE CENTER IN THE *USA*.
FSSSS
THOSE UGLY MOTHERS GONNA BE EXTREMELY ILL-TEMPERED AND ANXIOUS FOR *REVENGE*.
I JUST WANT TO RUB SALT IN THEIR WOUNDS ONE MORE TIME.
WHAT WAS *THAT* ALL ABOUT?
WHAT YOU MIGHT DESCRIBE AS A CALLING CARD, 'STOMP.
I WANT THEM TO KNOW *TWO* THINGS AT LEAST:
WE'RE OUT HERE, AND WE'RE *BAD*.
VROOM VROOM
LET'S HIT THE TARMAC, TEAM.
IT'S A BIG WORLD.
YOU ARE NOW LEAVING
SKRULLSVILLE
POPULATION: 0
DROP BY AGAIN, STRANGER!
AND WE ONLY JUST GOT STARTED.

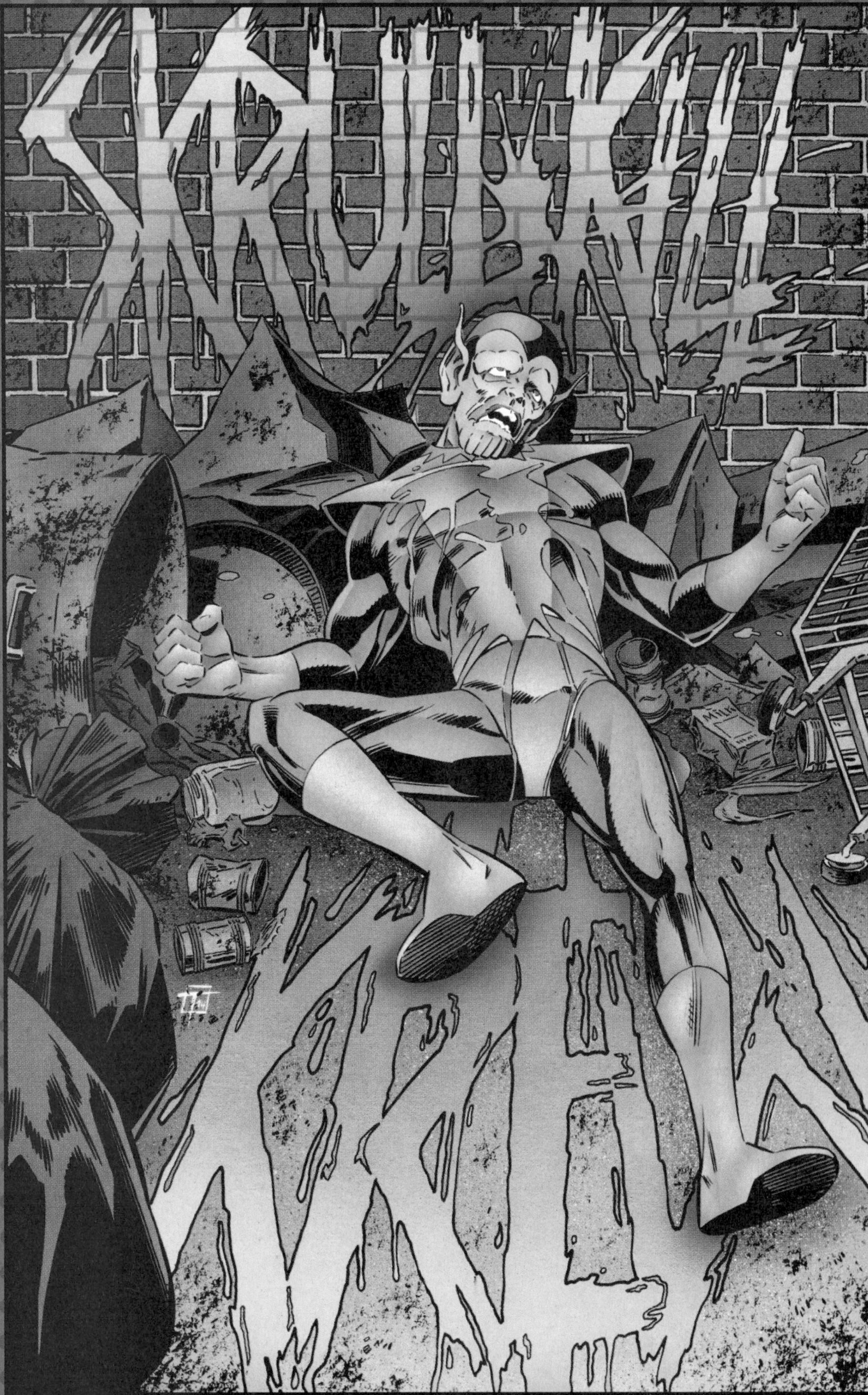

*Skrull Kill Krew* promotional artwork